The Chicana M(other)work Anthology

PORQUE SIN MADRES NO HAY REVOLUCIÓN

The Chicana M(other)work Anthology

EDITED BY
Cecilia Caballero,
Yvette Martínez-Vu,
Judith Pérez-Torres,
Michelle Téllez,
and Christine Vega

FOREWORD BY
Ana Castillo

THE UNIVERSITY OF
ARIZONA PRESS
TUCSON

The University of Arizona Press
www.uapress.arizona.edu

ISBN-13: 978-0-8165-3799-0 (paper)

Cover design by Leigh McDonald
Cover art by Christine Vega

Library of Congress Cataloging-in-Publication Data

Library of Congress Cataloging-in-Publication Data
Names: Caballero, Cecilia, editor.
Title: The Chicana motherwork anthology : porque sin madres no hay revolución / edited by
    Cecilia Caballero [and 4 others] ; foreword by Ana Castillo.
Description: Tucson : The University of Arizona Press, 2019 | Series: The Feminist wire
    books : connecting feminisms, race, and social justice | Includes bibliographical refer-
    ences and index.
Identifiers: LCCN 2018038444 | ISBN 9780816537990 (pbk. : alk. paper)
Subjects: LCSH: Mexican American mothers—Social conditions. | Mexican American
    women—Social conditions. | Women scholars—Social conditions. | Feminism.
Classification: LCC E184.M5 C394 2019 | DDC 305.48/86872073—dc23 LC record available
    at https://lccn.loc.gov/2018038444

Contents

Part I. Separation, Migration, State Violence, and Detention

Foreword

It is with enormous pleasure that I address the collection of scholarly writings included here. As a mother who raised her son for most of his life on her own, a writer and an educator, the daughter of a Mexic-Indian woman who took care of her family by working on assembly lines for more than four decades in Chicago, and as a Xicana, I welcome this volume wholeheartedly. In a way, it feels like being invited to a long-awaited sit-down luncheon or one of the informal potlucks I warmly recall with compañera-activists in days gone by. The experiences we shared at those gatherings about the work we had done all week—fighting the good fight as *mujeres en la lucha*—were not formally documented but fomented in part what would eventually be known as Chicana feminist thought.

"To think" is the key phrase here. *Cogito ergo sum*, as Descartes concluded. And in the end, it was and remains this singular line—a few words I was surely never familiar with at the start of the journey—that led me to take a road that no one, and surely nothing before such analysis formulated, had meant for me. And yet, whether rarely or disappeared, my own road had been tracked before.

If time is relative, then let us assume the groundwork for this collection was set by generations of prior thinking mothers—not all silent. Not at first, and not all. But the fundamental perspective embraced by the Chicana/Xicanista/Xicanx, holistic and inclusive (*bodymindspirit*), runs antithetical to the world we inhabit. More often than not, our proposals and efforts are diminished and even eventually dismissed. Most often, instead of seen as worthwhile reading for anyone interested in social change, our writings are reduced in importance with regard to the status quo, relegated to ethnic studies or women's and gender studies.

Contrary to the stubborn notion that we are a quiet, even complacent demographic, we have been speaking out for a very long time.

The conquest took place more than five centuries ago. Iztapapalotl wailed one night, "My children! What will become of my children?" It was a recorded omen of which the Emperor Moctezuma took note and rightly so. He heard a mother's cry and identified it with being representative of his empire. But on a pragmatic level, it was in fact women and their children who would be first most harshly oppressed as a result of the European invasion. The blood on these lands—South, North, and Central America and the attendant islands near and around—the sweat and tears of original peoples; the buried placentas and ombligos of newborns; the wails of madres sufridas and the war cries of guerrilleras; the prayers of sacerdotas, brujas' incantations, remedios de curanderas, y en hecho y en resumen, las madres-diosas—whether their words were written or rumored, echoed or muffled, all have served as the foundation of what we read in the following pages, as well as all the action produced by women of consciousness, day in and day out. From the decision to return to the classroom while our babies are still being breastfed, because we feel the need to continue guiding students; to running for public office while our children are dealing with adolescent angst at home; to volunteering with community organizations or human rights groups when our children no longer require our daily vigilance—Mother-Scholars are not all things to all at all times, but we are consistently conscious of our desire and will to leave the world a little less askew than how we came to it.

Consequently, the feminist who also identifies as a Chicana often goes ignored by dominant society. Despite our efforts on the part of thinking Brown women, until the mid-eighties (and I would put forth, to an extent in the present), the dialogue on the subject of feminism remains predominantly between Black and white people.

It was the desire and need to enter the dominated Black and white feminist dialogue and create a discussion that led me from the poems and novels I endeavored to investigating the various components that made up our identities: collective history; relationships as mestizas with the United States and Mexico; the legacy of religion, especially Catholicism; the ongoing bombardment and effects of racism against People of Color as the result of colonialism; and how writing as a relatively new form of communication for us as a group would help us unite in our efforts for social change. Although other like-minded writers were few, they were emerging in the eighties when I began my endeavor. We became a small but determined chorus. In the book that ensued, *Massacre of the Dreamers: Essays on Xicanisma*, I called a chapter "Un Tapiz," remarking on three books (one was my first novel) by three Chicanas. As I saw it, each book was addressing from a different tack the multilayers of patriarchal rules that had kept women of Mexican heritage out of the upper ranks of the public sphere, but more often, out of the public sphere altogether. We were not the most recent immigrant population, for the most part, even if we were first generation; we were not new to these lands. In terms of population, there were many of us, but whether in the media, government, or most prominent places, we were kept out.

"Learn what it is to be Toltec," the ancient ancestors instructed the young coming of age. To the girls, "Learn to weave, how to combine the colors." At first glance, someone today might see weaving as a domestic chore reserved for women who did not contribute much overall to the family's income. Weaving, however, was not just "women's work"; it was the basis of the economy for many groups. This tradition continued even into what would become the Southwest United States, where raising sheep and goats sustained Hispanic and Indigenous peoples. We are reminded of this inheritance when the editors here tell prospective readers, "We view the authors' journeys as Women of Color Mother-Scholars as interwoven." They recall the traditional Indigenous shawl, el rebozo, a lovely garment, historically identifying the wearer's ethnicity or tribe, having many functional uses and, as mentioned, being a fine economic staple. In the case of these writings, the woven rebozo is representational of the work they are building with like-minded Mother-Scholars.

Mother may be broadly defined. When a person becomes the guardian of another human being, particularly an infant or a child who requires nurturing in addition to protection and provisions, her whole perspective on society, in fact, on life's meaning, shifts. There may or may not be such as a thing as a mother's instinct; not all women have claimed to feel it. But that your life's view changes when you assume the role of caretaker is arguably true. It was this analysis of the ancestry I inherited, the world culture I was part of, and the immediate urgency of being a thinking mother that caused the writing of "Toward the Mother-Bond Principle," the ninth and penultimate chapter of *Massacre of the Dreamers: Essays on Xicanisma*. It was a call not solely to biological mothers but to everyone based on what is known in Buddhism as having "Mother Awareness." In the Buddhist belief system of reincarnation, we must consider that throughout our infinite past lifetimes, we have all been one another's mother. Anyone (and indeed, everyone) could have been your mother in another lifetime. This is the relationship we, therefore, should develop with each other, of unconditional love.

By the same token, each of us in one incarnation or another has been someone's child.

To have a fundamental perspective that informs us each that we are bonded to one another in every way on this planet isn't easy. It is not the way our current world works. People are divided by the various labels that we feel are our strongest suit to best beat out other labeled groups and individuals. Prominently, we are divided by class (or, today, just money, given the enormous salaries earned by athletes and celebrities), region, ethnicity and skin tone, use of language/s, and gender and sexual identification. Within those divisions are all kinds of subdivisions. From this place we teach the children in our care what is most critical to learn about achieving their goals as grown-ups. We are proud and thrilled when our little ones share their treats and toys. Later, we find ourselves urging them toward less generous ways and toward defending and protecting what is theirs.

The theme of this book, that of working mothers who support each other to navigate through the hostile waters of racism, patriarchy, institutional misogyny, daily microaggressions, and the many ways in which an educated woman may nonetheless experience economic hardship trying to support her family, isn't a revolutionary concept in the strict sense. Astute and strategic mothers who aim in community to protect and to provide for the next generation have been around since the big bang. It remains, however, a subject vital and urgent to our progress as human beings, and to the continuance of a healthy planet.

Ana Castillo, July 2018

Acknowledgments

Gracias to our children, Milagro, Alonzo, Luna, Emiliano, Tino, Janitzio Itztlaloc, and Joaquín, because this book would not exist if it were not for them and all they have taught us beyond the scopes of our imaginations. Thank you to our *madres*, Juana Duarte Caballero, Christina Luzanilla Uribe, Socorro Salazar Pérez, Rosaura Serratos, and María Cristina Guerrero Téllez. A nuestras *abuelitas*, Josefina García, Paula Cazares Guerrero, Maria Luisa Huante Linares, Teresa Madrigal Téllez, Socorro Martínez, Crescencia Rodríguez, Francisca (Panchita) Peralta Osegueda, Maria Vega Villarreal, Consuelo (Chelito) Rodriguez, Gracia Contreras Gutiérrez Duarte, and Cecilia Contreras Beltrán Caballero, and to our ancestors for leading the way and for their motherwork, which has sustained our communities, often at a great personal cost to themselves. We honor their labor and their love.

Thank you to our partners, our *comadres*, our students, our supporters, our sisters, and all our fellow Mothers of Color in academia, in the community, and in the home. Tlazo to the aunties and uncles, chosen familia, spirit kin who have helped raise us and raise our children. Without you all, we cannot do this work and walk in balance.

Tlazocamatli to the biggest mother that sustained us, Pachamama, Tonantzin, our earth mother. And to the other motherly ancestors.

We would also like to thank the three anonymous reviewers who reviewed our book proposal and the two anonymous reviewers of the full manuscript draft through the University of Arizona Press. Your sharp insight and analysis helped us clarify our vision for the book. Thank you to the editors of the Feminist Wire book series, Monica J. Casper, Tamura A. Lomax, and Darnell L. Moore, for your comments and generous support.

We thank our University of Arizona Press editor, Kristen Buckles, who believed in our collective from the very beginning.

Thank you to Sabbatical Beauty and the University of Arizona Commission on the Status of Women (CSW), whose funds assisted us with the completion of this project. Thank you to Jordan Beltran Gonzales for his copyediting work.

We want to thank the participants and communities at our various conference presentations, such as the National Women's Studies Association, the American Studies Association, the National Association of Chicano and Chicana Studies, Beyond Boundaries at Northern Arizona University, UCLA RAC, and many more, for expanding our project in new ways.

Finally, we want to thank all our contributors, who trusted this anthology as a space for their powerful testimonios and research. It was a deep joy to work with you all.

We are honored to share this path with our readers as we collectively envision and manifest better futures and reproductive justice for all mothers, parents, children, and families of color without fear. May this anthology inspire you to create, resist, build, and grow together in community.

The Chicana M(other)work Anthology

Introduction

Una Ofrenda para las Madres

Our labor is our prayer, our mothering is our offering.
—CHICANA M(OTHER)WORK COLLECTIVE

This edited collection of research, *testimonios*, and essays about Chicana and other Women of Color (WOC) mothering was born out of a collective dream, imagined together through tears, laughter, meals, and many, many conversations. Organized in four parts—(1) Separation, Migration, State Violence, and Detention; (2) Chicana/Latina/WOC Mother-Activists; (3) Intergenerational Mothering; and (4) Loss, Reproductive Justice, and Holistic Pregnancy—this book showcases research and testimonios by Chicana and other Women of Color Mother-Scholars and activists who center mothering as an act of transformative labor within academic and community spaces through an intersectional lens.[1]

The seed for the Chicana M(other)work collective was first planted by Michelle Téllez's writing on single Chicana mothering and academia (2013) and her introduction of the term "Chicana Motherwork" (2011, 2014). In late 2014, we all (Cecilia Caballero, Yvette Martínez-Vu, Judith Pérez-Torres, Christine Vega, and Michelle Téllez) met in person and presented together for the first time at the annual American Studies Association (ASA) conference, on a panel entitled "Mothers of Color in Academia." Since that ASA presentation, we have been working together as the Chicana M(other)work collective to amplify Chicana and other Mother of Color voices within academia and beyond through podcasting, publications, and presentations. Drawing from our first published article (Caballero et al. 2017), we define Chicana M(other)work as a strategy for collective resistance within institutions that continue to marginalize us. In our research, we found that much of the small but expanding body of scholarship on academic mothers narrowly focuses on white, middle-class, and married women (Evans and Grant 2008; Mason, Wolfinger, and Goulden 2013). For this reason, we draw attention to issues of heteropatriarchy, racism, and classism by highlighting the lived experiences of working-class Mothers of Color. Accordingly, we capitalize the phrase Mothers of Color (as well as Mother-Scholars) throughout our writing to emphasize this group as a distinct population.

Theorizing M(other)work

Chicana M(other)work is a concept and project informed by our shared gendered, classed, and racialized experiences as first-generation Chicana scholars from working-class, (im)migrant Mexican families.[2] Through Chicana M(other)work, we provide a framework for collective resistance that makes our various forms of feminized labor visible and promotes collective action, holistic healing, and social justice for Mother-Scholars and Activists of Color, our children, and our communities. Furthermore, rather than understanding Chicana identity as a singular monolith, we view it as ever evolving. Here we use the term "Chicana" conceptually to integrate our varying identitarian positionalities as cisgender mother-scholars who identify as Chicana, Xicana-Indigena, Chicana/x Latina, and Afro-Xicana. We are daughters of working-class Mexican migrant parents, and we are Chicana Mother-Scholars to Children of Color born in the United States. We use a Chicana feminist framework (Anzaldúa 1987; Delgado Bernal 1998; García 1997; Sandoval 2010; Téllez 2005; Villenas et al. 2006) as our theoretical grounding to explore and challenge white heteropatriarchy as it continuously marginalizes Women of Color in the academic pipeline (Harris and González 2013; Solórzano and Yosso 2006). While we self-identify as Chicana Mother-Scholars, however, we do not view our work as restricted to academic or domestic spaces; rather, the concept Mother-Scholar transgresses these spaces. Our work exists in the classrooms, community, with each other, and with our children. We view our care work and mothering, specifically "motherwork" (Collins 1994), as an interwoven political act that responds to multiple forms of oppression experienced by Mothers of Color in the United States.

We borrow the term "motherwork" from Patricia Hill Collins and modify it by embracing the term "other" through the use of parentheses. Chicana M(other)work calls attention to our layered care work from five words into one—Chicana, Mother, Other, Work, Motherwork. We see Chicana M(other)work as being inclusive to Women of Color (trans and cis), nonbinary Parents of Color, other-mothers, and allies because mothering is not confined to biology or normative family structures. We strive to build community within and outside academic institutions, and one way we do this is by mothering others and ourselves (Gumbs 2010; Gumbs, Martens, and Williams 2016). Building on Chicana feminists' critiques of institutional heteropatriarchal violence in the academy (Castañeda et al. 2014), Chicana M(other)work challenges increasingly corporatized neoliberal institutions by holding spaces accountable through activism when they are not supporting Mothers of Color and working-class families.[3] In these ways, we make it clear that Chicana M(other)work is not a project of assimilating or diversifying academia; on the contrary, we aim to transform it, for instance, by choosing not to hide our children, instead including them within our work for social justice. Furthermore, despite the possibility of our individual upward mobility with our doctoral degrees, we will always remain committed to our poor and working-class origins. As such, Chicana M(other)work is a call to action for justice within and outside academia.

For Patricia Hill Collins (1994, 2000), her theorization of mother-work centers race, class, gender, and other intersectional identities to challenge Western ideologies of mothers' roles. Collins's theoretical framework disrupts gender roles and defies the social structures and constructions of work and family as separate spheres for Black women; it acknowledges women's reproductive labor as work on behalf of the family as a whole rather than to benefit men. Motherwork also goes beyond the survival of the family by recognizing the survival of one's biological kin, as well as attending to the individual survival, empowerment, and identity of one's racial and ethnic community to protect the earth for children who are yet to be born. These concepts were instrumental for our own theorization of Chicana M(other)work.

As Chicana Mother-Scholars, our concept of Chicana M(other)-work is informed by the labor we perform in the neoliberal university model, which exploits our work as doctoral students, contingent faculty, and tenure-line faculty. Although women who are adjunct faculty now compose the new faculty majority in the United States, the difficulties of advancing in PhD programs and then into tenure-track and tenured careers are often framed as individual failings rather than fully recognized as institutional barriers that push Mothers of Color outside academia. In turn, the university is seldom held accountable for the institutional violence and exploitation faced by first-generation, low-income, and working-class Mother-Scholars of Color.

Institutional Barriers in the Academy

Institutional barriers in academia include (1) poverty-level stipends for graduate students, (2) exploitive wages for adjunct faculty, (3) unstable contingent employment, (4) little to no financial resources for childcare, (5) numerous unpaid service obligations, (6) conference presentations in non-child-friendly locations with expensive registration and travel fees, and (7) the expectation to attend professional networking events that often conflict with childcare and school hours. Moreover, a recent study shows that faculty family-leave policies benefit fathers and disadvantage mothers (Wolfers 2016). These issues compound further by the various degrees of everyday microaggressions that Mothers of Color receive from administrators, staff, faculty, and peers, all of which can cause psychological harm (Bell 1992, 1995; Solórzano 1998; Yosso et al. 2009). Taken together, these realities depict a dismal picture for Mothers of Color in academia.

When we place these substantial institutional barriers for Mothers of Color within the context of data about Women of Color in academia, we unsurprisingly find that very few advance along the pipeline of higher education and the professoriate in the United States. According to Ryu (2010), Women of Color made up 7.5 percent of full-time faculty positions in the United States in 2010 (as cited in Harris and González 2013, 2). More specifically, Women of Color represent 10.4 percent of instructors and lecturers, 9.9 percent of assistant professors, 6.6 percent of associate professors, and only 3.4 percent of full professors in U.S. colleges and universities (Harris and González 2013, 2). Women of Color are not only concentrated in the lower academic ranks, but they are also overrepresented in what are perceived as "less prestigious" academic institutions, such as community colleges (Snyder and Dillow 2010, 3). Among women graduate students—50 percent of PhD students—only 23 percent become tenure-track professors (Snyder and Dillow 2010, 2). Meanwhile, men with young children are 35 percent more likely than women with young children to secure tenure-track positions after completing their PhDs (Wolfinger 2013). Academic fathers, moreover, secure tenure about 20 percent more frequently than academic mothers (Mason, Wolfinger, and Goulden 2013). Together, this research shows that these numerous institutional issues directly affect the advancement of Women of Color Mother-Scholars in academia, whereas academic men benefit from and experience few obstacles from having children. The existing research about academic mothers demonstrates that motherhood goes hand in hand with second-tier positions. Mothers are an astounding 132 percent more likely than fathers to end up in low-paid contingent positions (Mason, Wolfinger, and Goulden 2013). The likelihood of a Mother of Color to receive a tenure-track position, let alone obtain tenure, is minimal (Castañeda and Isgro 2013). Combined with the invisible labor of mentoring Students of Color, providing undervalued service work for diversity initiatives, and maintaining family and community responsibilities, Mothers of Color are often institutionally pushed out because they rarely receive credit or compensation for their feminized labor, and they do not receive resources to adequately accommodate their motherwork.

Furthermore, the data about academic parents do not reflect the substantial gaps in the Chicanx and Latinx educational pipeline. For every 100 Chicanx and Latinx in kindergarten, 60 will receive a high school diploma, 11 will obtain a bachelor's degree, 3 will earn a graduate degree, and 0.2—or about 1 in 500—will receive a PhD (Pérez Huber et al. 2015; Solórzano and Yosso 2006). These numbers are sobering, especially when we apply an intersectional lens and consider how Chicana and Latina mothers constitute an even smaller percentage at all levels in the educational pipeline.

Since we are situated in academic spaces, our initial work was centered on ending this cycle of institutional violence against Chicanas, Latinas, and Mothers of Color in academia. As our work expanded, however, we realized that Chicana M(other)work is a useful framework in many spaces and that by taking agency, making our labor visible, building community, and prioritizing community and self-care, we can contribute to institutional change and collective resistance for Mothers of Color.

Storytelling for Social Justice:
Testimonio as Method

Testimonio is a story that is told from a place of intent and under-standing of social, political, and historical contexts (Delgado Bernal, Burciaga, and Flores Carmona 2012; Latina Feminist Group 2001). According to Lindsay Pérez Huber, testimonios historically emerged from the field of Latin American studies to document the lived experiences of oppressed groups and to denounce injustices (Booker 2002; Pérez Huber 2009). Pérez Huber offers a genealogy of testimonio and suggests that although no concrete definition of testimonio fits the complex, multilayered experiences of any oppressed group, testimonios have several characteristics of a method or framework. They may encompass, but are not limited to, narratives as a witness, a verbal journey, and knowledge creation. According to the Latina Feminist Group (2001), testimonios "create knowledge and theory through personal experiences, highlighting the significance of the process of testimonio in theorizing our own realities as Women of Color" (Pérez Huber 2009, 643).

It is imperative to understand that telling a testimonio has a larger purpose, where the private becomes profoundly political with the intent to raise social consciousness for readers (Latina Feminist Group 2001). By centering the power of storytelling, our personal histories are sites from which to theorize and understand how change can be used as a methodological tool (McClaurin 1999). Using Chicana and Black feminist theories on mothering with the method of testimonio, our methodology offers our experiences from locations of the Brown body (Cruz 2006) as a "bodymindspirit" (Lara 2003) memory. Our testimonios challenge the silence we hold, within ourselves, out of fear of not being "academic enough" or "mother enough," and allow us to reclaim space that would otherwise be marginalized by dominant discourse (Flores Carmona and Luciano 2014).

While not all testimonios within this anthology are a response to a Mother-Scholar identity in the academy—for example, some speak about experiences in the home, community, and activism—the use of testimonios is geared to offer a collective experience to identify how motherhood, mothering, adoption, pregnancy loss, and separation resonate with each story across this anthology. Furthermore, this book is structured with the rebozo in mind, a multifunctional shawl that is woven and strengthened from strands of fabric, used for generations by women. Each thread signifies and carries stories of our mothers and women in our lives, all condensed within a silky rectangular 3.5-meter-long scarf (Hernandez 2017). Our book similarly interweaves research and testimonios throughout to contextualize our theory and create a foundation for Chicana M(other)work. These testimonios provide an entryway for policy consideration and institutional transformation through collective resistance, where Women of Color—Chicana and Mothers of Color alike—are creating, writing, organizing, and pushing against our marginalization within institutions that fail to recognize our existence or needs as mothers and parents.

Rebozos and Coyolxauhqui: Threading Together Our Fragmented Identities

Our contributions, as Chicana M(other)work, are theoretical and epistemological, offering an understanding of motherwork through Chicana experiences. Therefore, we offer a definition of Chicana M(other)work as we attempt to witness and understand each other's testimonios as Chicanas in our struggle for change. Through everyday acts or tactics (Certeau 1984) of collective resistance against institutional violence, we are establishing an ethos of collective resistance.[4] Over time, these acts can help produce institutional and interpersonal cultural change in academia. By highlighting Chicana M(other)-

work as one example of collective resistance, we expect there will be an institutional response that recognizes the multiple identities we negotiate (e.g., working class, Women of Color, mothers, and scholars). We also believe that a Chicana M(other)work framework prioritizes mothers and Parents of Color who have been historically denied agency or ignored. We recognize that policy changes will fall short without collective work to empower Mother-Scholars and help them change the culture of the academy. In addition, since we do not view our work as confined to the institution, we believe this anthology and the ensuing discussion can also serve as calls to action in our everyday lives and communities, as some of our contributors and others demonstrate in their essays.[5]

Chicana M(other)work helps us thread together our intersectional and often fragmented identities. We borrow the term "rebozo" as a metaphor that informs our conceptualization and the organization of our framework as well as this anthology. The rebozo is woven together from very simple materials, such as cotton, that come from the earth. To weave, or to *tejer*, calls attention to the fragmentation—similar to the fragmentation within the words Chicana, mother, other, work, and motherwork—that we weave into one to become our Chicana M(other)work framework. Before being woven into a rebozo, the cotton is thin and fragile. When all the strands come together, the rebozo begins to take shape. The shawl holds our babies, our children, and is used to pull our hips together after giving birth. It can be used to cover, protect, and shield. With this in mind, we conceptualize and organize this book as a *trenza* (a braid) and build on Margaret Montoya's (1994) concept of "mascaras, trenzas y greñas" by weaving testimonios as Mothers of Color in between the research articles as well as including hybrid essays of both testimonios and research. We view the authors' journeys as Mother-Scholars of Color as interwoven like a braid: in that process of weaving, an understanding of our collective experience emerges.

We see our work as a political and feminist project that transforms the narrative for Chicana, Latina, and other Women of Color mothers and caregivers. When thinking about the weaving of our fragmented identities, we draw from the story of Coyolxauhqui in conversation with other Chicana *teoristas* (Anzaldúa 1987; Gaspar de Alba 2014; Luna and Galeana 2016; Moraga 1993, 1997). This fragmented image serves as the logo for the Chicana M(other)work collective, since we view our concept as a form of reclaiming our wholeness, birth, mothering, and stories of loss and separation (Vega 2016). Chicana M(other)work is informed by the story of Coyolxauhqui also because the institution does not account for the many ways in which our identities, as first-generation scholars and Mothers of Color, are split or further fragmented in academia. In response, Chicana M(other)work is about collectively attempting to heal these wounds and allowing us to view our labor as whole rather than fragmented. Like the rebozo, we pull ourselves together within and beyond these institutional spaces. Taken together, Chicana M(other)work incorporates the rebozo metaphor and Coyolxauhqui logo to call attention to how our identities are not only intersectional and fragmented but also interwoven, because we cannot easily compartmentalize the work we do within our communities, families, and academic spaces. Rather than isolating each form of labor and identity from the others, we accept that we can provide care work in all spaces.

Part of the work involved in threading together our fragmented identities requires speaking up and speaking back to institutions of power that silence us. In doing academic work, we are often explicitly and implicitly taught to silence and isolate ourselves for individualistic career advancement. Chicana M(other)work rejects this notion and highlights our agency and nonhierarchical collective power to dismantle heteropatriarchy and resist neoliberalism. Chicana M(other)work calls attention to the part of each one of us that was told not to get pregnant. Choosing to take control of our bodies and raise a family is healing and radical. To acknowledge someone as an academic Mother of Color, we validate her and the work she is doing through our micro-affirmations. By bearing witness to another academic mother, we can acknowledge each other's existence. All our labor— from the classroom and office to the community and home—is work that matters.

Ultimately, Chicana M(other)work is care work that includes the care we provide in our homes, classrooms, communities, and selves. Chicana M(other)work is expansive—for example, we do not mother alone but have help from partners, relatives, or friends—and inter-generational, because it includes the histories and *consejos* of our Chicana and Mexicana *abuelas*, mothers, *tías*, sisters, and other care-takers. Given that we also recognize our children as individuals with agency, and on many occasions, they have understood that "Mamá is studying," Chicana M(other)work is relational. It is also an imaginary, because we envision and are working toward mothering for libera-tion among interlocking systems of oppression. We refuse to continue living fragmented lives, and we will no longer be silent.

The Process: "Now Let Us Shift"

Transforming our collective dreams into a tangible project has taken us on a journey that we could not have planned or imagined. It has meant that we wake up to feed and dress our children, pack their lunches, and rush them to daycare or school so that we can make it on time to our sacred and early Chicana M(other)work conference calls. It has meant picking up and driving our children home from school while on a call with one another; indeed, our children recognize our faces on the screens and have begun to understand the collective space we have built. It has meant thinking deeply together about our experi-ences to inform the goals we have for this work. It has also meant that we do not always discuss work with each other and that we support each other through the layers of our actual lives, which include questions and critiques of our sex lives, or lack thereof, along with many other issues, such as divorce, custody issues, dating and relationships, and overall emotional support. All of our projects are born out of our mutual commitment, both to each other and to this project. We are the *ofrenda* to ourselves. We are the ofrenda to each other.

When we started receiving contributions following our call for papers (CFP) for this anthology in October 2016, we were overwhelmed with both shock and joy. The task of selecting eighteen chapters out of the eighty-six submissions was an honor, yet daunting and inspiring all at once. Although the research and testimonios we received could not all be included here, we acknowledge the many voices and experiences that are deeply embedded in this work. We know that the overwhelming response we received through our CFP reflects the radical need for this work. Given that most of the pieces would not make it into this printed form, we decided to create and publish a blog on our website to directly, and more expediently, start publishing the urgent voices and work that Mother of Color activists and scholars are doing. We view the anthology as another venue—in addition to our blog, podcast, and presentations—through which we can continue collaborating with other Mothers of Color within and beyond the academy to work toward transformation and social justice.

We also recognize, however, that this volume can read as cisgendered, heteronormative, and focused on the able-bodied. In our CFP, we welcomed contributions from women (cis and trans) and nonbinary people, as well as "from asexual, bisexual, gay, intersex, lesbian, gender non-conforming, pansexual, trans, and queer individuals." We have had to think deeply about why we did not receive any submissions from these perspectives. Was it because of who we are and how we present to others? This points to a need to examine the complexities and contradictions of doing work that is intersectional, including sexuality, especially because our work builds on our Women of Color feminist foremothers, such as Audre Lorde and Cherríe Moraga, who forged the path as queer Mothers of Color.[6] In what remains of this introduction, we present our ofrenda, the Chicana M(other)work anthology.

Separation, Migration, State Violence, and Detention

Part 1 recognizes how state violence disproportionately affects Black and Chicana/Latina mothers, particularly through police brutality, and often separates them from their children and families through incarceration, deportation and detention, and migration. These testimonios are especially urgent in the context of Trump-era violence—both state-sanctioned and individual white supremacist—against families at the U.S.-Mexico border. **Katherine Maldonado**, a PhD student and former gang-affiliated Chicana teen mother of three, reflects on "resistance as an act of bravery" and the ways in which she mothered back against state violence and the racism and classism of the child protective system, which led to her three children being briefly removed from her custody. **Gabriela Corona Valencia** shares her testimonio on the violence her own mother experienced in El Salvador, where the secrets carried within were of rape, survival, and the consequential stories of relatives found across borders. Valencia bridges stories of her mother and herself through her own pregnancy termination.

In **Gretel H. Vera-Rosas's** essay, she combines research with testimonio by mapping three coordinates that include her grandmother's home, the San Diego–Tijuana border, and California State University, Dominguez Hills, to show how intergenerational mothering and immigrant experiences collide and manifest in her experiences as a Mother-Scholar. **Grace Gámez** examines how formerly incarcerated or convicted mothers respond to the extralegal nature of their punishments by adapting preexisting skills, framed as "fierce mothering / motherhood," that allow them to survive and challenge common-sense notions around "ideal" mothering. Fierce mothering is a social position and practice characterized by the emotionally and socially complex experiences these mothers encounter. Finally, **Hortencia Jiménez** and **Nereida Oliva** provide a lens on how Latina mothers in community college challenge, contend, and negotiate roles of mothering, welfare, migration, movement, teaching, and incarceration to highlight how they come to "understand, conceptualize, and embody" their experiences as Mothers of Color in academia.

Chicana/Latina/Women of Color Mother-Activists

The chapters in part 2 recognize the numerous ways in which Chicana/Latina and other Mothers of Color are actively organizing and leading the next generation. Activist movements tend to have mothers and caregivers of color at the forefront, and yet their stories are often overlooked. This section is launched with a testimonio by **Trina Greene Brown**, who contests the continued exclusion and marginalization of Black activist mothers in the national feminist movement. Brown illuminates her struggle to secure maternity leave and childcare accommodations from a major feminist nonprofit organization. Yet despite these contradictions within the feminist movement, Brown writes about how this inspired her work as founder of Parenting for Liberation. Similarly, the **Mother-Scholars of Color (MSOC)** provide a collective testimonio study that highlights how they, as mothers and doctoral students of Guatemalan, Indian, Iranian, and Mexican descents, navigate their identities in personal and professional spaces that do not fully acknowledge their multiple identities. Through a thematic analysis of their counter-narratives, they debunk deficit perspectives of MSOC and advocate for more inclusive practices in higher education.

This section also includes a piece by **Victoria Isabel Durán**, whose theoretical framework Mama Academic Liberadora Activista (MALA) presents a foundation in homemade theory for Mamas of Color dedicated to liberatory work as academics and activists. This concept is rooted in ancestral knowledge with a vision of hope. **Cristina Herrera** and **Larissa M. Mercado-López** make a coauthored contribution to further examine Chicana mothering. Both authors share and challenge the narrow views of Chicana mothering and othermothering within a hostile climate in academia to offer their "reimagined notions of mothering in ways that sustain one another, promote meaningful productivity, and nurture emotional empowerment." Finally, in **Verónica N. Vélez's** essay, she examines ALIANZA, a Los Angeles–based Latina (im)migrant mother group devoted to improving conditions for Chicanx/Latinx children in public schools. In this study, Vélez highlights the interconnectedness between ALIANZA members' motherhood and migration experiences as well as with their political agency.

Intergenerational Mothering

Part 3 shows how mothers and caregivers often bear the weight of upholding their families and examines how mothering can break forms of intergenerational trauma and violence. Intergenerational mothering also reflects on the spirituality of being in touch with our families' cultural practices that come from a long lineage of ancestors. Spirituality in all its complexities has a central place in this section, where *pláticas* (conversations) across generations are a conduit for knowledge. The first essay, by **Alma Itzé Flores**, offers a pedagogical tool to understand Chicana mother-daughter pedagogies. She shows how teaching and learning take place especially in how mothers practice *educación* and engage in spirituality to encourage, bolster, and hold up their daughters in their pursuits of higher learning.

Likewise, a powerful narrative spanning poetic discourse, teachings, learning, and bearing witness to generational change appears in **Andrea Garavito Martínez's** piece on Chicana mother-daughter digital *conexiones*. Garavito Martínez offers what we know to be familiar pedagogies of the home: phone calls, *chisme*, check-ins, and *enseñanzas* from our mothers that range from *recetas* over the phone to critical conversations about pursuing professoriat positions to continue a migratory journey to teach. Incorporating creative writing and Indigenous knowledge, **Irene Lara** places Indigeneity at the core of her piece, rather than as an afterthought, in her ofrenda of sacred pláticas with the lineage of matriarchs, her daughters, and herself, all through feminine teachings of *plantitas*. Sacred pláticas between four generations of women remind us that we can disrupt the split between the mind, body, spirit: "We can create a 'bodymindspirit' Borderlands that strengthens our mothering-daughtering relationships with ourselves and one another, birthing *curandera-guerrera* decolonial feminism conocimientos along the way." Additionally, **Gabriela Spears-Rico** takes us deep into her painful experiences of childhood sexual violence, giving birth, further violence, and *ceremonia* as she evokes her matrilineal lineage as inheritance passed down from her ancestors. Through research, poetry, and storytelling, Spears-Rico theorizes a decolonial Xicana P'urhépecha way of being and worldview that blends her labor as a mother, researcher, and professor in multiple spaces.

Loss, Reproductive Justice, and Holistic Pregnancy

Finally, part 4 highlights both the privileges and the challenges of mothers who can and cannot physically bear children, while also recognizing that not all women choose to have children. **Corina Benavides López** provides a testimonio to break the silence around adoption and dismantle what she calls "adoption oppression," challenging the sympathy and pity she receives from others when sharing that her son is adopted. Her story also challenges the notion that only "biology is family and love" through examples of how she is cocreating a family full of radical love and resistance. **Mara Chavez-Diaz's** testimonio disrupts the unspoken pain of miscarriage and the implications of the racialized medical industrial complex. Her chapter links environmental disaster and racism with the ways in which Women of Color's bodies are erased and deemed disposable, yet, in her piece, she offers a radical lens toward birth justice that involves a decolonizing practice.

Mothers of Color in Academia (MOCA) is an active student collective whose focus is to enforce policies of change to meet the needs of Mothers of Color on their campus. Using a Chicana feminist praxis, the coauthors share three anecdotes about their endless efforts—along with their children—to disrupt embedded patriarchy in academia through various forms of resistance, making the presence of Mothers of Color on the campus visible and transformative. Finally, **Rose G. Salseda** writes about navigating her first pregnancy and (still)birth of her first child during her graduate program. Salseda advocates for increased access to medical care and reproductive justice for Women of Color, particularly for those who also experience infant loss. At the same time, she offers insight into how she was able to use the research skills she acquired through graduate school to help her "cope with the life-altering experiences of pregnancy, birth, and death."

Each of these powerful chapters illuminates that

Chicana M(other)work is intergenerational.
Chicana M(other)work means carving space.
Chicana M(other)work means healing ourselves.
Chicana M(other)work is an imaginary.
Chicana M(other)work makes our labor visible.
Our labor is our prayer, our mothering is our offering.

Notes

1. Here we use the term "intersectional" to borrow from Kimberlé Crenshaw's (1991) work, in which she refers to the crossing of varying identitarian positions that Women of Color experience, including race, class, and gender.

2. We use the term "(im)migrants" because we recognize ourselves as migrants living within colonial borders.

3. The Ad Hoc Committee on Institutional Violence (Castañeda et al. 2014) authored an important call to action about sexual and gendered violence in the field of Chicano studies. They assert, "Institutional violence is built into the functioning of all institutions; it shows up as unequal power and may cause harm through a slow process. It is not always visible in a specific event but it is always present, sanctioning and perpetuating a hostile environment. The structuring of unjust social relations requires the use of institutional violence and continually calls upon it[,] maintaining and legitimizing structured domination" (108–9).

4. We define "collective resistance" as an organized collective effort to push against institutional policies and norms that oppress individuals who do not fit the white, male, middle-class, and straight culture of the academy.

5. In one important publication, "Opinion: How to Tackle the Childcare-Conference Conundrum," Rebecca M. Calisi Rodriguez and the Working Group of Mothers in Science (2018) outline a list of concrete suggestions to better support mothers and their families in science and academia at large. The incredible reception and wide circulation of the essay demonstrates the need for better resources and institutional change.

6. Audre Lorde, famously self-described as "black, lesbian, mother, warrior, poet," in her essay "Man Child: A Black Lesbian Feminist's Response" (1979) examines her queer mothering relationship with her then-teenage son. Cherríe Moraga (1997) published a moving poetic memoir about her pregnancy, the first three years of her son's life, and what it means to be a queer Chicana feminist mother in *Waiting in the Wings: Portrait of a Queer Motherhood*. More recently, the anthology *Revolutionary Mothering: Love on the Front Lines* (Gumbs, Martens, and Williams 2016)

features several powerful essays about queer mothering, including Alexis Pauline Gumbs's "M/other Ourselves: A Black Queer Feminist Genealogy for Radical Mothering."

References

Anzaldúa, Gloria. 1987. *Borderlands / La Frontera: The New Mestiza*. San Francisco: Aunt Lute Books.

Bell, Derrick. 1992. *Faces at the Bottom of the Well: The Permanence of Racism*. New York: Basic Books.

Bell, Derrick. 1995. "Who's Afraid of Critical Race Theory?" *University of Illinois Law Review*, no. 4, 893–910.

Booker, Marja. 2002. "Stories of Violence: Use of Testimony in a Support Group for Latin American Battered Women." In *Charting a New Course for Feminist Psychology*, edited by Lynn H. Collins, Michelle R. Dunlap, and Joan C. Chrisler, 307–21. Westport, CT: Praeger.

Caballero, Cecilia, Yvette Martínez-Vu, Judith C. Pérez-Torres, Michelle Téllez, and Christine Vega. 2017. "'Our Labor Is Our Prayer, Our Mothering Is Our Offering': A Chicana M(other)work Framework for Collective Resistance." *Chicana/Latina Studies: The Journal of MALCS* 16 (2): 44–75.

Calisi Rodriguez, Rebecca M., and the Working Group of Mothers in Science. 2018. "Opinion: How to Tackle the Childcare-Conference Conundrum." *Proceedings of the National Academy of Sciences of the United States of America* 115 (12): 2845–49, published ahead of print, March 5, 2018. http://www.pnas.org/content/early/2018/03/01/1803153115.

Castañeda, Antonia, Marie "Keta" Miranda, Marisol Moreno, Ana Clarissa Rojas Durazo, Audrey Silvestre, and Nadia Zepeda (The Ad Hoc Committee on Institutional Violence and Focused Issue Editors). 2014. "Ending Heteropatriarchal Institutional Violence in Chicano Studies: A Reflection on Our Path." *Chicana/Latina Studies: The Journal of MALCS* 13 (2): 104–17.

Castañeda, Mari, and Kirsten Lynn Isgro, eds. 2013. *Mothers in Academia*. New York: Columbia University Press.

Certeau, Michel de. 1984. *The Practice of Everyday Life*. Translated by Steven Rendall. Berkeley: University of California Press.

Collins, Patricia Hill. 1994. "Shifting the Center: Race, Class, and Feminist Theorizing about Motherhood." In *Mothering: Ideology, Experience, and*

Agency, edited by Evelyn Nakano Glenn, Grace Chang, and Linda Rennie Forcey, 45–66. New York: Routledge.

Collins, Patricia Hill. 2000. *Black Feminist Thought: Knowledge, Consciousness, and the Politics of Empowerment*. 2nd ed. New York: Routledge Press.

Crenshaw, Kimberlé Williams. 1991. "Mapping the Margins: Intersectionality, Identity Politics, and Violence Against Women of Color." *Stanford Law Review* 43 (6): 1241–99.

Cruz, Cynthia. 2006. "Testimonial Narratives of Queer Street Youth: Toward an Epistemology of a Brown Body." PhD diss., University of California, Los Angeles.

Delgado Bernal, Dolores. 1998. "Using a Chicana Feminist Epistemology in Educational Research." *Harvard Educational Review* 68:555–82.

Delgado Bernal, Dolores, Rebeca Burciaga, and Judith Flores Carmona. 2012. "Chicana/Latina Testimonios: Mapping the Methodological, Pedagogical, and Political." *Equity and Excellence in Education* 45 (3): 363–72.

Evans, Elrena, and Caroline Grant, eds. 2008. *Mama, PhD: Women Write about Motherhood and Academic Life*. New Brunswick, NJ: Rutgers University Press.

Flores Carmona, Judith, and Aymee Malena Luciano. 2014. "A Student-Teacher Testimonio: Reflexivity, Empathy, and Pedagogy." In *Crafting Critical Stories: Toward Pedagogies and Methodologies of Collaboration, Inclusion and Voice*, edited by Judith Flores Carmona and Kristen V. Luschen, 75–92. New York: Peter Lang.

García, Alma M. 1997. "Voices of Women of Color: Redefining Women's Studies." *Race, Gender, and Class* 4 (2): 11–28.

Gaspar de Alba, Alicia. 2014. *[Un]framing the "Bad Woman": Sor Juana, Malinche, Coyolxauhqui and Other Rebels with a Cause*. Austin: University of Texas Press.

Gumbs, Alexis Pauline. 2010. "We Can Learn to Mother Ourselves: The Queer Survival of Black Feminism 1968–1996." PhD diss., Duke University, Durham, NC.

Gumbs, Alexis Pauline, China Martens, and Mai'a Williams, eds. 2016. *Revolutionary Mothering: Love on the Front Lines*. Oakland, CA: PM Press.

Harris, Angela P., and Carmen G. González. 2013. Introduction to *Presumed Incompetent: The Intersections of Race and Class for Women in Academia*. Edited by Gabriella Gutiérrez y Muhs, Yolanda Flores Niemann,

Carmen G. González, and Angela P. Harris, 1–16. Boulder: University Press of Colorado.

Hernandez, Alexandra. 2017. "El Rebozo." *Chicana/Latina Studies: The Journal of MALCS* 17 (1): 126–27.

Lara, Irene. 2003. "Decolonizing Latina Spiritualities and Sexualities: Healing Practices in Las Américas." PhD diss., University of California, Berkeley.

Latina Feminist Group. 2001. *Telling to Live: Latina Feminist Testimonios*. Durham, NC: Duke University Press.

Lorde, Audre. 1979. "Man Child: A Black Lesbian Feminist's Response." *Conditions: Four* 2 (1): 30–61.

Luna, Jennie, and Martha Galeana. 2016. "Remembering Coyolxauhqui as a Birthing Text." *Regeneración Tlacuilolli: UCLA Raza Studies Journal* 1 (2): 7–32.

Mason, Mary Ann, Nicholas H. Wolfinger, and Marc Goulden. 2013. *Do Babies Matter? Gender and Family in the Ivory Tower*. New Brunswick, NJ: Rutgers University Press.

McClaurin, Irma. 1999. "Salvaging Lives in the African Diaspora: Anthropology, Ethnography, and Women's Narratives." *Souls: A Critical Journal of Black Politics, Culture and Society* 1 (3): 25–39.

Montoya, Margaret E. 1994. "Máscaras, Trenzas, y Greñas: Un/masking the Self While Un/Braiding Latina Stories and Legal Discourse." *Harvard Women's Law Journal* 17:185–220.

Moraga, Cherríe. 1993. *The Last Generation*. Boston: South End Press.

Moraga, Cherríe. 1997. *Waiting in the Wings: Portrait of a Queer Motherhood*. Ithaca, NY: Firebrand Books.

Pérez Huber, Lindsay. 2009. "Disrupting Apartheid of Knowledge: 'Testimonio' as Methodology in Latina/o Critical Race Research in Education." *International Journal of Qualitative Studies in Education* 22 (6): 639–54.

Pérez Huber, Lindsay, María C. Malagón, Brianna R. Ramirez, Lorena Camargo Gonzalez, Alberto Jimenez, and Verónica N. Vélez. 2015. *Still Falling Through the Cracks: Revisiting the Latina/o Educational Pipeline*. CSRC Research Report 19. Los Angeles: UCLA Chicano Studies Research Center.

Ryu, Mikyung. 2010. *Minorities in Higher Education: 24th Status Report*. Washington, DC: American Council on Education.

Sandoval, Gabriela. 2010. "Motherwork Revisited: A Critical Personal Narrative by a Queer Chicana Choice Mama." Paper presented at the American Sociological Association Annual Meeting, Atlanta, GA, August 14, 2010.

Snyder, Thomas D., and Sally A. Dillow. 2010. *Digest of Education Statistics 2009*. NCES 2010–013. Washington, DC: National Center for Education Statistics, Institute of Education Sciences.

Solórzano, Daniel G. 1998. "Critical Race Theory, Race and Gender Microaggressions, and the Experience of Chicana and Chicano Scholars." *International Journal of Qualitative Studies in Education* 11 (1): 121–36.

Solórzano, Daniel G., and Tara J. Yosso. 2006. *Leaks in the Chicana and Chicano Educational Pipeline*. Latino Policy and Issues Brief 13. Los Angeles: UCLA Chicano Studies Research Center.

Téllez, Michelle. 2005. "Doing Research at the Borderlands: Notes from a Chicana Feminist Ethnographer." *Chicana/Latina Studies: The Journal of MALCS* 4 (2): 46–71.

Téllez, Michelle. 2011. "*Mi Madre, Mi Hija y Yo*: Chicana Mothering Through Memory, Culture and Place." In *Latina/Chicana Mothering*, edited by Dorsía Smith Silva, 57–67. Toronto: Demeter Press.

Téllez, Michelle. 2013. "Lectures, Evaluations, and Diapers: Navigating the Terrains of Chicana Single Motherhood in the Academy." *Feminist Formations* 25 (3): 79–97.

Téllez, Michelle. 2014. "Personal Is Political: Chicana Motherwork." *Feminist Wire*, March 6, 2014. https://thefeministwire.com/2014/03/chicana-motherwork/.

Vega, Christine. 2016. "Coyolxauhqui: Challenging Patriarchy by Re-imagining her Birth Story." *InterActions: UCLA Journal of Education and Information Studies* 12 (1). https://escholarship.org/uc/item/4f47x7bh.

Villenas, Sofia, Francisca E. Godinez, Dolores Delgado Bernal, and C. Alejandra Elenes. 2006. "Chicanas/Latinas Building Bridges: An Introduction." In *Chicana/Latina Education in Everyday Life: Feminista Perspectives on Pedagogy and Epistemology*, edited by Dolores Delgado Bernal, C. Alejandra Elenes, Francisca E. Godinez, and Sofia Villenas, 1–9. Albany: SUNY Press.

Wolfers, Justin. 2016. "A Family-Friendly Policy That's Friendliest to Male Professors." *New York Times*, June 24, 2016. http://www.nytimes.com/2016/06/26/business/tenure-extension-policies-that-put-women-at-a-disadvantage.html.

Wolfinger, Nicholas H. 2013. "For Female Scientists, There's No Good Time to Have Children." *Atlantic*, July 29, 2013. http://www.theatlantic.com/sexes /archive/2013/07/for-female-scientists-theres-no-good-time-to-have -children/278165/.

Yosso, Tara J., William A. Smith, Miguel Ceja, and Daniel G. Solórzano. 2009. "Critical Race Theory, Racial Microaggressions, and Campus Racial Climate for Latina/o Undergraduates." *Harvard Educational Review* 79 (4): 659–90.

Part I

Separation, Migration, State Violence, and Detention

Gang-Affiliated Chicana Teen Momma Against Systemic Violence

A Testimonio Challenging Dominant Discourse Through Academic Bravery

Katherine Maldonado

For twenty-three years, my Brown mestiza body has resided amid poverty, racism, and patriarchy.[1] As a fifteen-year-old Chicana, I experienced intersectional forms of violence that pushed me to believe that I was a teenager incapable of creating life. Society and its institutions taught me that a Brown woman's body is ignorant and only dwells in the head. I slowly learned, however, that the body is smart and reacts equally viscerally to events from the imagination as to real events (Anzaldúa 1987). I position my Brown body as an agent and a producer of knowledge because the contemplation of my body is essential in the development and evaluation of an epistemology of Chicana thought and culture (Cruz 2001). This orientation allows me to value my knowledge. Each violent act that I have experienced throughout my socialization as a gang affiliate, a mother, and an academic enables me to show how my body resists the forms of violence I continuously live through. For this work, I focus on state violence and how my children and my pursuit of education inspire the bravery in me to resist that violence.

My experience and struggle with the "matrix of domination" (racism, classism, sexism) gives me what Gloria Anzaldúa calls the gift of *la facultad*, the "capacity to see in surface phenomena the meaning of deeper realities, to see the deep structure below the surface" (Anzaldúa 1987, 38; Martinez 2002, 168).[2] The facultad engenders an oppositional consciousness that provides a deeper understanding of intersectional identities of Women of Color. The objectification of my body as a young mother activated my own facultad to understand how violence has affected my life trajectory. As a young mother, my multiple identities triggered physical violence, gang violence, symbolic violence (i.e., controlling images and negative stereotypes), and state violence via the education and child welfare systems. I have experienced, and continue to experience and resist, this institutional violence as a student in high school, then in college, and now as a doctoral student while parenting three young children.

The focus of this chapter is the state-sponsored institutional violence perpetrated by the child welfare system. My testimonio highlights the interactions of institutions that exert structural violence through processes that often stigmatize and perpetuate violence gradually across the life trajectory. In these social processes, Chicanx children are disproportionately represented in child welfare systems in the United States. Child welfare agents often negatively evaluate Chicanx culture (Church, Gross, and Baldwin 2005) and stigmatize Chicana mothers and their families. Thus, I argue that being a Chicana mother, and specifically a teen mother, who has been negatively stereotyped and who has experienced structural violence both systemically and indirectly, I have resisted and responded to these structurally violent conditions at the individual and collective levels of consciousness.

I have learned to navigate multiple cultures and to adopt a mode of thinking in which "nothing is thrust out, the good, the bad, and the ugly, nothing ever rejected, nothing abandoned" (Anzaldúa 1987, 79). This mode of thinking gives *nacimiento* to a phenomenon that

I call "mothering resistance as an act of bravery," a process in which motherhood, rather than debilitating, drives resistance to oppression. Because I was a gang-affiliated Chicana teen mother, society (e.g., researchers, media, educators, community, and even family) tried to diminish my experiences, label me deviant, stigmatize me, and ignore my mental, emotional, physical, and intellectual needs. Yet, all this occurred in the context of motherhood, a role that calls for a woman to be a nurturer, protector, leader, and model. As a mother fulfills this role for her children, she too benefits, because the drive to succeed strengthens and nurtures her drive to challenge multisided forms of violence. In this testimonio, I show how the beautiful yet painful struggle of motherhood fuels resistance and courage when all odds are against a Chicana mother.

Testimonio Methodology

My experiences as a Chicana growing up in South-Central Los Angeles afforded me particular facultades that have helped me navigate the social realities stemming from institutional and interpersonal forms of violence. For Anzaldúa (1987), the facultad is a gift that allows you to see deeper social realities, a fully embodied epistemological process that gathers information from context and relations. Thus, a Brown body is central in any consideration of an epistemology of Women of Color (Cruz 2001). If I am not able to transform my lived experiences into knowledge and use them as a process to unveil new knowledge, I will never be able to participate rigorously in a dialogue as a process of learning and knowing (Freire 1970). Knowledge and power work together to regulate the things we can and also to create new perceptions about our social actions and thoughts, which in turn create cultural norms.

Testimonio moves us into a realm of knowledge creation that is grounded in lived experience; it is a method that Women of Color use that "exposes brutality, disrupts silencing, and builds solidarity" (Delgado Bernal, Burciaga, and Flores Carmona 2012, 363; Anzaldúa 1990). This method was first used to communicate the sociopolitical forces in Latin America, and it continues to be used as a political tool involving a critical reflection on personal experience to construct social change (Behar 1993; Burgos-Debray 1984). Testimonio is a methodological process that requires one to recover previous experiences and unfold them into narratives that disclose personal, political, and social realities (Delgado Bernal, Burciaga, and Flores Carmona 2012). To emphasize, the method "evokes the process by which we contemplate thoughts and feelings, often in isolation and through difficult times" (Latina Feminist Group 2001, 1). I kept my experiences in my memory, then I wrote them down and stored them in safe places, waiting for the appropriate moment to return to them for review and analysis, to speak out and share them with others, and this testimonio is certainly an appropriate moment.

My testimonio highlights the injustices I have suffered and the effects they have had in my life. The recollection and recapturing of my journey enables me to transform my past experiences, create a new present, and enhance the future (Brabeck 2001; Cienfuegos and Monelli 1983). Since my "body holds the stress and tensions of my daily life, I am sharing the stories of body breakdowns" (Latina Feminist Group 2001, 12). My personal experiences navigating the child welfare system reveal an epistemology of truths that emphasizes how I came to understand violence as a continuous process that does not desist, even as I find myself in a position of power and privilege as a student in the University of California system. As Sofia Villenas (1996, 726) states, "This story demonstrates that some Chicanas do not move from marginalization to new positions of privilege associated with university affiliation, as if switching from one seat to another in the bus." What is certain is that testimonio is not meant to be hidden nor kept secret. The objective is to bring to light a marginalized point of view and, in the process, express the need for an urgent call for action; testimonio is intentional and political.

The Personal Is Political

I have spent many weeks thinking about the appropriate ways to write a testimonio in which I share the painful and beautiful experience of my life as a mother while also bringing awareness of institutional injustices to an academic audience. I struggle every time I start, and my mind goes blank. I become paralyzed because I am unsure of the words that best describe my journey of violence and resistance. The stories I share capture moments that I have yet to fully heal from, moments that scarred me for life: from the joyful times of giving birth and nurturing my young children, to the agonizing times I endured legal separation from them, when my soul felt dead, and the only thing that kept me from pulling the trigger of a gun to my head was my children's existence. In this testimonio, I write about unspeakable wounds. I write this story crying, with anger and with hate, but most of all with love and passion.

Teen Mother in the Hood

It was January 2010, two weeks before my sixteenth birthday, when my mother decided to take me to the doctor and introduce me to birth control. Our visit went well, and before we left, a nurse practitioner wrote a prescription and gave it to my mother. A few minutes later, and without formal introduction, a different nurse came into the waiting room, grabbed the handwritten prescription, and ripped it into tiny pieces. In a loud tone, she said, "You can't get on birth control. You are already pregnant." I felt confused. I did not know how to react. I heard my heartbeat pound in my ears, and I became scared. The tears I shed signaled two opposing feelings: I was afraid, but I was also happy. My mom looked at me with anger and said, "Te lo dije, cabrona." I had failed the only person to whom I had always looked for approval. We scheduled my first ultrasound amid "Awwws" and "Congratulations! You are such a baby." The ride home was silent. I held my head down as my mom radiated anger and frustration. After arriving home, I locked myself in my room, and for the first time I touched my stomach. "How could there be someone living in me right now? What am I going to do with my life?"

I was fifteen years old and two months pregnant. I did not feel ready to raise a child but was never given the option of abortion. During my first ultrasound, I not only saw a small peanut-shaped body, but also heard a heartbeat. I came to the realization that something was growing inside me. I was excited to be afforded the opportunity to be a mother, to shape and mold another being, and I was also fearful because I was a teenager with nothing to offer but love. This realization pushed me to do everything possible to give my child, a son, what he deserved. I wanted to challenge the stereotypes that everyone had applied to me. During this time, I began questioning how education could be a vehicle to offer my son a different life from the one I was living.

At my school, rumors about me and my pregnancy went around. Many people congratulated me, while others looked at me with despair. School friends asked if I was going to leave high school and go to the "pregnant school" (i.e., continuation school), where a lot of the women who became pregnant attended. Why was I not seen as a "regular" student who could succeed alongside my peers? I was seen as a "fuckup" even before I got pregnant. I was a member of a female gang. My partner was also a gang member. We both engaged in heavy drug use and violence.

My life involved navigating the streets, which included police harassment and rival gang approaches. I remember getting patted down by police officers every time I walked to the store, with my huge belly, to get food to satisfy my late-night cravings. One time, when I was nine months pregnant, walking home with my partner from school, eight young men approached us. One person pulled out a gun. They all surrounded us. It was the first time I feared not for myself but for my son. Incidents like these made me hyperaware of my identity as a young mother (to be) and gang affiliate.

I woke up on a Sunday at three in the morning with pain. I lasted approximately forty hours in labor and gave birth to a healthy boy. I cried and held him in my arms. His arrival changed me completely. He gave me a motivation that I never felt before. I was learning how to be a mother, and it was the hardest experience of my life. During his first-week checkup, I spoke on the phone with my grandmother, who lives in Sonora, Mexico. She told me, "Mija, ya quiero ir a conocerlo a mi primer bisnieto." I responded, "Pues abuelita, recuperese para que venga. Necesito de su ayuda." One week later, on September 17, 2010, my grandmother passed away. My grandmother never got to meet my son, but that last conversation I had with her reassured me that I was capable of raising him.

In the midst of this emotional roller coaster, I went back to school two weeks after my son's birth. Looking back, I wonder if anyone questioned my mental health at the time. I was a new mother, trying to learn how to function with only three hours of sleep per night, accept my grandmother's death, and catch up and keep up with schoolwork. My struggles were intense. On the one hand, I became numb to my pain, which meant that I put off dealing with it until later to cope with the demands of daily life. School became a place of distraction, where I could feel capable and focused. Keeping busy enabled me to get by. My son became my primary motivation; I gave everything, my all for him. I got straight As in high school, became involved in volunteer work, took advanced classes at the local community college, became high school president, and was accepted to nine universities, including UCLA.

Many scholars have constructed teenage pregnancy as a "problem," strongly pathologizing young mothers (Cherrington and Breheny 2005) and treating their pregnancy as a disease that requires treatment (Woodward, Fergusson, and Horwood 2001). Consequently, these academics have shaped a narrative that strongly stigmatizes the process of birthing for Latina mothers. Today, stereotypes of "bad mothers" include the teenage mother, welfare mother, drug-using mother, gang-affiliated mother, and, to a lesser extent, the single mother and working mother (Moloney et al. 2011), all of which I fall under. As if this were not enough, gang-involved Latinas, whose stories of stigma often outpace empirical research, face added consequences for being gang affiliated while also being mothers (Moloney et al. 2011). As part of this racialized group, Latinas are more likely to face negative stereotypes if they become teen mothers (López and Chesney-Lind 2014). Other scholars, however, have conducted research showing that motherhood can be positively transformative for young women. For example, it can drive mothers either to recommit to or engage dedicatedly for the first time in their education (Moloney et al. 2011; Angwin and Kamp 2007).

"Catching a Case" at UCLA

In July 2015, I was twenty-one years old, enrolled as an undergraduate, and the mother of two boys (ages five and one). I was in the middle of a GRE study group at UCLA when I received a phone call. My partner had taken our one-year-old son to the UCLA hospital because of an accidental iron burn. He said, "They are investigating us. The police are asking questions. You need to come now. They think we burned him purposely." I left my study group, and as soon as I arrived, I was interviewed by the doctors and police officers. I told them exactly what had occurred. My son had gotten burned by an iron that had accidentally fallen onto his leg while both boys were on the bed. When I had taken him to the doctor, they had wanted to charge me $481 because our health insurance was inactive. So instead, I had taken him to his great-grandmother's house, and she had cared for his burn. The following day, I took my son back to his childcare center at UCLA, but the teachers there stated that he could not come back without a doctor's note. For that reason, my partner took our son to the hospital; we knew that they would give a doctor's note even though we did not have health insurance.

I was frustrated that the teachers, hospital staff, and police thought we might have purposely harmed our child. While at the hospital, I was followed by university police the entire time. I asked the officers many times why we were being investigated. One officer noted my frustration as I was questioning a doctor about discrimination against us. She said, "It is not because you are Hispanic, but we need to protect the children." I continued questioning. What was the actual reason that this accident warranted a referral to Child Protective Services? They released us from the hospital, and I thought the nightmare was over, but it was only the beginning.

We arrived home to our UCLA family housing at 2 a.m. Soon after, Los Angeles County sheriffs knocked on our door. I opened, and the first thing I noticed was that they had their hands on their guns. They interviewed us about the iron accident. One of the first questions they asked was about our gang affiliations. Again, I asked myself, what really made this accident worthy of CPS involvement? After the sheriffs left, university police arrived an hour later to investigate because they also had to report the incident. At 4 a.m., a social worker arrived and informed us that he was an emergency social worker who was called into situations where children might be in immediate danger. He, too, interviewed us. We explained everything in detail, and the social worker saw that the home was clean, the children were sound asleep, and nothing in the home environment was abnormal. He explained that the investigation was standard procedure and that our case would be closed if no evidence indicated a threat to our child.

Two weeks later, I received a visit from another social worker, an Asian woman with only six months of experience in the field. She asked me loaded questions such as "How do you parent, being that you are so young?" and "What do you think about your partner's criminal record?" (which, by the way, involved only one minor incident). In addition, she reported false information about our case to her agency, including that we struck "the children with belts and hangers. These neglectful acts on the part of the child's parents endanger the child's physical health, safety and wellbeing, create a detrimental home environment" (Code 300, page 4 of case). In what was this caseworker really interested? The safety of the children or our backgrounds as individuals and our gang affiliations?

On August 19, 2015, I received a call from the UCLA childcare center informing me that police officers were taking my children for inspection. I did not know why that was happening. Without my consent, they were taking my children. For what? They conducted a full inspection of their bodies, with x-rays, and a mental health assessment. Everyone agreed that the children were healthy and that the burn was accidental. The officers told me, "You'll be good. The kids look all happy and good. We've seen really worse cases." I remember feeling relief, telling myself that this was just protocol. When everything was over, and I said, "Okay, kids, we're getting ready to go," the social worker said, "Ms. Maldonado, the kids are being placed under foster care. My boss and I have ordered an emergency removal."

At that moment, my heart dropped. I could not believe what I was hearing. For weeks, I had believed that all these procedures were simply part of the protocol so that they could confirm that my kids were safe with me. I cried, telling the social worker, "How could you do this to them? They are not safe with anyone besides me." I wanted to get on my knees, to beg her not to take my children. They had never been away from me. They had never been under a stranger's care. She took my children as they were crying. I tried holding a straight face and told my five-year-old son to please take care of himself and his brother and never to separate from each other. They both looked scared, but I had to show them strength so that they could walk away feeling okay.

I could not believe that my children had been taken away from me after everything I had done to be a loving mother, dedicating my entire life so that my children wouldn't encounter the unsafe streets I had navigated, so that they could have a quality education and everything they needed. As we drove home, I asked myself, What did I do wrong? Where did I fail as a mother? Why was this happening to me? My children did not deserve to go through this. They were being attacked instead of protected. I got home and curled up in a corner, grabbing my knees tight into a fetal position. I cried. I pulled my hair. I wanted to die, but I thought about my kids the entire night. How could they be sleeping in a foster home when their beds were at home for them? How could the social worker and others rip away my parental rights when I had birthed those children and done all the things required of a mother. My educational achievements meant nothing. My soul felt dead. I was angry toward the system because its power hurt my children and me. The system had failed us yet again. And this time, it felt undefeatable.

A few days later, I wrote the following in my journal during the court hearing: "My professor just led a prayer in the middle of this place. As I hugged my children tight, he prayed for my family and all the families fighting for custody. I see some mothers crying, black and Brown kids running around. I know what I am feeling right now is not something new, as I see others grieving the same way, but why are we going through this? Why is this floor full of people that look like the neighbors I grew up with in South Central? I wish I could hug all the children, all the mothers and tell them WE will be okay, but the reality is that we will not. My lawyer just told me that what I am being accused of has been taken to another level, and they want to take full custody and place my kids under adoption. What have I done wrong to go through this? Is there really a god looking after me? Will the prayer be heard? At this moment, I feel hate, and abandoned, as if a god truly did not exist for me. It's like hate has been injected in to my veins, and I think about running away to escape, but I can't. And at this moment my skin has absorbed too many tears."

I presented evidence to show that my partner and I were good parents, but the case continued for six months.[3] Thankfully, I had a public defender who believed in me and fought for me to regain custody. I will never forget this lawyer's words in the court hearing: "Your honor, these teen parents come from the bottom. Look at the mother; she is now at UCLA. They deserve to be with their children." It was with her help that all the evidence I presented enabled me to regain custody, albeit with conditions (obtain drug testing, participate in counseling, and attend parenting classes). Soon after, I found out that I was pregnant with my third child. It was emotionally and practically challenging and traumatizing to meet the case conditions while being pregnant. The judge ordered that the children's father, my partner, move out of the home. Later, over time, I realized that I could no longer continue a relationship with the father of my children. I became and have learned how to be a single mother of three boys.

Parents whose children are involved with the child welfare system are largely poor and of color (Lee 2016); however, even parents with college degrees are vulnerable to child welfare involvement if they cannot achieve middle-class status. Approximately 60 percent of Latina teen mothers live below the poverty line, and 69 percent still live in poverty after their children reach the age of three (National Campaign 2012). Consequently, nearly two-thirds of teen mothers receive public assistance (National Campaign 2012). Additionally, the children of teen parents are twice as likely to be placed in foster care as children born to older parents (National Campaign 2012), and ethnically diverse children are assessed more punitively (Church, Gross, and Baldwin 2005). "The differential treatment of ethnically diverse children, as manifested through more frequent removal of these children from their homes, is largely the result of unwarranted, inaccurate, and racist assumptions, held by child welfare workers, judges, and others in the system, of parental inadequacy and family instability" (Close 1983, 14). Whether overt or covert, institutional discrimination is a major driving force behind the unequal distribution of children's (and thus their parents') life chances (Church, Gross, and Baldwin 2005).

A Chicana's Academic Bravery

Despite graduating from UCLA and gaining acceptance into a PhD program, I continue to face, and thus must resist, state violence. The surveillance I experienced as a teen mother persists, as every day I fear that my children will accidentally fall, and I will "catch a case" with child welfare again. My current experiences as an educated Chicana show that Brown bodies are socially controlled. I cannot fight this control by hiding. I cannot survive poverty alone; I rely on the state for support. I cannot stand up for myself and others with silence. So I consciously choose to put my body under surveillance by the same institutions that have marginalized me. My "body is a map for oppression, a map of institutional violence and stress, of exclusion, objectification, and abuse" (Latina Feminist Group 2001, 12). My involvement with the child welfare system reflects what Michel Foucault (1975, 198) calls panopticism; I have existed under "an organization in depth of surveillance and control." I have internalized this "unnoticeable" disciplinary power; this self-surveillance controls my life. Thus, I write to raise consciousness about the ways in which Chicana mothers are caught up in systems of power, systems in which our Brown bodies are socially controlled.

Relative to other racial/ethnic groups, including other Latinx, Chicanx have low educational attainment. For every 100 Chicanx in the educational pipeline, 60 will receive a high school diploma; 11, a bachelor's degree; 3, a graduate degree; and 0.2, a doctoral degree (Yosso 2006a, 2006b). The numbers for mothers are even lower. Among all ethnic groups, only 40 percent of teen mothers receive a high school diploma. Less than 2 percent of all teens who have a baby before eighteen ever graduate college (National Campaign 2012). Among women who have children after enrolling in community college, 61 percent fail to attain their degrees (National Campaign 2012). These statistics hint at the struggles involved in academic achievement for Chicanx and mothers. They do not reveal, however, how we Chicana mothers manage to succeed educationally despite the odds against us. Though we constantly face obstacles, we do not halt our educational journey. We stand strong so that our children will not face what we had to. Thus, "Motherwork goes beyond maintaining the family, securing the survival of one's own biological kin. It also involves maintaining one's own survival and the survival, empowerment, and identity of a mother's racial/ethnic community" (Caballero et al. 2017, 47).

Conclusion

In the telling of my story, I reveal an experience of structural violence, a process far too complex to ignore the resistance I responded with. The injustices I experienced were not caused by my own failings but by systemic biases about who I am. The system's biases shaped the way I was/am treated and perpetuate intergenerational inequalities in that the harder I have to work to protect myself and my children against those biases, the more my life chances and those of my children are curtailed. My body is a constant reminder that knowledge fully saturated with history and social life is driven by resistance (Cruz 2001). This epistemological orientation challenges the historical and ideological representations of Chicana mothers (and other Mothers of Color) as "careless" parents who choose to raise children in poverty and prefer to depend on welfare. As one who has been labeled an "unfit" mother and a "risk" to my children, I want to interrogate the social relations of power and track the abuse I encounter. I am tired of being scarred and of witnessing the scarring of people I hold dear to my heart. This testimonio has helped me unveil the workings of power in institutional cultures (specifically, in the child welfare system), its human costs, and how individual people—in this case, Chicana mothers—can and do overcome the ravages of power dynamics and abuses (Latina Feminist Group 2001, 14).

For centuries, writers have drawn from traumatic life experiences for inspiration, as a means of transformation and healing (Baker and Mazza 2004). Writing about my life forces me to ask, "What is the meaning of it all?" (Wakefield 1990, 18). While I have no precise definition of what it means to be coherent, understandable, or meaningful in writing about my emotional upheaval (Baker and Mazza 2004), writing this testimonio has been a source of liberation for me. It has been not only liberating in the process of telling, but also political in its production of awareness, because there is a revolutionary aspect of literacy—in this case, knowing the way things are (Reyes and Rodriguez 2012; Freire 1970). By sharing my personal struggles and exposing my vulnerabilities, I tell you about the multiple worlds I inhabit. This transformational resistance demonstrates my desire for social justice, as I negotiate and struggle with social structures and create meaning from interactions to engage in a praxis that influences individual and collective change (Solórzano and Delgado Bernal 2001). I will always be a woman of wounds, full of scars, with reminders of those who have hurt me. Yet, I am also and will always be a brave Chicana mother. Every day, my children wake up to kiss my scars, and in so doing, they remind me that bravery is activated through love.

Notes

1. Mestiza refers to a woman whose identity is a product of at least two cultures (Anzaldúa 1987).
2. The "matrix of domination" is a theoretical approach to understanding domination by exploring the interlocking systems of oppression related to race, class, and gender, among other forms of marginalized identities (Collins 2002).
3. The evidence included letters of support from professors, former teachers, mentors, and employers (everyone who had witnessed my parenting); parent-teacher conference reports from my children's school to show that no concerns about my parenting had been reported; and medical records to show that I had provided my children proper medical care.

References

Angwin, Jennifer, and Annelies Kamp. 2007. "Policy Hysteria in Action: Teenage Parents at Secondary School in Australia." In *Learning from the Margins: Young Women, Social Exclusion and Education*, edited by Julie McLeod and Andrea C. Allard, 95–107. London: Routledge.

Anzaldúa, Gloria. 1987. *Borderlands / La Frontera: The New Mestiza*. San Francisco: Aunt Lute Books.

Anzaldúa, Gloria, ed. 1990. *Making Face, Making Soul / Haciendo Caras: Creative and Critical Perspectives by Feminists of Color*. San Francisco: Aunt Lute Books.

Baker, Kathleen Connolly, and Nicholas Mazza. 2004. "The Healing Power of Writing: Applying the Expressive / Creative Component of Poetry Therapy." *Journal of Poetry Therapy* 17 (3): 141–54.

Behar, Ruth. 1993. *Translated Woman: Crossing the Border with Esperanza's Story*. Boston: Beacon.

Brabeck, Kalina. 2001. "Testimonio: Bridging Feminist Ethics with Activist Research to Create New Spaces of Collectivity." Paper presented at Bridging the Gap: Feminisms and Participatory Action Research Conference, Boston College, Newton, Massachusetts, June 22–24, 2001.

Burgos-Debray, Elisabeth, ed. 1984. *I, Rigoberta Menchú: An Indian Woman in Guatemala*. London: Verso.

Caballero, Cecilia, Yvette Martínez-Vu, Judith C. Pérez-Torres, Michelle Téllez, and Christine Vega. 2017. "'Our Labor Is Our Prayer, Our Mothering Is Our Offering': A Chicana M(other)work Framework for Collective Resistance." *Chicana/Latina Studies: The Journal of MALCS* 16 (2): 44–75.

Cherrington, Jane, and Mary Breheny. 2005. "Politicizing Dominant Discursive Constructions About Teenage Pregnancy: Re-locating the Subject as Social." *Health* 9 (1): 89–111.

Church, Wesley T., Emma R. Gross, and Joshua Baldwin. 2005. "Maybe Ignorance Is Not Always Bliss: The Disparate Treatment of Hispanics Within the Child Welfare System." *Children and Youth Services Review* 27 (12): 1279–92.

Cienfuegos, Ana Julia, and Cristina Monelli. 1983. "The Testimony of Political Repression as a Therapeutic Instrument." *American Journal of Orthopsychiatry* 53 (1): 43–51.

Close, John Sylvester. 1983. "A Study of the Development of Linear Patterning Among Young Economically Disadvantaged Children of Three Ethnic Groups." PhD diss., University of Connecticut, 1976. Ann Arbor, MI: University Microfilms International.

Collins, Patricia Hill. 2002. *Black Feminist Thought: Knowledge, Consciousness, and the Politics of Empowerment*. New York: Routledge.

Cruz, Cynthia. 2001. "Toward an Epistemology of a Brown Body." *International Journal of Qualitative Studies in Education* 14 (5): 657–69.

Delgado Bernal, Dolores, Rebeca Burciaga, and Judith Flores Carmona. 2012. "Chicana/Latina Testimonios: Mapping the Methodological, Pedagogical, and Political." *Equity and Excellence in Education* 45 (3): 363–72.

Foucault, Michel. 1975. *Discipline and Punish: The Birth of the Prison.* Translated from the French by Alan Sheridan. London: Penguin.

Freire, Paulo. 1970. *Pedagogy of the Oppressed.* New York: Herder and Herder.

Harding, Sandra. 1991. *Whose Science? Whose Knowledge? Thinking from Women's Lives.* Ithaca, NY: Cornell University Press.

Latina Feminist Group. 2001. *Telling to Live: Latina Feminist Testimonios.* Durham, NC: Duke University Press.

Lee, Tina. 2016. "Processes of Racialization in New York City's Child Welfare System." *City and Society* 28 (3): 279–97.

López, Vera A., and Meda Chesney-Lind. 2014. "Latina Girls Speak Out: Stereotypes, Gender and Relationship Dynamics." *Latino Studies* 12 (4): 527–49.

Martínez, Theresa A. 2002. "The Double-Consciousness of Du Bois and the 'Mestiza Consciousness' of Anzaldúa." *Race, Gender and Class* 9 (4): 158–76.

Moloney, Molly, Geoffrey P. Hunt, Karen Joe-Laidler, and Kathleen Mackenzie. 2011. "Young Mother (in the) Hood: Gang Girls' Negotiation of New Identities." *Journal of Youth Studies* 14 (1): 1–19.

National Campaign to Prevent Teen and Unplanned Pregnancy. 2012. *Teen Pregnancy and Childbearing Among Latina Teens.* Washington, DC: National Campaign to Prevent Teen and Unplanned Pregnancy.

National Women's Law Center and Mexican American Legal Defense and Educational Fund. 2009. *Listening to Latinas: Barriers to High School Graduation.* Washington, DC: National Women's Law Center and Mexican American Legal Defense and Educational Fund.

Reyes, Kathryn Blackmer, and Julia E. Curry Rodríguez. 2012. "*Testimonio*: Origins, Terms, and Resources." *Equity and Excellence in Education* 45 (3): 525–38.

Solórzano, Daniel G., and Dolores Delgado Bernal. 2001. "Examining Transformational Resistance Through a Critical Race and LatCrit Theory Framework: Chicana and Chicano Students in an Urban Context." *Urban Education* 36:308–42.

Villenas, Sofia. 1996. "The Colonizer/Colonized Chicana Ethnographer: Identity, Marginalization, and Co-optation in the Field." *Harvard Educational Review* 66 (4): 711–31.

Wakefield, Dan. 1990. *The Story of Your Life: Writing a Spiritual Autobiography.* Boston: Beacon Press.

Woodward, Lianne, David M. Fergusson, and L. John Horwood. 2001. "Risk Factors and Life Processes Associated with Teenage Pregnancy: Results of a Prospective Study from Birth to 20 Years." *Journal of Marriage and the Family* 63 (4): 1170–84.

Yosso, Tara J. 2006a. "Madres por la Educación: Community Cultural Wealth at Southside Elementary." In *Critical Race Counterstories Along the Chicana/Chicano Educational Pipeline*, 21–56. New York: Routledge.

Yosso, Tara J. 2006b. "Why Use Critical Race Theory and Counterstorytelling to Analyze the Chicana/o Educational Pipeline." In *Critical Race Counterstories Along the Chicana/Chicano Educational Pipeline*, 1–20. New York: Routledge.

2

Aquí Se Respira Lucha

A Mother-Daughter Herstory of Amor, Dolor, y Resistencia

Gabriela Corona Valencia

El amor vive en dos países al mismo tiempo.
—YESIKA SALGADO, *CORAZÓN*

A few years ago, my mother came up to me and told me there was going to be a meteor shower later that night. Although I do not remember the exact day, month, or time of this interaction, I do recall being depressed, exhausted, and impatient because of school and the toxic relationship I was in. We planned on watching the meteor shower together and made sure to conserve our energy for the night. Around 10:00 p.m., we walked out to the front lawn of our house, wrapped up in blankets, and sat on some old chairs to wait for the sky show. As we waited, we talked about our family, friends, and school. All of a sudden, we started seeing bright spots shoot across the sky. My mother was mesmerized. I was in awe. I would look away periodically to stare at my mother's eyes, glowing with excitement—it was as if she had witnessed magic for the first time. Years later, my mother still brings up this experience. "Esa es unas de mis memorias favoritas," she says with that same glow in her beautiful hazel eyes.[1] "A mi nunca se me va olvidar, ma," I respond. How comforting it is to know that something as infinite as the sky will eternally connect my mother and me.

New Moon: Struggling to Be Seen

From 1979 to 1992, the Salvadoran Civil War claimed the lives of thousands of civilians. In *Harvest of Empire*, author Juan González states, "Central America's victims perished mostly at the hands of their own soldiers or from right-wing death squads, and invariably from weapons made in the U.S.A., since in each country our government provided massive military aid to the side doing most of the killing" (González 2011, 131). Seeing lines of dead bodies on the road while walking to school was a norm my mother had to live with. When the violence started escalating, and she felt she was in immense danger, she made the difficult decision to travel up to el norte. The last time she saw my grandmother was while sitting in the back of a truck full of people desperate to get to el otro lado, where they were promised a life of money and safety. My mother's daughter was standing next to my grandmother, crying uncontrollably as she watched the vehicle drive away. Although the destination seemed like a dream come true, the journey to get there was a nightmare. My mother vividly remembers the stops the driver would make near motels. She remembers the way he would open the back of the truck, force a young girl from the group out, then see that girl limp back to the car a couple of hours later. She remembers how fast she had to run from border patrol officers, and how she almost thought the journey was over when she fell into a hole, but an elderly woman from the group pulled her out from *las greñas*, screaming at her to keep running. The long dark hair she was often admired for was cut short to make herself look more Americana. Starting a new life in the United States meant shifting her identity and persona to survive; however, becoming a "new" Ana did not mend the broken heart she had over leaving everything she knew behind.

I was aware that my mother migrated to the United States from El Salvador at a young age. Did I understand her reasons? Not at all. Did I feel connected to this part of my culture? Menos. Since she was not open about her migration story and the family she had left behind in her homeland, I felt a major disconnection when it came down to proclaiming my Salvadoran culture. I used to lie about my family history and about the Spanish I spoke at home. Since I did not know anything about my cultural roots, I believed I had the liberty to be anything I wanted. Now that I look back at it, I feel ashamed and embarrassed for denying the connection to my cultural identity for so long. I regret not taking the time sooner to understand the emotional barriers my mother carried with her. As I was growing up, I used to resent how sheltered I was and overbearing she was toward me. Every time I asked to go out, she would bombard me with a million questions like, "Who are you going out with? Have I met them yet? Why have I not met them yet? Are you sure that is where you are going? Where do they live? Can you please write down their phone numbers and addresses in case of an emergency?" At the time, I thought these questions were an attempt to restrict some of my independence; I realize now, however, that she was trying to make sure I was always okay because she was terrified of my experiencing anything similar to what she had been through.

After opening up about her migration story throughout the years, my mother started giving me details about the life she had led as a young girl in El Salvador. I recall once getting in trouble for something when she suddenly broke down crying. She told me that she was going to carry certain secrets to her grave, and that no one would ever understand the suffering she had been internalizing. We fell into a ten-second silence until I asked her very timidly, "Te violaron, ma?" She cried some more and started telling me stories about the father she hated and the other men who were nothing more than cochinos. The man she'd had to reluctantly call her father had sexually abused her daily until he died of cancer when she was eleven years old. After being angry with her for so long for being too overprotective and possessive of me, I started to understand her reasons. The last thing she wanted was for me to experience the same horrors she'd had to endure. Even though her protective habits made me feel as though I were trapped in a bubble, that bubble made it possible for her to keep me out of harm's way, or so she thought. Most importantly, she wanted me to learn different ways to distance myself from a group that is often known to dehumanize the lives of women: men.

Aside from being sexually violated by her father, she was harassed by the men from his side of the family, and at fifteen years old, she encountered a death squad leader who began abusing her; this man soon became the father of her daughter Laura. This pattern of abuse perpetuated by family members and surrounding people within the community was examined more thoroughly in a study exploring the experiences of sexual abuse survivors in Central America. The authors note that "the prevalence of CSA [child sexual assault] in the three Central American countries included ranges from 5% to 8%, and most of the abuse took place before the women's 11th birthday. Perpetuators of the abuse were most often known to the victim and her family and as shown in El Salvador were more likely to include the father, stepfather, or strangers" (Speizer et al. 2008, 460). In my mother's case, escaping the abusive environments she was surrounded by was a nearly impossible task since people were afraid to confront the abusers, who had reputations as being dominant and dangerous. Although the women in her family lived in fear every day, standing up to the abusers was not a choice; the women wanted to avoid "punishments" at all costs. Surviving was a priority, and if that meant submission and obedience, then that is what they offered, regardless of the detrimental effects it had on their lives.

Giving birth to Laura at fifteen years old forced my mother to be a teenager and a guardian at the same time. Even though she despised the man who abused her, having Laura around made her feel less alone. Her family turned their backs on her because they believed she was irresponsible for what had happened; no one knew the details of the awful reality my mother experienced at the hands of her abuser. After she gave birth, she was forced to live with this man and his family. Since he was a guerrillero who had developed many enemies throughout the Civil War, she would often be caught in the middle of violence. She was left with the responsibility of cooking for him and other guerrilleros, often fearing their violent behavior or the cruel possibility of being raided and executed by their opponents.

Waxing Crescent Moon:
Parte de Mi Aquí, Parte de Mi Allá

Laura was someone I knew existed but hardly understood my connection to as I was growing up. My mother would remind me from time to time that I had another sister in El Salvador, but I never asked questions about why she was not with us or whether I would ever get the chance to see her in real life; since Laura was not brought up often, I did not think she had a major role in our family. When I started college, I was enrolled in various Chicanx studies courses, and some of the major projects I was assigned required me to interview my parents to gain a better understanding of their homeland experiences and migration trajectories. When I started asking my mother questions about her life in El Salvador and the family she had left behind, I began to comprehend the various types of motherhood roles she had embarked on with Laura on one side of the border and us on the other. In "'I'm Here, but I'm There': The Meanings of Latina Transnational Motherhood," Pierrette Hondagneu-Sotelo and Ernestine Avila explain, "Central American and Mexican women who leave their young children 'back home' and come to the United States in search of employment are in the process of actively, if not voluntarily, building alternative constructions of motherhood" (1997, 549). My mother expressed to me that leaving Laura behind was one of the most difficult decisions she had ever had to make, but the journey to el norte was too dangerous; many migrants had been murdered or had gone missing. If something had happened to Laura along the way, she would have never forgiven herself for it.

Laura contacted me through Facebook in December 2015. She sent me a message explaining that she was looking for her mother, and after asking some relatives about the names of her half-siblings, she had come across my profile. The message was about a paragraph long. I had to read it nearly ten times to fully grasp the reality that this was the first time I was communicating with the sister I had thought existed only through stories and dreams. After about twenty minutes, I finally responded to her, saying that she had found the right person and that I would put her in contact with our mother. "Sabia que tu tenias que ser mi hermana . . . tienes los ojos de nuestra mama," she said. When I approached my mother with the news, she sat down in the dining room as the kids from the childcare she owns were cleaning up their play area. She was having trouble finding the right emotions to express. When she finally got behind the screen and saw Laura's face, the tears started rolling, and the apologies started spilling. The emptiness my mother had been feeling for decades seemed to start filling in throughout the following weeks as she and Laura began sharing the experiences that occurred during their time apart.

In recent months, my mother has brought up the idea of traveling to El Salvador to visit Laura. Since Laura's plans to travel here fell through because of her financial situation, my mother is determined to try anything possible to see her. Sometimes I fear the possibility of going through my life without ever seeing Laura in person. I hear her voice every time she talks to our mother, and I can sense the pain and loneliness she feels knowing that her solitude could have been aided by being around a supportive family. For a long time, she believed that our mother had abandoned her because she had considered her a burden to a better life. Our mother's connection to her side of the family never existed since they were toxic and abusive, and although they had told our mother that they would take care of Laura, they often marginalized her from family events and made her feel as though she did not belong.

First Quarter Moon: When Pain Helps You Start Growing and Glowing

I found out I was pregnant in March 2015. I took a pregnancy test in the restroom a couple of minutes before class started. When I saw the test come out positive, I could not help but think the worst about myself. "Great! Everything you ever wanted in life is never going to happen. You are the biggest disappointment to your family," my brain yelled at me. I had this type of reaction because for as long as I could remember, my family had carried the idea that I would be the first one to graduate from college. Every day I would get reminders from them telling me to be careful with what I do because I needed to focus on graduating. The pressure I felt to make my family proud made me think of my pregnancy as a mistake instead of as a moment to celebrate. I walked to my class with my head hanging low, holding back an ocean of tears. During the seventy-five-minute lecture, the words went straight over my head as I pondered the choices I had and whether I was brave enough to make one. Since there were two pregnancy tests in the box I had bought, I took temporary comfort in believing that the first test was defective; there was no way I could be pregnant. As soon as we were dismissed, I rushed back to the bathroom, peed on the stick, walked back and forth, and waited. Positive. That was it. My life as I knew it was over.

As soon as I was done with classes for the day, I decided to drive over to my former partner's house and break the news to him. I wanted to be strong. I wanted to be fearless. But my heart already hurt because I knew the reaction I was going to get from him was not going to be a good one. He was playing video games when I arrived. Our relationship was toxic, and we always failed to communicate in a healthy manner, so I struggled to find the right moment to tell him what was happening. He was in the middle of fighting off zombies with a controller when I just blurted out, "I am pregnant." He kept playing, but I could see his face drop. His brother was in the other room, and I could tell he wanted me to remain calm so no one would hear what we were saying. He set the controller down, and after a couple minutes of silence, I knew that there was no way he would want to go through with the pregnancy; at the time, I was twenty years old, and facing something like this alone terrified me to the core. I felt ashamed, irresponsible, and dumb. In "Guadalupe the Sex Goddess," Sandra Cisneros states, "So much guilt, so much silence, and yet a yearning to be loved; no wonder young women find themselves having sex while they are still children, having sex without sexual protection, too ashamed to confide their feelings and fears to anyone" (Cisneros 1997, 48). I wanted to be loved, and I thought sharing myself with this person was going to grant me that; I was wrong. After saying that it was going to be nearly impossible to raise a child at this point in our lives, I got in my car and drove off, dreading the decision and actions I would take in the next couple of days.

My sister drove me to a clinic a few days after I found out I was pregnant. When I told her what was going on, she did not know whether to be happy or sad for me since I was expressionless and numb. Once we got to the clinic, I tried to convince myself that this was only a checkup. I wanted to know the important details: How far along was I? Was I healthy? What were my options? What were some of the dangers and consequences that came with each option? Once the nurses were conducting the ultrasound, I tried convincing myself that going through with the pregnancy would be possible; in the end, the self-convincing was not enough for me. I refused to look at the ultrasound screen, even after the nurses' continuous encouragement.

The decision to terminate my pregnancy is one that I think about constantly. I remember the conversation I had with my mother years prior, when she told me she was going to take certain secrets to her grave; I thought this was one of my own secrets that I would never share. A year after the abortion, I was depressed, anxious, and so angry. I was picking fights with everyone. I hated being around people. More than anything, I hated myself. There was a week when my energy was so heavy, and the disagreements with my mother started intensifying. I ended up blurting out, "Ma, aborte el año pasado y todavia me duele." Her face softened, and she started asking me questions. It took her a while to be able to accept that her bebé was a sexually active woman who made serious decisions regarding her reproductive health. Sometimes I feel as though she wishes we could turn back time to when our bodies and sex were not the recurring topics in our conversations. Regardless of her obvious discomfort with the confirmation of my sexual activity, she reminded me that no one was allowed to consider me less of a person because of my decisions. To my surprise, she made it known that I was in control of my body and that I deserved to treat it like the treasure it was.

Full Moon: Feeling Enough for Myself, Feeling Enough for Each Other

Over the past couple of years, I constantly compared myself to my mother. I considered myself weak because I was not brave enough to continue with my pregnancy at twenty years old, while my mother had given birth to Laura at fifteen years old. After disclosing these feelings to her, she explained to me how she had the complete opposite opinion. In her eyes, learning about my loss made her feel more connected to me because of the way I handled the entire ordeal so independently. An event that I thought was going to make me lose my mother instead made us friends. I recently came across a form I'd had to sign regarding my pregnancy. I showed it to my mother, wondering what she was going to say. She read it very carefully and with the softest voice asked me whether I would like to keep it or throw it away. I decided that I wanted to keep it in a box, because no matter how much it hurt, that experience would always be a part of me, and I wanted to be able to hold on to items that can help me remain connected to the past me who was terrified of going through such an event. I wanted to visit and remind her that we pulled through; we are doing just fine because our mother's love has been the most potent medicine for our wounded bodies, minds, and spirits.

Even after all the hardships my mother has been through, I do not want people to read her story and see her as a victim. Instead I want them to recognize that she is a beautiful, resilient, empowered woman who continues to hustle and to radically love a world that has not always been so kind to her. Being open about this side of our family history required an immense amount of remembering, processing, and accepting. Some wounds are still open, but when you have people helping you mitigate the unexpected pains throughout time, the process of healing becomes a bit more bearable. My mother's love and compassion continue to surprise me, because after all she has been through, she refuses to let the negative past influence the way she interacts with her family, her community, and herself. Gloria Anzaldúa once said, "I will have my serpent's tongue—my woman's voice, my sexual voice, my poet's voice. I will overcome the tradition of silence" (1987, 81). Together, the tongues of my mother and I will move mountains. Together, we will let our tongues flow through the veins of those who hear our stories in the future. Together. She and I. Always.

Notes

Chapter title: "Aqui se respira lucha" is one of my favorite phrases from the song "Latinoamerica" by Calle 13. To me, it accurately represents the resiliency my mother and I carry every day.

1.   To challenge the dominant English language and pay tribute to my culture and family, I do not italicize, set in boldface, or translate the Spanish within my work.

References

Anzaldúa, Gloria. 1987. *Borderlands / La Frontera: The New Mestiza*. San Francisco: Aunt Lute Books.

Cisneros, Sandra. 1997. "Guadalupe the Sex Goddess." In *Goddess of the Americas*, edited by Ana Castillo, 46–52. New York: Riverhead Books.

González, Juan. 2011. *Harvest of Empire: A History of Latinos in America*. New York: Penguin Books.

Hondagneu-Sotelo, Pierrette, and Ernestine Avila. 1997. "'I'm Here, but I'm There': The Meanings of Latina Transnational Motherhood." *Gender and Society* 11 (5): 548–71.

Salgado, Yesika. 2017. *Corazón*. Los Angeles: Not a Cult Press.

Speizer, Ilene, Mary Goodwin, Lisa Whittle, Maureen Clyde, and Jennifer Rogers. 2008. "Dimensions of Child Sexual Abuse Before Age 15 in Three Central American Countries: Honduras, El Salvador, Guatemala." *Child Abuse and Neglect* 32 (4): 455–62.

3

Coordinates

A Testimonio on Urban Migration, Mothering, and Teaching

Gretel H. Vera-Rosas

When my mother migrated from Mexico City to Gardena, California, in the late 1980s, she gave us careful instructions to say that she had been given a scholarship to study the latest coloring techniques at a cosmetology academy in Monterrey, Nuevo León. I assume that, for Mom, a made-up story of a divorcée cosmetology student getting a scholarship was more acceptable (and socially valuable) than a mother leaving her two daughters to find work in a different country. After all, part of the tale we told was that she came to visit us once a month from Monterrey. Regardless if Mom, like many working-class women, was accustomed to participating in the workforce and sharing mothering responsibilities with her own mother and sisters (especially after her divorce), migrating meant prolonged temporal and spatial separation from her daughters, which some people might interpret as maternal abandonment, since pervasive cultural notions of good mothering have been tied to and shaped by not only the ideology of the conjugal-heterosexual-nuclear family but also by the idealization of motherhood, which assigns the biological mother as the natural, selfless, and primary caregiver (Roberts 1993; Collins 1994; Hays 1998). As a decolonial feminist, I have come to understand my mother's need to "reframe" her absence as her being conscripted by gender norms and assumptions of what it means to be a good mother. Her lie, therefore, was not just a way of protecting herself against condemnation; it was a reflection of her own values as a mother and a woman in a society and culture structured by patriarchal ideologies of maternal propriety and femininity.

As a young girl, I was indelibly marked by my mother's departure, and later, by my own experience of migration and illegality as an undocumented high school student. Unlike children who grew up in rural areas with heavy migratory flows, whose perceptions of the United States were informed by transgenerational and community migration stories (Sertzen and Torres 2016), for me migration as a lived experience or concept was not part of my everyday grammar until my mother left on January 29, 1988 (a day after my eleventh birthday). People did not migrate from our working-class neighborhood in northwest Mexico City. If they did, their cases were rare and not part of transgenerational circuits of migration. Research shows that the displacement of Mexican urbanites to the United States became an emerging social phenomenon only after the expansion of export-led development and the economic crises of the 1980s (Hernández-León 2008; Hamilton and Villarreal 2011). In our case, mom was the first (and until today the only) in her family to venture North. Growing up, we had no family stories of migration; our U.S. referents came from dubbed American television shows and movies. Even now, when I hear "With a Little Help from My Friends," I am transported back to my grandmother's bedroom, where we religiously watched *The Wonder Years*. This particular show fueled my imagination of the United States as a place of symmetry, school lockers, nuclear families, and green front yards, but never as a place of racial-economic violence and firmly rooted transnational Mexican/Latinx communities.

Early in my academic journey, *la maternidad y la ilegalidad*, as categories of analysis, gave meaning to the raw material of my life and reconfigured my relationship to my subjects and objects of study. Being the daughter of a transnational single mother shaped and exposed me to alternative ways of "doing family." And that experience has informed my interests in thinking critically about and making space for nonnormative mothering practices. Today, as a Mother-Scholar working at a minority-serving institution, I write and teach about raced motherhood and the many ways in which legal and racial regimes expose us to premature death; but more importantly, my work renders visible the "motherwork" (Collins 1994) and radical connections that prevent us from falling over or that pull us back from the precipice. Like my mother, I try to imagine a *there* and *then* in which hope, as potentiality, moves us toward a life otherwise, toward alternative futures in which, as Audre Lorde powerfully wrote, our children's dreams "will not reflect the death of ours" ([1978] 1995, 31).

In this chapter, I weave *testimonio*, research on motherhood, and migration to map three different coordinates: (1) my grandmother's home in Mexico City, (2) the San Diego–Tijuana border, and (3) California State University, Dominguez Hills, where I teach.[1] I use the term "coordinates" not only to refer to geographic location, but also to call attention to the word as a verb; that is, as the act of negotiating and making of "arrangements so that two or more people or groups of people can work together properly and well."[2] By doing so, I tie certain forms of motherwork to specific classed and racialized geographies. Tracing these coordinates (as place and action) enables me to write an intimate narrative of family, maternal embodiment, and location that explores the meaningful ways in which immigration and motherwork manifests in my relationship with my mother, in my experience as a Mother-Scholar on the tenure track, and in teaching student-moms.

N 19° 29' 40.115" W 99° 11' 15.247": A House, a Home, and Transgenerational Mothering

I grew up in *the place of the anthills*, Azcapotzalco, a municipality in northwestern Mexico City. My maternal family arrived in La Reynosa, a working-poor colonia located north of Azcapotzalco's historic center, in the 1950s. My grandmother's house was built on a *terreno* her father, Fernando, and one of his brothers purchased for two adjacent houses. Fernando was a widower and a gardener who raised his only daughter, Francisca, on his own. My great-grandfather felt it was his paternal obligation to ensure that his daughter had a place to root herself: *para que no anduviera rodando de un lado a otro.* I was almost five years old when my parents separated, and my mom, sister, and I moved into my grandma's house. My grandparents made room for us in a house crowded with cousins, aunts, and uncles (and a parrot who always warbled along with my grandma's morning singing). In that house, I frequently woke up to the sounds of my grandma's voice, since she often sang as she watered her plants and swept the sidewalk before going to morning Mass at the church of the Sacred Heart. Prior to marrying my father, my mother's labor inside and outside the home was necessary for the economic survival of her family. As the second eldest of nine, she cared for her younger siblings and started working in the informal economy at ten years old. In the 1960s, by the time Mom was a teenager, she was part of a female workforce in the textile industry in Mexico City.

It was in this house that in 1988 my mother left my sister and me under the care of her parents and her sister Magda. One of the most poignant memories I have of Mom before her departure is of her doing our laundry while we celebrated my eleventh birthday the night before she left for the United States. She refused to join us in the living room because she did not want to leave my grandma with a pile of dirty clothes. Many years later, when as an undocumented high school student I first heard León Chávez Teixeiro's song "La mujer, se va la vida, compañera," it brought back the image of my mom dealing with her pain and uncertainty by doing laundry, *fregando ropa a mano.* The song renders audible the emotional and domestic labor that women do in their working-class neighborhoods to keep life afloat. Deciding to leave her children was a monumental decision, one that my mother describes as the most painful experience of her life. But, perhaps, she did not want her life to go "down the hole like muck in the sink" (Chávez Teixeiro [1998] 2013). And against her fear, *mi madre* took her chances.

Yet, Mom Was Not Alone

Unbeknownst to us, she was part of a wave of immigrants that was increasingly female and urban. Frequently, these women were mothers who left their children behind under the care of "middle women." According to Joanna Dreby, these middle women are caregivers, who tend to be primarily maternal grandmothers, who are perceived as the most appropriate persons to care for children in the absence of the biological mother (2010). In many ways, these transnational familial relationships of care continue to reinscribe child rearing to women through the maternal line. Transnational motherhood, as a new transnational family formation, has been produced by many factors, including changing labor demands (e.g., the globalization of care work), political unrest, civil wars, and economic restructuring (Hondagneu-Sotelo and Avila 1997; Menjívar, Abrego, and Schmalzbauer 2016). But circumstances that are not always economic or political also influence a mother's decision to migrate. At times, these women are also driven by the desire for adventure, the search for sexual and gender freedom, as well as the need to escape domestic violence or to reconstruct their lives after a divorce (Sanz Abad and García-Moreno 2016).

Pierrette Hondagneu-Sotelo and Ernestine Avila argue that the alternative arrangements transnational mothers make to care for their children at a distance disrupt and contradict both Latina and U.S. white middle-class dominant ideas of good mothering and monolithic notions of family. Affected by long distances of time and space, transnational motherhood also breaks away from the middle-class model of mother-child isolation and the working-class practice of mother-child integration in the workplace (1997). While these new arrangements disrupt many traditional notions of motherhood by posing a radical break with "deeply gendered and temporal boundaries of family and work," as Hondagneu-Sotelo and Avila argue, "this form of motherhood continues a long historical legacy of People of Color being incorporated into the United States through coercive systems of labor that do not recognize family rights" (552, 598). Feminist scholarship on gender and migration shows that, since the 1980s, transnational mothers not only represent a change in migratory patterns and the continuation of hyperproductive surplus extraction from mothering Bodies of Color, but their mothering practices and experiences reveal new and mediated forms of maternal embodiment and affect that challenge us to rethink the meaning of normal motherhood.

La casa de mi abuela anchors me to the maternal (my grandmother, mother, and middle women). It is also the place where Mom learned to suffer graciously and to navigate everyday life with dignity and creativity. In that crowded and oftentimes noisy home, we learned about the power of prayer, song, and gardening. My mother's experiences as a working-class child and mother need to be understood outside the meanings and inscriptions of normative childhood and motherhood. Though the capitalist middle-class nuclear family and solo motherhood emerged as an ideality and as a response to economic and social conditions after industrialization, extended family kinships have contributed to the economic and emotional well-being of the working poor. "While among the elite[,] extended family systems preserve inherited wealth" (Andersen and Taylor 2008, 396), for those who have experienced slavery, white-settler colonialism, urban poverty, and migration, extended or fictive kinships have functioned as adaptations to conditions of violence, as well as nonnormative ways of caring for one another and crafting lives that are whole (Davis 1981).

In La Reynosa, Mom learned that through resiliency, conflict, and solidarity with her friends and neighbors, working-class sociality is made material. Those lessons she carried with her across the border.

N 32° 32′ 37.78″, W 117° 1′ 46.126″: Crossings, Migrant Motherhood, and Theorizing in the Flesh

While my mother, like many immigrants, had promised that she would be gone for only a year, life is complicated, and sometimes, like rules and laws, promises have to be broken. Three years after Mom's departure, my sister and I arrived in Tijuana, the westernmost city of Mexico, in August 19, 1990, to reunite with her. For us, traveling north brought us closer to her, but for our grandma and aunt, the journey meant a greater separation. Both had been the middle women who took care of us for three years. Now, they had traveled on bus for three days only to deliver us to our mother. I remember arriving and waiting outside la Central de Autobuses de Tijuana until my tiny mother appeared in the distance: a five-foot-tall woman dressed in red. I remember the four of us walking and watching a punk-goth teenager dancing as her friends smoked cigarettes. I remember the four of us talking in the darkness as we tried to fall asleep in a hotel room.

. . . And Then, the Next Morning, My Mom, Sister, and I Crossed the Border

National borders, like motherhood and childhood, are historically contingent social constructs. For many families, the Tijuana–San Diego border represents an interface that simultaneously marks our separation and our refusal to be separated. El Parque de la Amistad, a half-acre cement plaza sitting in a high, steep bank of Border Field Park, crystalizes this dynamic. Despite the watchful presence of the border patrol and the materiality of the steel poles that run a few feet into the ocean until they disappear, relatives divided by the border gather to visit through the fence. The landscape of this park is one of public intimacy and affect constrained by and exceeding regulation. For Jonathan Xavier Inda, the nonvalue of immigrant life can best be apprehended at two sites: the hypermilitarized cartography of the U.S.-Mexico border and the policing of the reproductive bodies of undocumented mothers (2007). For instance, in anti-immigrant legislation and mainstream media, the undocumented immigrant mother is portrayed as a "mother of anchor-children," and as such, she is conceived as a cultural threat and a social failure (Vera-Rosas 2014). Within this context, the notion of "theory in the flesh" provides us with a critical viewpoint to rethink maternal bodies, border crossing, and illegality outside the lens of criminalization because the theory reveals the complex history of racialization in the United States and its consequences.

A theory in the flesh, Cherríe Moraga writes, is "one where the physical realities of our lives—our skin color, the land or concrete we grew up on, our sexual longings—all fuse to create a politic born out of necessity" ([1981] 2015a, 19). Theory in the flesh regards emotional reckoning with the contradictions of our lives and the source of our oppressions. For Moraga, this is a theory of identification with and empathy for her mother's oppression: "I had no choice but to enter into the life of my mother" ([1981] 2015b, 23). Her claim is by no means a praise of the maternal that ignores how certain parts of our mothers' heritages have functioned to prevent us from knowing ourselves. A theory in the flesh, however, is a theory of coexistence and interconnectivity through which the daughters of the oppressed learn to claim the parts of their mothers' heritages that will help them survive and envision a life-affirming future "born out of what is dark and female" (29). Moreover, to theorize in the flesh is to heal and reawaken in us the faith of our mothers. As Moraga explains, it is about radically "believing that we have the power to actually transform our experience, change our lives, save our lives" ([1981] 2015c, xl). As such, it is a theory of maternity and materiality, of affect and embodiment, a corporeal politics of location.

"I am the very well-educated daughter of a woman who, by the standards in this country, would be considered largely illiterate," Moraga states ([1981] 2015b, 22). The sentence resonates with me because Moraga refuses to measure her mother against a dominant logic that assumes that mothers with little formal education are ignorant or uncultured. She defines her mother as "a fine story-teller," underscoring this as one way through which her mom transferred knowledge to her. Moraga's refusal is politically important particularly in a sociocultural context in which working-poor and immigrant mothers time and again are labeled as unfit parents or as responsible for the achievement gap of their children. Take for instance the NPR news piece "Mexican-American Toddlers: Understanding the Achievement Gap," aired on *All Things Considered* in 2015, which summarizes the "achievement gap" as the product of "weak parenting in the U.S. context." Based on a study by the Institute of Human Development at the University of California, Berkeley, the report claims that while white middle-class mothers prioritize their children's preliteracy skills, Latinx parents, particularly immigrant mothers with low levels of education, do not encourage their children to speak early and do not read to them daily. Toddlers are more likely to show a "robust growth if their moms [work] outside the home" because, the report contends, they are exposed to middle-class forms of parenting that are more innovative. Exposure to middle-class values, it argues, will essentially help children of immigrants to better assimilate to American culture.[3]

These arguments are not new. On one hand, they restate a deficit-oriented perspective that blames parents rather than structural conditions; on the other, they center reading while ignoring other practices of the home space that promote literacy (Villenas 2009). This epistemological debate, Tara J. Yosso explains, has been shaped by race and racism; and it has ignored the accumulated assets and community cultural wealth Students of Color and their parents bring to academic settings (2005). For those of us who grew up in families with little to no formal education, resources like song, popular culture, family stories, and, in my case, gardening functioned as nonlettered forms for the transmission of knowledge, identity, and cultural memory. Moreover, as working-class and immigrant children, as Yosso affirms, we develop understandings of the familial that extend beyond consanguineal kin. These alternative forms of kinship, such as intergenerational communal mothering or immigrant fictive family networks, "model lessons of caring, coping and providing (educación), which inform our emotional, moral, educational and occupational consciousness" (79).

By continuing to frame the achievement gap through the lens of lack, the findings presented in the NPR report reinscribe the cultural practices of the white middle-class mother as the norm, while situating home practices of the racialized foreign-born mother at the bottom of the hierarchy. These racist and classist discourses have historically been central to the construction of poor Mothers of Color as deficient parents. In the specific case of immigrant women, maternal irresponsibility is not only couched in terms of the "educational achievement gap" of their kids but also in anti-immigrant discourses portraying these women as lawbreakers and as mothers of "anchor children," and therefore as threats to the nation. Thus, by the standards in this country, *I am the daughter of a woman who is considered a bad mother, a working-poor immigrant, a border crosser.*

As someone marked by the experience of migration, family separation, and illegality, I have entered this country and academia as my mother's daughter. Chicana educational scholar Cindy Cruz contends that for us to reclaim our narratives and develop radical projects of liberation and transformation, we must understand the Brown body and its regulation (2001). Engaging also with Moraga's theory in the flesh, Cruz suggests that "our production of knowledge begins in the bodies of our mothers and grandmothers, in the acknowledgement of the critical practices of women of color before us" (658). For me, this project manifests in my instance to claim the undocumented immigrant mother as a figure that can enable us to formulate a dream of alternative futures, "while establishing a continuation between the past and present policing of racialized maternity" (Vera-Rosas 2014). This claim is often asserted in my classes, where I work with my students to expose the ways in which motherhood is a rich site of investigation and a focal point for questions about our bodies, subjectivities, labor, and knowledge production.

N 33° 51′ 48.134″ W 118° 15′ 19.011″: Academia and Maternal Lines of Flight

In my Women in Society courses, students learn that the debasement of the feminine and the simultaneous negation and glorification of the mother (and her labor) have been central to feminist debates on motherhood and the maternal. Our discussions emphasize the importance of a feminist politics of maternity that resists two seemingly opposing myths: the antifeminist notion of women as vessels of reproduction, and the radical feminist myth of women as vessels of patriarchal order (Guenther 2006; Galindo 2006). Students learn to recognize the urgency for a politics of maternity that, in María Galindo's words, "recuperates the place of the mother, where women change from being objects of reproduction to subjects of maternity" (2006).

As work and educational sites, academic institutions reproduce a culture that demands and necessitates the exploitation of female labor, witnessed through the unequal demands for teaching, service, and mentorship. Scholarship on the experience of academic mothers reveals that motherhood is perceived as tarnishing one's professional status. And the lack of support for Mother-Scholars and student-moms makes very difficult the integration of career and homelife without penalty or stigma (Téllez 2013; Loveless 2014). For me, enacting a feminist politics of maternity demands a refusal to see mothering as detrimental to my professional life. It requires making visible the emotional and maternal labor that I perform without guilt or shame. A feminist politics of maternity pushes me to continue to theorize and embody motherhood as a collective social practice that can generate radical connections with others. It also demands that I actively support and advocate for student-parents. My transition from being a daughter of a transnational mother theorizing about immigrant maternity to becoming an academic mother has not been easy. Yet, this becoming has presented new maternal lines of flight.

My pregnancy and early years of maternal life were marked by the uncertainty of the academic job market, the realities of being an adjunct instructor, and the emotional and economic demands of being the partner of someone diagnosed with bipolar disorder. Besides the exhaustion and sleep deprivation that parenting brings to one's life, my first year of maternal life was extremely hard because assuming motherhood on my own terms was a difficult process for me. And it has been an identity that I have learned to embrace slowly. I was also uncertain of how to love and support a partner with a mental health history. Through trial and error, I have learned to set boundaries and develop an ethics of care that is attentive to my needs as a mom and as a first-generation professor while also being present for those who need me and value my emotional, pedagogical, and intellectual labor.

During those days, I often told my mother that the pregnancy glow bypassed me. I was physically exhausted from coping with my teaching load, driving to two different campuses three times a week while my belly kept expanding, drafting endless documents for job applications, and going back to work a month after giving birth. Studies have shown that there are racial and gender dimensions to adjunct positions in academia. The precariousness of the academic job market has disproportionately affected underrepresented groups, particularly Women of Color, since their numbers have increased as contingent labor but not necessarily as tenure-track or tenured faculty (Flaherty 2016). Thus, for working-class, first-generation adjunct professors with massive student debt, as Tressie McMillan Cottom explains, "the prescription for poverty—educational attainment—has become a condition *for* poverty" (2014). Moreover, as Michelle Téllez underscores, "family formation—specifically, marriage and babies—explains why more women are, overall, less likely than men to enter tenure-track positions" (2013, 88–89).

Despite the hierarchies within and between academic institutions and the overvaluation of research over teaching, I always envisioned working with nontraditional students at a public teaching institution. This became a reality when I was offered a tenure-track job at California State University, Dominguez Hills. As a Hispanic-serving institution and a public teaching university, CSUDH is composed of a mostly nontraditional student body: first-generation students, transfer students, student-parents, and older adults (more than sixty years old). Additionally, it is a mostly female campus. As a result, every semester at least one-third of my students are Black or Latina student-moms. According to Katarzyna Marciniak and Bruce Bennett, "Teaching is regarded in many contexts as a feminized practice associated with compassion, empathy, and perhaps, child-rearing. Moreover, as a form of domestic labor, pedagogy is gendered, consigned to the culturally degraded status of 'women's work' and as such, a disregard for teaching is completed by the overvaluation of masculine intellectual ambition and celebrity scholarship" (2016, 13). While the association of teaching with female labor does have negative consequences for female scholars, particularly Women of Color, for me teaching has always been transformative.

Teaching student-moms enables me to provide mentorship and support based on my research and the common experience of being mothers in academia. Statistically, low-income, first-generation student-moms face often insurmountable challenges in completing a college degree; and even if they are outstanding students, they have a lower graduation rate (Nelson, Froehner, and Gault 2013; Noll, Reichlin, and Gault 2017). Student-moms, much like Mother-Scholars, are often categorized as bad subjects. That is, they are frequently perceived as not being serious and as caring more about their family than their performance within the university. The permanence of mothers in academic institutions is challenged by a lack of flexibility and the absence of policies that can potentially ease and ensure the process of graduation or tenure. On top of this, my student-parents frequently complain about how some instructors demand that they leave their family life and personal problems at home. This is not surprising since the prevailing expectation in academia is that one must not be distracted by the mundane tasks of everyday existence. This demand assumes, of course, that the university is an institution devoid of power relations, which oftentimes prevents us from fully thriving as people with intersectional identities.

Despite the challenges that emerge from a heavy teaching load, I like the promise of the classroom. While the association of teaching with the feminine and the maternal is a vexed relationship, Deborah Lea Byrd and Fiona Joy Green argue that, whether or not one is a mother, engaging in maternal pedagogies can help us counter dominant ways of teaching and the oppressive culture of mainstream academic institutions (2011). Maternal pedagogies augment critical pedagogies by claiming the maternal as a site of labor, embodiment, and praxis. Thus, for me, claiming the maternal is about expectancy and potentiality. As a Mother-Scholar, I have tried to theorize and teach "in the flesh," to practice a politics of maternity that challenges and disrupts familial and academic normative relations and that makes motherhood a subject of coordination and action.

Conclusion

My mother has an obsession with my hands: it is the product of her preoccupation with transforming the conditions and realities of my life. She believes that the condition of one's hands partially tells the story of one's life. She is a woman who knows, like many working-poor women do, that work imprints your body in very specific ways, that, as time passes, your body deteriorates depending on what you do for a living. As a result, my hands reflect a life of minor physical labor (thus a successful generational change in her eyes). But the soft texture of my hands says little about how I was marked by my experience as a first-generation college student who was once undocumented. It belies the fact that I am the daughter of a woman who started working at the age of ten: a working-poor Mexican immigrant, single mother with only a sixth-grade education who left my younger sister and me under the care of my grandmother to come to the United States in the late eighties.

As such, my research and work within and outside academia are driven by a desire to understand my personal experience as part of transnational processes of displacement, which make single Mothers of Color hypervulnerable to dispossession and criminalization. Despite differences in our relative subject positions and levels of education, my mother, my student-moms, and I still carry the stigma of "bad motherhood" in different ways. We are all marked by our race and class, and we are forced to navigate the expectations and strictures of normative motherhood. The softness of my hands also betrays the extent to which, regardless of my educational achievement, this form of privilege has not spared me from the stigma of being a working Mother of Color who must juggle the demands of academia with what is expected of me as a mother and as a partner. Neither has this new professional status spared me from the sexism, racism, and classism that permeates institutions of higher learning. Throughout this chapter, I have traced different coordinates to show how location affects the directions of my inquiry, my projects, and my understanding of motherhood as a collective social practice that can generate radical connections with others. More importantly, my testimonio demonstrates, as Chilean filmmaker Patricio Guzmán has so poetically stated, *que uno afirma lo que ama.*

Notes

1. I draw on testimonio as a subaltern method that marginalized groups have used to insert themselves into history. Testimonio, as situated knowledge, disrupts and challenges the assumption of the knowing subject as unmarked by sociohistorical and economic processes. I also play with repetition and structure as narrative strategies to disrupt the conventions and strictures of academic writing.

2. See *Merriam-Webster Learner's Dictionary*, s.v. "coordinate (*v.*)," accessed August 3, 2018, https://www.merriam-webster.com/dictionary /coordinate.

3. See Claudio Sanchez, "Mexican-American Toddlers: Understanding the Achievement Gap," NPR, April 7, 2015, http://www.npr.org/sections /ed/2015/04/07/397829916/mexican-american-toddlers-understanding -the-achievement-gap.

References

Andersen, Margaret L., and Howard F. Taylor. 2008. "Extended and Nuclear Families." In *Sociology: Understanding a Diverse Society*, 396–99. 4th ed. Belmont, CA: Thomson Wadsworth.

Byrd, Deborah Lea, and Fiona Joy Green. 2011. Introduction to *Maternal Pedagogies: In and Outside the Classroom*. Edited by Deborah Lea Byrd and Fiona Joy Green, 1–17. Bradford, ON: Demeter Press.

Chávez Teixeiro, León. (1998) 2013. "La Mujer, Se Va la Vida, Compañera." *De Nuevo Otra Vez*. Originally released July 29, 1998. Pentagrama. CD.

Collins, Patricia Hill. 1994. "Shifting the Center: Race, Class, and Feminist Theorizing About Motherhood." In *Mothering: Ideology, Experience, and Agency*, edited by Evelyn Nakano Glenn, Grace Chang, and Linda Rennie Forcey, 43–65. New York: Routledge.

Cruz, Cindy. 2001. "Toward an Epistemology of a Brown Body." *International Journal of Qualitative Studies in Education* 14 (5): 657–69.

Davis, Angela. 1981. *Women, Race, and Class*. New York: Random House.

Dreby, Joanna. 2010. *Divided by Borders: Mexican Migrants and Their Children*. Berkeley: University of California Press.

Flaherty, Colleen. 2016. "More Faculty Diversity, Not on Tenure Track." *Inside HigherEd*, August 22, 2016. https://www.insidehighered.com/news/2016/08/22/study-finds-gains-faculty-diversity-not-tenure-track.

Galindo, María. 2006. "Evo Morales y la Descolonización Fálica del Estado Boliviano." *Mujeres en red*, June 2006. http://www.mujeresenred.net/spip.php?article612.

Guenther, Lisa. 2006. *The Gift of the Other: Levinas and the Politics of Reproduction*. Albany: SUNY Press.

Hays, Sharon. 1998. *The Cultural Contradictions of Motherhood*. New Haven, CT: Yale University Press.

Hamilton, Erin R., and Andrés Villarreal. 2011. "Development and the Urban and Rural Geography of Mexican Emigration to the United States." *Social Forces* 90 (2): 661–83.

Hernández-León, Rubén. 2008. *Metropolitan Migrants: The Migration of Urban Mexicans to the United States*. Berkeley: University of California Press.

Hondagneu-Sotelo, Pierrette, and Ernestine Avila. 1997. "'I'm Here, but I'm There': The Meanings of Latina Transnational Motherhood." *Gender and Society* 11 (5): 548–71.

Inda, Jonathan Xavier. 2007. "The Value of Immigrant Life." In *Women and Migration in the U.S.-Mexico Borderlands*, edited by Denise A. Segura and Patricia Zavella, 134–57. Durham, NC: Duke University Press.

Lorde, Audre. (1978) 1995. "A Litany for Survival." In *The Black Unicorn Poems*, 31–32. Reissue ed. New York: Norton.

Loveless, Natalie S. 2014. "Maternal Ecologies: A Story in Three Parts." In *Performing Motherhood: Artistic, Activist, and Everyday Enactments*, edited by Amber E. Kinser, Kym Freehling-Burton, and Terri Hawkes, 149–70. Bradford, ON: Demeter Press.

Marciniak, Katarzyna, and Bruce Bennett. 2016. Introduction to *Teaching Transnational Cinema: Politics and Pedagogy*. Edited by Katarzyna Marciniak and Bruce Bennett, 1–36. New York: Routledge.

McMillan Cottom, Tressie. 2014. "The New Old Labor Crisis." *Slate*, January 24, 2014. http://www.slate.com/articles/life/counter_narrative/2014/01/adjunct_crisis_in_higher_ed_an_all_too_familiar_story_for_black_faculty.html.

Menjívar, Cecilia, Leisy Abrego, and Leah Schmalzbauer. 2016. *Immigrant Families*. Cambridge: Polity Press.

Moraga, Cherríe. (1981) 2015a. "Entering the Lives of Others: Theory in the Flesh." In *This Bridge Called My Back: Writings by Radical Women of Color*, 4th ed., edited by Gloria Anzaldúa and Cherríe Moraga, 19. Albany: SUNY Press.

Moraga, Cherríe. (1981) 2015b. "La Guera." In *This Bridge Called My Back: Writings by Radical Women of Color*, 4th ed., edited by Gloria Anzaldúa and Cherríe Moraga, 22–29. Albany: SUNY Press.

Moraga, Cherríe. (1981) 2015c. "La Jornada: Preface, 1981." In *This Bridge Called My Back: Writings by Radical Women of Color*, 4th ed., edited by Gloria Anzaldúa and Cherríe Moraga, xxxv–xxlii. Albany: SUNY Press.

Nelson, Bethany, Megan Froehner, and Barbara Gault. 2013. *College Students with Children Are Common and Face Many Challenges in Completing Higher Education*. IWPR Report C404. Washington, DC: Institute for Women's Policy Research. https://iwpr.org/publications/college-students-with-children-are-common-and-face-many-challenges-in-completing-higher-education-summary/.

Noll, Elizabeth, Lindsey Reichlin, and Barbara Gault. 2017. *College Students with Children: National and Regional Profiles*. IWPR Report C451. Washington, DC: Institute for Women's Policy Research. https://iwpr.org/wp-content/uploads/2017/02/C451-5.pdf.

Roberts, Dorothy. 1993. "Racism and Patriarchy in the Meaning of Mother-hood." *Faculty Scholarship* 595. http://scholarship.law.upenn.edu/faculty_scholarship/595.

Sanz Abad, Jesús, and Cristina García-Moreno. 2016. "Me Fui, Aunque No por Cuestiones Económicas: Migraciones a España de Mujeres Cubanas y Ecuatorianas por Motivos Extra Económicos." *Latin American Research Review* 51 (2): 128–49.

Sertzen, Pamela K., and Rebeca M. Torres. 2016. "Dibujando el 'Otro Lado': Mexican Children's Perceptions of Migration to the United States." *Journal of Latin American Geography* 15 (2): 55–77.

Téllez, Michelle. 2013. "Lectures, Evaluations, and Diapers: Navigating the Terrains of Chicana Single Motherhood in the Academy." *Feminist Formations* 25 (3): 79–97.

Vera-Rosas, Gretel H. 2014. "Regarding 'the Mother of Anchor-Children': Towards an Ethical Practice of the Flesh." In "Decolonial Gestures," edited by Jill Lane, Marcial Anativia-Godoy, and Macarena Gómez-Barris, special issue, *E-misférica* 11 (1). http://hemisphericinstitute.org/hemi/en/emisferica-111-decolonial-gesture/verarosas.

Villenas, Sofía. 2009. "Knowing and *Unknowing* Transnational Latino Lives in Teacher Education: At the Intersection of Educational Research and the Latino Humanities." In "At the Intersection of Transnationalism, Latina/o Immigrants, and Education," special issue, *High School Journal* 92 (4): 129–36.

Yosso, Tara J. 2005. "Whose Culture Has Capital? A Critical Race Theory Discussion of Community Cultural Wealth." *Race Ethnicity and Education* 8 (1): 69–91.

Fierce Mamas Rising

Navigating the Terrain of Motherhood as Formerly Incarcerated or Convicted Women

Grace Gámez

But when we are silent
We are still afraid
So it is better to speak
Remembering
We were never meant to survive
—AUDRE LORDE, *LITANY FOR SURVIVAL*

For those of us who live at the edge of the shoreline, life means that precarity is a way of being: waves roll in, sometimes gently lapping at, and other times urgently crashing against, the shore. The waves remind us not just that change is constant, but how close we are to power with the capacity to destroy or alter our lives. This work is an invitation to those who live at the edges of society to rise and claim your birthright to a full and just life. But foremost, this work is a love offering to fierce mothers: mothers who confront agonizing dilemmas, holding the forces that desire to lay waste to our lives at bay, many times only with our love. Fierce mamas dare to dream of a world beyond our own, audaciously raising our children to dream dreams that transcend those the world imagines for them. From this daunting reality, we survive what is meant to destroy us, create new ways to envision and interact with the world, and invent forms of resistance to forces that seek to bury us before our time.

I developed the concept of fierce mothering from a storytelling project I conducted with mothers, primarily Black and Latina, who were formerly incarcerated or convicted. The project broadly considered the reverberations of being system involved, with the goals of gaining a nuanced understanding of the consequences of indefinite punishment and retrieving mothers' everyday practices of resistance. Because the project was inspired by my own experience in the punishment system, the stories gathered reflect and echo my own.

Each mother who participated in the project told stories riddled with pain and sadness but also tenacity—and a fierce reclamation of identity. Yraida Guanipa did the single longest stretch of time in prison of any of the mothers I interviewed. Her children were babies when she was incarcerated, and her story touches on every cog of the system that binds and oppresses people who run afoul of the law—particularly Women of Color. From mandatory minimums and harsh sentencing guidelines, to the distance of prisons from family, making regular contact impossible—Yraida's story features it all. And her resistance to her own unmaking as a mother, her expression of individual agency—even as she was without technical individual rights—illustrates the concept of fierce mothering.

Fierce mothering stands in opposition to, and in spite of, state constructions of good and bad mothers. It is an articulation of feminism that arises from lived experience. Mothers who are formerly incarcerated or convicted frequently perform their roles in between a rock and a hard place. Moments of nonchoice characterize their lives, and at tender junctures in their mother roles, they often make impossible decisions.[1] Fierce mothering is characterized by those impossible choices and agonizing dilemmas through which mothers see their authority, expertise, and analysis evolve and sharpen. Fierce mothers redefine commonsense notions surrounding justice, rights, freedom, and the institution of motherhood.[2]

Women who are incarcerated are viewed as having departed from the hegemonic standard of motherhood and become questionable in their roles as mothers, often to the point of being labeled "bad" mothers. While the challenges of parenting behind bars have been widely studied, a paucity of research examines the experiences and challenges of mothers *after* incarceration or probation, and the literature is devoid of attempts to view this population outside the confines of the good/bad mother dichotomy. Through the story of Yraida, this chapter provides insight into how mothers who were formerly incarcerated or convicted navigate and negotiate their roles, not as "good" or "bad" mothers but as fierce mothers.[3]

Good Eggs or Bad Apples?

The United States holds the record for the largest number of people incarcerated among all nations in the world. As of 2015, this amounted to an estimated 6.7 million people under state or federal supervision, including prison, jail, probation, and parole (Glaze and Kaeble 2016). Incarceration in all its forms has become an American institution. And like many of America's violent institutions and practices, it has a disparate impact on women, People of Color, the poor, and those suffering from mental illness and other medical conditions, such as drug and alcohol addiction. Women are the fastest-growing population under correctional control, outpacing their male counterparts by two times the rate (Glaze and Kaeble 2014). Latina and Black women are incarcerated at close to two and three times the rate of white women, respectively (Guerino, Harrison, and Sabol 2011).

One of the most significant social consequences of the escalating number of women in prison is that they are more likely than men to have been removed from their roles as custodial parents of children under the age of eighteen (Glaze and Maruschak 2010). Therefore, children whose mothers are incarcerated are more likely to experience a disruption in their caretakers than are children whose fathers are incarcerated (Dallaire 2007). Mothering from prison or jail is complicated. Traditional notions of "active" parenting are largely impossible (White 2009; Enos 2001; Owen 1998). One way in which mothers maintain relationships with their children is through visitation. Children being unable to visit or prevented from visiting has negative emotional, behavioral, and psychological repercussions for both children and mothers (Arditti and Few 2008; Poehlmann 2005; Young and Reviere 2006). Despite these challenges and consequences, the mothers in this project credited motherhood as the reason they were able to survive prison and its aftermath.

The reality of a formerly incarcerated or convicted woman's status and her identity as a mother often come in conflict with each other. She is a mother but is often unable to perform the role according to society's standards, which produces "role strain." As Phyllis E. Berry and Helen M. Eigenberg write, these mothers are "expected to follow standards of behavior that are universal for mothers, but due to [her detention,] . . . she cannot meet these standards in normal ways" (2003, 104). This population is difficult to even recognize as mothers when identified with supercharged labels such as "convicted felon," "criminal," "ex-convict," "drug addict," "drug trafficker," or "prostitute." These stigma-laden designations dominate and overwrite that of "mother" (Faith 1993; Girshick 1999; Zalba 1964). Formerly incarcerated or convicted women are seen as having doubly failed—both as women and as mothers (Beckerman 1991; Hairston 1991; Jones 1993). Once within the web of the punishment system, including ancillaries such as child welfare agencies and the Department of Economic Security, women find that their engagement with motherhood is intimately controlled and shaped by the state. Nevertheless, women affected by the punishment system continue to identify as mothers and look for ways to perform their roles to the degree they are capable. With "fugitive movements," they circumvent and defy conditions and restrictions placed on them to engage in their children's lives in what were once considered "normal" ways, prior to their contact with the punishment system.[4] In effect, they steal back their roles moment by crafted moment.

Some of These Women Are Fierce

The concept of fierce mothers disrupts the dichotomy of the good/ bad mother paradigm. The struggle becomes part of the lens through which women see their selfhood and power evolve. They bring the energy of hard-won survival to their mother roles and beyond. For many of the women involved in this project, an increasing confidence in their roles as mothers formed the impetus behind their social justice activism.

Chandra Talpade Mohanty argues that feminism is sustained by "imagined communities of women with divergent histories and social locations, woven together by the political threads of opposition to forms of domination that are not only pervasive but also systemic" (1991, 4). Thus, what allows for the imagined community to coidentify, ally, and collaborate is a "common context of struggle" (7). In this way, fierce mothers who shared their stories with me formed an imagined community—even though Women of Color receive longer sentences, face more serious limitations on maintaining contact with their children as a result of financial constraints, and struggle with more job instability than their white counterparts; this community shared a common commitment to freedom and an understanding that freedom will remain forever out of reach if any one of us is left behind.[5]

Another significant layer of fierce motherhood is a genealogical restatement of motherhood. It emerges from situated knowledge, which Donna Haraway (1988, 579) describes as offering "a more adequate, richer, better account of a world, in order to live in it well and in critical, reflexive relation to our own as well as others' practices of domination and the unequal parts of privilege and oppression that make up all positions." Formerly incarcerated and convicted mothers similarly create and offer knowledge born from a unique relationship with the state. This knowledge addresses how women navigate their roles as mothers alongside state violence and how they survive those conditions mentally and emotionally as individuals.

Phoebe, one of the project participants, demonstrated how the knowledge and skills produced by surviving conditions that are not of your own making are passed down and built on. She spent a significant amount of time in the care of her maternal grandmother when her mother was employed outside the home. Phoebe said her grandmother was "like a second mom," who taught her what it meant to be a present, supportive, and resilient parent. She watched her grandmother offer support and care for her uncles when they cycled in and out of the system, and she observed her mother driving her grandmother to the prison for visits and connecting her uncles to services when they got out. Phoebe's mother learned from her own mother that sometimes the people we love make poor choices, but poor choices do not bar care, love, or support—all of which she offered to her daughter when Phoebe ran afoul of the law. According to Phoebe, navigating difficult moments as a parent requires patience and sacrifice, with an end goal of ensuring your child feels supported and cared for. This passed-down knowledge has informed Phoebe's own parenting style.

A related concept is "othermothering," which is the practice of nurturing children in the place of or alongside biological mothers. Othermothers can be grandmothers, aunts, cousins, older siblings, uncles, and caretakers who are not blood related (Collins 2000; James 1993; Wane 2000). Communal mothering, or othermothering, was a tradition and strategy many of the mothers I interviewed relied on. In two instances, older siblings acted as caretakers of younger siblings. The first example came from Yraida, whose mother had passed away when Yraida was a young child. One of her much older sisters not only raised her but also acted as a grandmother to Yraida's two sons when Yraida was incarcerated. The sister also provided emotional care for Yraida during her long term of incarceration.

The second example of othermothering by siblings comes from Lisa. When her husband abandoned her and their five minor children during her seven-year sentence in a Florida federal prison, Lisa relied on her oldest son, then seventeen, to care for his younger siblings, who resided in New York. Two female neighbors who kept an eye out for the family and sent Lisa pictures and updates of the children made the situation a collective effort.

Rather than reverting to familiar constructs that categorize and pathologize people, fierce mothers challenge us to support *all* the ways in which women mother. The idealistic script of motherhood structures social expectations of women. Consequently, an ideal, or good, mother is one who is self-sacrificing and able to devote herself solely to caretaking. Most women are written outside this ideal, but mothers with a conviction history fall far outside the parameters of the normative construct. Regardless, the women who participated in this project retained strong opinions based on their understanding of the makings of a good or bad mother.

Primarily, the women reported that good mothers meet the needs of their children and offer their presence, support, and unconditional love. In terms of what made a bad mother, many of the women highlighted situations of neglect or abuse; even in this, however, their analysis was nuanced. For example, Yraida said, "Mother's aren't bad by nature, not even animals are. Sometimes when mothers do something to their children, it is because they are going through a depression or they've been injured a lot in their own lives." Yraida's story, which follows, recounts her journey into the system, how she theorized that experience, and how she applied that knowledge to her life and activism.

Surviving the Punishment System

The sentencing doesn't end with you. It doesn't even end with your life. Your sentence goes to your children and even your grandchildren.

—YRAIDA GUANIPA

"Hustler" is often used to refer to a person who traffics in the underground street economy for survival (e.g., selling illicit drugs, doing sex work, running cons). But the term also describes a person who is willing to do what is necessary to meet a goal or a need. Hustlers are uncompromisingly determined to succeed; they refuse to be deterred when obstacles arise. Instead they look for the open windows when doors are closed; they are adept at navigating choppy and dangerous waters. They use ingenuity to "hustle up" resources for survival. Yraida was a hustler while incarcerated, and she remained so when she got out. Her singular determination to be with her children motivated every action inside and outside the prison—from filed motions to radical blogging and organizing. Yraida used her entire arsenal to reunite with her family.

At the start of our interview, I asked Yraida what pseudonym she wanted to use, and she said, "I want you to use my name; I want to be public about it. People need to know, and people like me, the formerly incarcerated, need to be open about that." Yraida is currently pursuing her doctorate in human resource management at a university in Miami, Florida. She also founded her own nonprofit organization, the Yraida Guanipa Institute, located in south Miami. The organization is dedicated to helping formerly incarcerated people reestablish their parent-child relationships after release.

My interview with Yraida was largely focused on her sons and how her role as a mother changed once she came in conflict with the punishment system. Yraida said, "As a mom we play so many roles, a friend, a teacher, caregiver, everything. It is challenging to fulfill the expectations of your children, especially after being incarcerated." She gave the example of being unable to participate in her son's school activities because of her criminal record, which meant that she couldn't join the PTA, get directly involved with the sports/band booster club, or chaperone events.

Yraida was convicted on federal drug conspiracy charges in 1996. In 1995, she was the general manager of a mail facility in Miami, a position she had held for seven years. When a package came in for a regular customer who spoke only Spanish, Yraida was asked to verify its arrival over the phone, and she did so without knowing it contained a large quantity of cocaine. When she was indicted on charges of attempted possession and distribution of cocaine, she pleaded not guilty. She said, "My entire involvement in this crime was the phone call." A year later, however, she was convicted on federal charges of attempted possession and conspiracy to distribute and was sentenced to thirteen years in prison, with five years of supervised probation. Her sons were toddlers at the time, ages one and two. Yraida fully cooperated in the investigation, had no criminal background, and was married, stably employed, and involved in her church and community—ostensible markers of what it means to be a "good" mother, and yet in the eyes of the state, Yraida was rendered undeserving, as none of these factors was taken into consideration during sentencing.

Yraida's federal charges made her ineligible for parole under the Sentencing Reform Act of 1984.[6] Good conduct was her only recourse for reducing her sentence, but she soon learned that a legal code established by the Bureau of Prisons had changed the calculation. While incarcerated, Yraida filed motions to contest this legal code, and her case was eventually heard before the 11th Circuit Court in northern Florida. Though the court decided against her petition, it represents her tenacity in advocating for herself and others affected by this injustice.[7]

Every decision Yraida made while incarcerated was done with her sons in mind. She says that she survived prison because of her sons' love. When Yraida went to prison, her family went from a two-income household to a single-income home. Her husband began working sixteen-hour days six days a week to manage the family's expenses. Her children were cared for by the half-sister who had raised Yraida after her own mother died. The family's emotional and financial circumstances were further strained by the fact that Yraida was sent to a "prison camp" three hundred miles away, which made consistent family visitation an insurmountable hardship.

Yraida understood her family's financial constraints but also knew the importance of maintaining a mother-child relationship. She saw other mothers in the same facility suffering under the same family restraints she was, and she used her frustration as motivation to look for help. After exhausting multiple legal channels, Yraida staged a hunger strike. The prison's response was five days in solitary confinement followed by transfer to a facility two hundred miles farther away to serve the remainder of her sentence. As a result of the now five-hundred-mile distance and associated costs, Yraida saw her boys only four times during the ten and a half years she was incarcerated. The visits were limited by the prison to thirty minutes each.

Even after repeated devastating failures, Yraida did not give up the effort to help her sons visit and to ensure that the women she was incarcerated alongside had the same visitation right. She responded to the increasingly difficult challenge by getting more creative. As she changed her focus to people outside the system, she still encountered regulations that interfered with her goal, but she decided to write to church and civil rights organizations and ask if they would be willing to sponsor a bus for children of mothers incarcerated at the facility in which she was housed. Eventually, she found an organization willing to provide this service and was able to arrange transportation for her two sons and forty-six other children to visit their mothers for an entire day. It took eight years to achieve this win.

When I asked Yraida why she had worked so hard and taken so many risks (including a second hunger strike that had nearly killed her), she said, "I always wanted to make sure my boys knew I loved them immensely and that my mistake would not destroy the unconditional love I have for them." She called them three times a week, wrote letters, and crocheted gifts for them, but nothing takes the place of seeing and holding your children and vice versa. The time apart fractured their relationship. She described the toll in tears:

> Serving a sentence of ten and a half years changes you, your children—everybody. I was a stranger to my children when I came out of prison. When I was inside I was dreaming. I was dreaming how it was gonna be when I came back home, and when I was released, they rejected me. That's the word: rejection. They wanted me to leave. I don't blame them. I was not part of their life. I mean, can you imagine only seeing your children four times in ten and a half years? Eight years after my release, I'm still struggling to have a healthy relationship with my boys.

Yraida continued to talk about the challenges that presented themselves after incarceration and through her last several years on federal probation. Even though she was outside the prison walls, probation made her home part of the surveillance system. Her young sons, who barely knew her, started fearing her because of what living with her meant. She said, "My probation officer wore a gun when she came to the home, and even though it was under her blouse, you could still see it. My kids would just run inside the room, and they would not go out. It was hard." Yraida also talked about what time is like now, out of prison and off probation. She said,

> There is a life sentence in having a record. It doesn't go away. I am afraid that if my kids do something good or become famous, they will always tell them, "Your mother was in prison." If they want to run for politics, forget it, they will say, "We see your mother was in prison." ... So the sentencing doesn't end with you. It doesn't end even with your

life. Your sentence goes to your children and even your grandchildren. If my grandchildren become successful, somebody will bring the subject up. It will be like, "Oh, your grandmother was in prison!"

As we concluded our conversation, I asked Yraida what freedom meant to her. She said, "It is very simple: to be free means to be able to be a mom." I thought about her definition of freedom, and about all the stories she had shared with me. Being a mom means being able to freely engage in all areas of your child's development and interests, to actively support their dreams and desires, to be fully present. And it also means being able to realize the full potential of who *you* are in that role. If you've never experienced the unfreedom of state-sanctioned violence, you may not connect being a mom with being free. I realized, however, that her definition of freedom, "to be a mom," isn't simple for people like us, whose obstacles are layered and pronounced, and it will never be.

We Dream of Freedom

It is important to share how I know survival is survival and not just a walk through the rain.

—AUDRE LORDE

The proscriptive understanding of "good" mothers assumes there is only one way to express love, care, and devotion for one's child. Formerly incarcerated or convicted mothers carry heavy emotional burdens exacerbated by social and legal norms, which produce diverse barriers. Fierce mothers learn to navigate spaces and shoulder burdens to protect and shield their children, even if this means being absent from important moments, like school plays, first steps, graduations, and perhaps even their children's lives. What characterizes and sets apart fierce motherhood from other ways in which motherhood has been theorized is persistently having to make critical parenting decisions under conditions of duress. The messiness of life is what fierce mothers actively engage in, which is sanitized from parochial models of mothering.

Social exclusion, demonization, and the associated grief that formerly incarcerated or convicted mothers face produce a different way of viewing and living in the world.[8] Fierce mothers as a concept dismisses normative thinking around motherhood and creates a rupturing space to understand our roles as mothers from the perspective of multiplicity, difference, and resistance.

The story of Yraida reveals the obstacles mothers face postpunishment and demonstrates how mothers navigate and negotiate barriers under conditions of unfreedom in order to perform their roles as mothers. To create a livable life, fierce mothers learn to live and mother unapologetically; they live, love, and otherwise operate outside the binary of the good/bad mother scripts. They resist the social norms that label them "bad" mothers, push back against de facto discrimination, and defy imposed obstacles to claim their right to be mothers *in spite of* the state. Part of the reason that mothers in this project were able to persevere is because they audaciously clung to the idea of hope. Hope is central to revolutions of oppressed and marginalized communities, and it is fundamental to what it means to be human.

The U.S. punishment system and its corollaries function by attacking hope, without which the soul ceases to exist. Yraida's story in particular undermines the argument that the purpose of the punishment system is to produce "worthy" subjects. If that were true, people with conviction histories would be allowed to participate in the democratic process and to readily access employment and other social safety nets postpunishment. Instead, the punishment system operates to reproduce state power, subordination, and domination.

In *Abolition Democracy*, Angela Davis (2005, 34) encourages us to "think about different versions of democracy," and to expect relief from suffering and injustice, because hope can reach beyond physical and psychological conditions. It can act as the connection between identifying what requires change and what means are necessary to facilitate change, and therefore hope is able to mobilize. Hope is political, didactic, and performative; it holds the promise of a new understanding of democracy, justice, and freedom.

Notes

1. Fierce mothering moves beyond an understanding of motherhood that is limited to reproductive rights and reproductive healthcare, complicating how we understand the idea of "choice." As Silliman and colleagues argue in *Undivided Rights*, "choice implies a marketplace of options," where women have the right to decide what happens to and in their bodies (2004, 6). Furthermore, choice suggests that women have options regarding how, if, or to what extent they perform their roles as mothers. I found that fierce mothers respond to the absence of choice (nonchoice) through creative insurgency; they generate possibilities in the absence of institutional reproductive liberty and claim their rights and identities as mothers and activists.

2. Several common tropes come to mind when we imagine mothers and motherhood, largely because American culture dictates how mothers should "show up"—racially, physically, and sexually. Liberal/Ideal Motherhood is characterized by selflessness, and it is the model of mothering that all mothers are regulated and judged by. Women of Color and women who have been system involved—to name two categories of "otherized" women—are viewed as always already failing in their roles as mothers. Adrienne Rich (1977) argues that the "patriarchal institution of motherhood is not the human condition[; rather motherhood] has a history and ideology" (33). Thus, this construct of

mothering can be undone—we can choose to be our own definers and to create paths that are affirming and life giving.

3. "Formerly incarcerated" is used to refer to people who have spent time in prison or jail. "Convicted" refers to people who have a misdemeanor or felony conviction on their record and who have had to serve time on probation. "System involved" refers to both populations and can also include families who have navigated prison, jail, the Department of Economic Security, and/or the Department of Child Safety (formerly Child Protective Services).

4. In "The Case of Blackness," Fred Moten writes, "Fugitive movement is stolen life, and its relation to law is reducible neither to simple interdiction nor bare transgression" (2008, 179).

5. Drawn from "All of Us or None," by Bertolt Brecht. He writes, "Everything or nothing. All of us or none. One alone his lot can't better. Choose the gun or fetter. Everything or nothing. All of us or none" (1945, 140).

6. Part of the Comprehensive Crime Control Act of 1984, Pub. L. No. 98–473 § 218(a)(5), 98 Stat. 1837, 2027 (repealing 18 U.S.C.A. § 4201 et seq.).

7. Yraida Leonides Guanipa v. Warden Carlyle Holder, 05–15137 (11th Cir. 2006). Access the complete ruling here: https://law.justia.com/cases /federal/appellate-courts/ca11/05-15137/200515137-2011-02-28.html.

8. Robin Kelley (2002), in discussing Richard Wright's *Native Son*, writes, "Black people did not have to go out and find surrealism[,] for their lives were already surreal. . . . [I]t was the forced exclusion of black people that produced a different way of looking at the world and feeling it" (183).

References

Arditti, Joyce, and April Few. 2008. "Maternal Distress and Women's Reentry into Family and Community Life." *Family Process* 47:303–21.

Beckerman, Adela. 1991. "Women in Prison: The Conflict Between Confinement and Parental Rights." *Social Justice* 18 (3): 171-83.

Berry, Phyllis E., and Helen M. Eigenberg. 2003. "Role Strain and Incarcerated Mothers: Understanding the Process of Mothering." *Women and Criminal Justice* 15 (1): 101–19.

Brecht, Bertolt. 1945. "All of Us or None." *Poetry: A Magazine of Verse*, December 1945, 140–41.

Collins, Patricia Hill. 2000. "Mammies, Matriarchs, and Other Controlling Images." In *Black Feminist Thought*, edited by Patricia Hill Collins, 76-106. New York: Routledge Press.

Dallaire, Danielle. 2007. "Incarcerated Mothers and Fathers: A Comparison of Risks for Children and Families." *Family Relations* 56:440–53.

Davis, Angela. 2005. *Abolition Democracy: Beyond Empire, Prisons, and Torture*. New York: Seven Stories Press.

Enos, Sandra. 2001. *Mothering from the Inside: Parenting in a Women's Prison*. Albany: SUNY Press.

Faith, Karlene. 1993. *Unruly Women: The Politics of Confinement and Resistance*. Vancouver, BC: Press Gang.

Girshick, Lori B. 1999. *No Safe Haven: Stories of Women in Prison*. Boston: Northeastern University Press.

Glaze, Lauren E., and Danielle Kaeble. 2014. *Correctional Populations in the United States, 2013*. Washington, DC: Bureau of Justice Statistics.

Glaze, Lauren E., and Danielle Kaeble. 2016. *Correctional Populations in the United States, 2015*. Washington, DC: Bureau of Justice Statistics.

Glaze, Lauren E., and Laura M. Maruschak. 2010. *Parents in Prison and Their Minor Children*. Washington, DC: Bureau of Justice Statistics.

Guerino, Paul M., Paige M. Harrison, and William J. Sabol. 2011. *Prisoners in 2010*. Washington, DC: Bureau of Justice Statistics.

Hairston, Creasie Finney. 1991. "Family Ties During Imprisonment: Important to Whom and for What?" *Journal of Sociology and Welfare* 18:87-104.

Haraway, Donna. 1988. "Situated Knowledges: The Science Question in Feminism and the Privilege of Partial Perspective." *Feminist Studies* 14:575-99.

James, Stanlie M. 1993. "Mothering: A Possible Black Feminist Link to Social Transformation." In *Theorizing Black Feminisms: The Visionary Pragmatism of Black Women*, edited by Stanlie M. James and Abena P. A. Busia, 32–44. London: Routledge.

Jones, Richard S. 1993. "Coping with Separation: Adaptive Responses of Women Prisoners." *Women and Criminal Justice* 5 (1): 71–91.

Kelley, Robin. 2002. *Freedom Dreams: The Black Radical Imagination.* Boston, MA: Beacon Press.

Mohanty, Chandra Talpade. 1991. "Cartographies of Struggle." In *Third World Women and the Politics of Feminism,* edited by Chandra Talpade Mohanty, Ann Russo, and Lourdes Torres, 1–50. Bloomington: Indiana University Press.

Moten, Fred. 2008. "The Case of Blackness." *Criticism* 50 (2): 177–218.

Owen, Barbara. 1998. *"In the Mix": Struggle and Survival in a Women's Prison.* Albany: SUNY Press.

Poehlmann, Julie. 2005. "Incarcerated Mothers' Contact with Children, Perceived Family Relationships, and Depressive Symptoms." *Journal of Family Psychology* 19 (3): 350–57.

Rich, Adrienne. 1977. *Of Woman Born.* New York: Bantam.

Silliman, Jael, Marlene Gerber Fried, Loretta Ross, and Elena R. Gutiérrez. 2004. *Undivided Rights: Women of Color Organize for Reproductive Justice.* Cambridge, MA: South End Press.

Wane, Njoki. 2000. "Reflections on the Mutuality of Mothering: Women, Children and Othermothering." *Journal of the Association for Research on Mothering* 2 (2): 105–16.

White, Regina Lynn. 2009. "Giving Back Not Giving Up: Generativity Among Older Female Inmates." PhD diss., University of Tennessee, Knoxville.

Young, Vernetta D., and Rebecca Reviere. 2006. *Women Behind Bars: Gender and Race in U.S. Prisons.* Boulder, CO: Lynne Rienner.

Zalba, Serapio R. 1964. *Women Prisoners and Their Families.* Los Angeles: Delmar Press.

Herstories of Sobrevivencia

Chicanx/Latinx Community College Student-Mothers (Re)claiming and (Re)defining the Educational Pipeline and CalWORKS

Nereida Oliva and Hortencia Jiménez

While the Chicanx/Latinx population has grown steadily in the last decades, their educational attainment remains relatively low.[1] Scholars have found that "Latinas/os continue to face issues of access, remediation, financial aid challenges, retention, (low) expectations, and mentorship options from faculty and other leadership who recognize their specific challenges, strengths, and potential to thrive as college-level students" (Rodríguez and Oseguera 2015, 129). Latinx student-mothers face additional challenges, ranging from lack of childcare, unwelcoming campus climates, and limited institutional support programs and services (Oliva and Jiménez 2017). The Institute for Women's Policy Research (IWPR) notes that of the 4.8 million undergraduate students, 26 percent are parents. The largest share (45 percent) of student-parents attends community colleges, and of those, the majority are Mothers of Color. Over half of Black women at community college are parents (53.7 percent), while Latinx and American Indian mothers make up 40 percent of the total community college student-parent population (Reichlin Cruse 2015).

Research on student-mothers accentuates the importance of an education and how it can alter quality of life for the mothers and their children (Christopher 2005; Jones-DeWeever and Gault 2008; Sidel 2006; Van Stone, Nelson, and Niemann 1994). Thus, exploring how Chicanx/Latinx community college student-mothers navigate multiple institutions grounded in systems of oppression is crucial to improving their families' futures. For community college student-mothers, systems of oppression operate in contradictory ways in "terms of their potential to be oppressive institutions that marginalize Latino students, but also how these institutions offer the potential of real hope and opportunity" (Oliva, Pérez, and Parker 2013, 142). Chicanx/Latinx community college student-mother experiences and realities are a reflection of the policies and practices that affect their academic and personal lives. For some Latinx/Chicanx community college student-mothers in our research, the personal is the political, as a higher education would not be as easily accessible without cash aid from programs such as California Work Opportunity and Responsibility to Kids (CalWORKS).

This chapter is organized into five parts: first, we provide a snapshot of Latinx in higher education. We then briefly examine the history of welfare reform legislation. Next, we discuss the framework of *sobrevivencia* and our methodology (Galván 2006). Thereafter, we examine the herstories of three Chicanx/Latinx student-mothers who navigate CalWORKS while furthering their educations.[2] We end with a discussion and a call to action for community colleges to implement an organizational culture that centers the experiences of student-parents.

Chicanx/Latinx Access to Higher Education

The Chicanx education pipeline reveals the "leaks" and patterns that influence the educational attainment of this specific ethnic group (Pérez Huber et al. 2015). Educators, scholars, and policymakers have used this pipeline to develop and implement policies addressing issues found among Chicanx/Latinx students. Out of one hundred Latinx students who begin elementary school together, 17 percent will attend a community college (Pérez Huber et al. 2015). Patricia Gándara (2015) notes that one in every five women in the United States was Latina in 2015, and by 2060, it is estimated that Latinas will compose nearly one-third of the country's female population. Although the number of Latinas in higher education has increased dramatically, degree attainment for the group remains significantly low. The Center for American Progress noted that in 2010, 30 percent of white women held a bachelor's degree or higher, compared with 14.9 percent of Latinas (Ahmad and Iverson 2013).

These statistics regarding the educational attainment and success of Latinx raise concern and warrant closer examination. For Latinx, college access and educational attainment is complex and intricate. Societal, cultural, and familial traditions and beliefs highly influence their educational experiences (Valdés 1996). Hernández-Truyol (2008, 1287) explains that "the complicated amalgam of pressures that emanates from both outside and inside—the majority culture and *la cultura Latina*—result in Latina invisibility, marginalization and subordination in all their communities," including in higher education. Dominant deficit ideologies about Chicanx/Latinx often create challenges and barriers for accessing a postsecondary education (Valencia 2010). These deficit ideologies maintain that low academic achievement for Chicanx/Latinx students is a direct result of family factors and beliefs regarding education, insisting that Chicanx/Latinx parents do not care about or value education (López 2001). For example, Chicanx/Latinx K–12 students are often perceived as passive and not interested or invested in their education, and thus they are not placed in college preparatory classes in high school (Thompson, Warren, and Carter 2004). Currently, Chicanx/Latinx students are often the first in their family to pursue postsecondary education and tend to be unfamiliar with college admissions and survival processes (Auerbach 2002; Zarate and Pachon 2006). Other factors, such as language, immigration, and economic status, also exacerbate their poor experiences within higher education (Gonzalez 2016).

Community colleges enroll the majority of Students of Color (SOC) in higher education, in part because of the colleges' low cost, but also because they provide the "opportunity" to enter and participate in higher education (Gaxiola Serrano 2016, 240). According to the Pew Research Center, 48 percent of Chicanx/Latinx college students begin at a community college, the highest percentage of any racial/ethnic group attending two-year institutions (Krogstad 2016). Yet, transfer rates for Latinx community college students are relatively low (Castro and Cortez 2016). Low degree attainment for Latinx can be linked to lack of academic preparation by K–12 institutions, lack of access to proper information about college choice and the admissions process, financial barriers, and inadequate support systems (Zarate and Burciaga 2010).

While a growing body of research focuses on Chicanx/Latinx in higher education, scant attention is given to Latinx student-mothers. Not only must community college student-mothers meet the intense demands of work, school, and motherhood, they also must continuously engage in the energy-intensive labor of seeking public benefits and school support services, which are difficult to find, understand, apply to, and qualify for. Keeping in mind that only 26 percent of students attending a two-year institution attain a degree or certificate within six years, our research seeks to center and explore the experiences of a significant but overlooked community college student (Reichlin Cruse 2015).

The Personal Responsibility and Work Opportunity Reconciliation Act

In the mid-1990s, the social welfare system was restructured in a way that altered the safety net for many poor families throughout the United States (Hays 2003). The Personal Responsibility and Work

Opportunity Reconciliation Act (PRWORA), better known as "welfare reform"—signature legislation of the Clinton Administration—passed in 1996. The legislation ended the cash assistance program Aid to Families with Dependent Children and replaced it with Temporary Aid to Needy Families (TANF). Several studies note that the "success" of the new welfare reform legislation was not to move low-income families into living-wage careers but to push low-income families off welfare rolls (Acs and Loprest 2004; Cherlin et al. 2002). PRWORA was primarily designed to send a message to the poor regarding personal morality rather than to develop more effective, evidence-based interventions to provide Americans with a basic standard of living (Maréchal 2015). Bok (2004) notes that in some states, clients were limited or barred from pursuing higher education because the "work-first" model did not support college attendance as counting toward federal work-participation rates. The limitations of PRWORA and TANF led many low-income families to require supplemental benefits to make ends meet (Deparle 2009).

The passage of welfare reform legislation complicated the lives of many, particularly low-income, working-class single mothers wanting to achieve a college education, because now they faced additional stipulations of mandatory job training to obtain cash aid. As a result, these welfare policies created additional barriers for parents trying to access them, particularly the poor.

Rather than acknowledging structural and institutional barriers to achieving a college education, the literature points to personal responsibility as the primary barrier for single mothers (Polakow et al. 2004). Vyvian C. Adair (2001) contends that single mothers are less likely to benefit from changes in welfare policies because these changes limit access to the jobs and job training that the policies are intended to provide in the first place. Student-mothers' academic enrollment in rural community colleges is contingent on a combination of other programs, such as financial aid, public assistance programs, and employment income, including subsidized housing, Medicaid, the Special Supplemental Nutrition Program for Women, Infants, and Children (WIC), food stamps, TANF, Head Start, and the earned income tax credit (EITC).

In 1997, the state of California created the CalWORKS legislation. The primary purpose of this state initiative is to help families with children become self-reliant through services such as temporary cash aid, childcare, and job training. During the 2000–2001 school year, forty-seven thousand CalWORKS recipients attended California community colleges (Mathur et al. 2002). CalWORKS students are more likely to be Women of Color and single mothers (Romo and Segura 2010, 179). Mathur, Reichle, Strawn, and Wiseley (2002) examined the educational outcomes, employment rates, and earnings of participants in CalWORKS who were enrolled in a California community college but also left the college during the 1999–2000 school year. Additionally, the study compared the educational attainment of CalWORKS recipients to that of all women disenrolling from a California community college during the same period. The researchers found that completing a vocational certificate increased earnings. Their findings also suggested that CalWORKS recipients were more likely to have a long-term full-time job upon graduating from a community college.

To explore how that works out in the lived experiences of Latinx student-mothers, we focus in the next section on the sobrevivencia narratives of Alejandra, Rosa, and Aracely, each of whom grew up surviving on government assistance and/or are currently receiving some type of aid.

Framework

The term "sobrevivencia" is used by Chicana feminist scholars to honor and celebrate their experiences and challenges amid the complexities of everyday realities. Ruth Trinidad Galván explains that sobrevivencia is "not survival, but that beyondness" (2006, 163). That "beyondness" encapsulates the often unspoken raw and honest emotions and thoughts Chicanx and Latinx experience as a result of their everyday trials and tribulations. Understanding that "beyondness" of which Galván speaks helps capture the various ways in which Chicanx and Latinx use their resources and ancestral ways of knowing and teaching to literally and figuratively navigate and negotiate multiple and intersecting systems of oppression. The Chicanx/Latinx community college student-mothers in this study demonstrate sobrevivencia as they learn to navigate and negotiate the education system and safety net programs such as CalWORKS. Their sobrevivencia offers a multifaceted and needed understanding of the community college student-mother experience, capturing what higher educational practitioners and educators perhaps cannot "see" because they use frameworks that do not center or address issues of race, class, gender, and other forms of oppression, nor the experiences of students who are also parents.

Methodology and Findings

To highlight herstories of sobrevivencia, we present in-depth accounts of three Chicanx/Latinx student-mothers: Alejandra, Rosa, and Aracely.[3] At the time of the interview, all three participants were enrolled full time at Pacific Coast Community College and were receiving some type of financial assistance (e.g., CalWORKS, financial aid, EOPS). Alejandra, a twenty-four-year-old married mother of four children (ages seven months and two, three, and six years), also works part-time on campus. She aspires to be a social worker and to transfer to a California state university. Rosa, a thirty-one-year-old single mother of a five-year-old girl, lived with her parents at the time of the interview. She is passionate about guiding students and plans to be a high school or college counselor. She will graduate from Hartnell College with an AA degree in sociology. Aracely is also pursuing a sociology degree and would like to earn a PhD. She is a thirty-one-year-old single mother of four children, ages thirteen, ten, five, and two. Aracely was working part time in the Extended Opportunity Program and Services (EOPS) office at Hartnell College at the time of the interview.

The data for the three student-mothers were gathered from four focus groups we conducted with thirteen student-mothers in the academic year 2016–2017.[4] Participants in the focus groups were recruited through fliers posted all over campus and word of mouth from other students as well as from faculty and counselors. The participants identified themselves as Mexican and Mexican American. The youngest participant was twenty-four, and the oldest, thirty-one. All participants had at least one child; their children's ages ranged from seven months to thirteen years. None of the participants had completed a four-year degree. All three earned less than twenty-five thousand dollars a year and received some form of assistance from welfare.

Narratives of Sobrevivencia: Chicanx/Latinx Student-Mothers' Pathways to Higher Education Through Public Assistance

Alejandra

Alejandra enrolled at Pacific Coast Community College in fall 2014 and has been attending since. As a mother of four children, she recognized that her academic achievements were made possible by the help and support of programs such as CalWORKS, but, she clarified, "It's not the way that some people think it is." CalWORKS, like other services, has eligibility guidelines and requirements for student participants. Initially, Alejandra was not interested in receiving help and support from CalWORKS, preferring to work, and she told the social worker, "I don't wanna go to school. I'm gonna work." She worked extensive hours for minimal pay in the fields until one day, Alejandra said, she had an "epiphany" while at work and told herself, "This is not my life." Soon after this insight, Alejandra eagerly and excitedly reached out to the caseworker who had informed her about CalWORKS. This time around, however, the social worker was not as enthusiastic and helpful, saying, "Well, you can't just change your mind. . . . I have to change your case," to which Alejandra responded, "Isn't that your job?"

The caseworker eventually provided Alejandra with assistance and informed her of what paperwork she needed to submit to the college and to the CalWORKS program. To complete the application process, Alejandra had to provide check stubs and documents to verify income eligibility as well as take proficiency exams to measure her academic ability and potential. Alejandra felt overwhelmed by these demands and "almost gave up." Her perseverance and persistence paid off, however, and she was awarded CalWORKS benefits so that she could complete her general education at Hartnell College. To complete her coursework within the time frame given, Alejandra took "eighteen, twenty-two, twelve units during the summer," the same full-time course load she took during the regular academic term. Being a full-time student required her to remain focused on her studies while also parenting four young children. Her various roles and responsibilities required Alejandra to adopt schedules and routines that enabled her to complete coursework but also prioritize spending time with her children and partner. Though this was not an easy task, Alejandra completed her general education requirements with a 2.8 grade point average and is now on her way to a four-year university to prepare to be a social worker.

Alejandra's sobrevivencia affords her the strength, courage, and resilience to challenge and resist institutions grounded in systems of oppression. In articulating how her experiences at the community college reflected the ways in which such institutions perpetuate intersecting and multiple forms of oppression, Alejandra held those institutions and the individuals within them accountable for their oppressive ideologies and practices. Rather than "blaming the victim," herself, Alejandra stated, "I was supposed to be impoverished for the rest of my life, and my kids too. My kids are supposed to be in gangs. To the government, to anybody else, I'm not supposed to be anybody or anything. I feel like I have been able to prove that wrong." Valencia (2010) explains that "blaming the victim" is a characteristic of the deficit-thinking model, in which Students of Color are believed to be deficient and are blamed for their educational disadvantages, while programs and policies address and remedy those deficiencies without changing the architecture of schools and other institutions that create and perpetuate educational inequities for marginalized groups. Alejandra is very much aware of deficit ideologies regarding her and her children, but she is also able to articulate how she challenged such ideologies by completing the general education requirements at Pacific Coast Community College so that she could pursue a career helping other student-mothers in similar situations. She aspires to be a resource for others and plans to commit to sharing her knowledge and experience, further resisting the institutions that would keep her and others in their place.

Alejandra's sobrevivencia stands in opposition to and amid institutions, policies, and practices that, on the one hand, helped her access a postsecondary education while raising four children, but, on the other, racialized and gendered her community college experience as a first-generation student-mother. As a result, her sobrevivencia adds complexity to the community college student profile typically discussed in the literature. More importantly, Alejandra's herstory of sobrevivencia humanizes how policies and practices affect the everyday lives of community college student-mothers.

Rosa

Rosa is a thirty-one-year-old single mother of a five-year-old. When Rosa enrolled at Pacific Coast Community College, she received Cal-WORKS for two semesters, but after staff members discovered that Rosa had an associate's degree from a for-profit institution she had previously attended, they disqualified her from the program. Rosa explained the first time she applied for CalWORKS: "Being on welfare was a big stigma in my family, you know, '*no somos huevones*,' you know; they thought being on welfare is being lazy. You're taking from other hard-working people. That's how I was raised, but when it came down to it, it's like, I did work, I worked, I want to work but I'm gonna die if I don't eat, if I don't feed my child. I'm gonna be on the street if I can't pay rent." Rosa understands the stigma associated with welfare and the dominant narrative of the welfare recipient as "lazy." The term "welfare queen" was used in Ronald Reagan's 1976 presidential campaign to stigmatize and chastise economically disadvantaged racial and ethnic minorities, immigrants, and, particularly, Black single mothers. The "queen" symbolically transmitted prejudicial, derogatory racial, gender, and class subtexts, conveying the message that public assistance programs were overburdened by undeserving people and pathologizing parenting by African American and Latina mothers (Kohler-Hausmann 2017). Similar racially coded language and terms are still being used to promote deficit ideologies in discourses regarding various social justice issues, such as mass incarceration, immigration, and reproductive rights (Alexander 2010; Zavella 2016).

Rosa did not want to be perceived as lazy, a belief that she had internalized early in life. She challenges the narrative of the lazy welfare mother with her sobrevivencia herstory, noting that she has worked and now needed CalWORKS to provide for her daughter. Rosa was "mortified" at the thought of having to go to the welfare office because she did not know what to expect once she got there, and she was concerned that someone would recognize her. She said, "People are going to recognize me, you know; do I dress in sweats to blend in with everybody else? What is the dress code? I just don't know." Rosa was overwhelmed with the thought of being recognized at the welfare office. This was coupled with the stress of having to figure out how to present herself once there. Michel Foucault's (1991) work on disciplinary power is useful in understanding how the deserving welfare recipient is constructed. Foucault describes three types of disciplinary power: hierarchical observation, normalization, and examination. The latter helps explain how welfare recipients are constructed through the examination of personal case files and supporting documentation. At the welfare office, the caseworker needed additional information about Rosa; as she comments, "They tell you, we need all these documents and then you are going to have an appointment, and you bring all these documents, and they're like, well, you need this, this, and this too." The making of Rosa's case file involved an examination of her life, making her private life visible and open to judgment by the caseworker. Foucault writes that the documentary techniques of the examination makes each individual a "case" in which "he may be described, judged, measured, compared with others" (Foucault 1991, 191).

Low-income People of Color like Rosa must constantly submit to invasive monitoring of their private lives to receive benefits to which they are legally entitled. Nathalie Maréchal (2015) observes that one of the features of the twenty-first-century welfare system is the widespread use of surveillance techniques on poor people who receive certain types of public benefits. This is a form of state criminalization of the poor by controlling and monitoring their lives and marking them as Other (Maréchal 2015, 65). For Rosa, this process was invasive and embarrassing because, as she said, "they want almost your DNA because they do fingerprints and everything now, mugshots. I feel so embarrassed. I feel like they are doing this on purpose to make me feel bad, you know." Rosa is "not asking for handouts" and "will work" to get the assistance she needs. Rosa's sobrevivencia is central in deconstructing and challenging the lazy welfare recipient. This required a mental shift for Rosa, who said she had "to learn how to take myself from a different mind frame, like, I'm not lazy. I'm on welfare, but I'm going to school, I'm a mom, I'm a single mom now, I'm working." Her story of sobrevivencia involves working through her raw emotions, feelings, and thoughts. It involves challenging the beliefs she has internalized about being a welfare recipient and coming to terms with the fact that she is not lazy and is deserving of public assistance.

Aracely

Unlike Alejandra and Rosa, Aracely was able to tap into additional resources at Hartnell College from the beginning of her education. A thirty-one-year-old single mother of four children, Aracely used her sobrevivencia strategies to take advantage of every opportunity offered at Pacific Coast Community College, where she obtained financial resources and services to further her education. These included EOPS options offered to students disadvantaged by educational, language, social, and economic factors. Aracely was also part of Cooperative Agencies Resource for Education (CARE), a program given to students who are recipients of CalWORKS and are single heads of household. To qualify for CARE, students like Aracely also need to be enrolled in EOPS. Aracely shared her experience making use of financial resources:

> I'm a CalWORKS student. I get the help from the Monterey County; they help me pay for my books. I'm also a CARE student. [They] help me pay for my meals here at Hartnell College. I'm also an EOPS student and . . . I get the priority registration, sign up for my classes. I do apply for scholarships even though some things I won't get, but I know that I did the effort and I took the time to apply for them. Whatever

comes, it's welcome, it helps a lot. Last month I went to a field trip and I got two hundred dollars just for going on a Saturday, and I didn't want to, but I needed those two hundred dollars. I knew they were going to help me.

As a CalWORKS, CARE, and EOP student, Aracely is able to get most of her books for free and obtain priority registration. When possible, she joins field trips to get a stipend. In addition, Aracely's daughter attends preschool at the Child Development Center on the main campus, which the young girl "loves." Aracely's sobrevivencia strategy is to constantly be on the lookout for resources she can apply for, including scholarships. Her sobrevivencia exemplifies initiative, leadership, perseverance, and self-advocacy in seeking financial resources. Aracely is aware of programs on campus and actively seeks them. We recognize, however, that many student-mothers are unaware of the programs and services at Pacific Coast Community College and are currently struggling.

These narratives offered by Alejandra, Rosa, and Aracely illustrate their commitment and desire to continue their education against all odds, even with the limitations on safety net programs and services at Pacific Coast Community College. Their herstories of sobrevivencia point to voices of strength, hard work, resourcefulness, and perseverance—for them, giving up is not an option. Their sobrevivencia therefore compels them to do whatever possible to make it through school and life as community college student-mothers.

Discussion

The narratives shared above contextualize "both the problematic and effective aspects" (Romo and Segura 2010, 173) of social safety net programs such as CalWORKS. CalWORKS provided Alejandra, Rosa, and Aracely the services and support they needed to complete the general education requirements for transferring to a four-year institution, while also providing for their families. Yet, accessing Cal-WORKS services and benefits involved intense emotional turmoil derived from initial contact with CalWORKS caseworkers and from the negative stigma attached to being a welfare recipient. Alejandra, Rosa, and Aracely have unapologetically disrupted both the educational and the welfare systems and (re)claimed the conventional narratives about Latinx community college students and mothers. Sobrevivencia pushes the mothers beyond the stigma of being welfare recipients and critiques the policies and practices that heavily influence their educational experiences, so that they can hold institutions accountable for perpetuating and sustaining social and educational inequities. Sobrevivencia enables us to delve into the "messiness" of the Chicanx and Latinx community college student-mother experience without jeopardizing their experiences, epistemologies, and pedagogies. Chicanx and Latinx community college student-mothers' sobrevivencia encompasses and recognizes mothering as a source of knowledge, or *sabiduria*, resistance, and healing. The narratives of sobrevivencia presented in this chapter broaden the existing profile of the community college student experience and call for dialogue on how to continue supporting Chicanx/Latinx community college students and student-mothers. By centering the Chicanx/Latinx community college student-mothers' herstories of sobrevivencia, administrators, policymakers, and educators can increase their awareness of policies and practices that shape the educational access and experiences of this particular student population. To be specific, the herstories of sobrevivencia presented in this chapter warrant a critical evaluation of the connection and disconnection between theory and practice through the lenses of those most affected by both theory and practice.

In addition to programs like CalWORKS, institutions can support Chicanx/Latinx community college student-mothers by providing child-friendly spaces on campus, on-campus childcare in the mornings and evenings, and campus activities centered on student-parents, such as Family Movie Night. At the national level, there is a growing effort to bring visibility to student-parents in institutions of higher education. The National Center for Student Parent Programs is at the forefront in researching and publishing work on student-parents as well as in organizing the Student Parent Support Symposium for the past twelve years to promote support services for college and university student-parents. In spring 2017, the National Center for Student Parent Programs launched the Hands on Hats Campaign for Student Parent Awareness to highlight student-parents who are graduating from colleges across the nation. Our institution, Pacific Coast Community College, participated in this campaign.

As Chicanx/Latinx faculty and former student-mothers, we have a strong commitment to bringing attention to a growing population of student-parents at the community college, through both our research and our teaching positions at Pacific Coast. We are optimistic that our research and our active participation in campus committees will move the conversation forward at our college, shaping an organizational culture receptive to student-parents by creating and implementing initiatives that can further support student-parents' success.

Notes

1.   Chicanx/Latinx is used to classify individuals of Latin American ancestry. This term also acknowledges and embraces all gender and sexual identities. The term signifies both singular and plural. In direct quotations or in formal titles of publications or organizations, original terminology is preserved. Where the reference is gender specific, gendered Spanish endings (*o/a*) apply.

2.   We feel the term "herstories" captures the core and purpose of this chapter, which is to center the lived experiences and realities of Chicanx/Latinx community college student-mothers. The term aligns with Chicana feminist epistemologies, our guiding principles. Herstories challenge and "talk back" to dominant narratives of Chicanx/Latinx by highlighting their knowledge, strength, and resiliency.

3. The participants requested that their actual names be used. Direct quotations capture each respondent's voice, nuances, and views.

4. All the stories and lived experiences shared during the focus groups were powerful, but we chose to highlight three narratives to provide a more intimate and personal illustration of the sobrevivencia of Chicanx/Latinx community college student-mothers.

References

Acs, Gregory, and Pamela Loprest. 2004. *Leaving Welfare: Employment and Well-Being of Families that Left Welfare in the Post-Entitlement Era.* Kalamazoo, MI: Upjohn Institute for Employment Research.

Adair, Vyvian C. 2001. "Poverty and the (Broken) Promise of Higher Education." *Harvard Educational Review* 71 (2): 217–39.

Ahmad, Farah, and Sarah Iverson. 2013. *The State of Women of Color in the United States: Too Many Barriers Remain for this Growing and Increasingly Important Population.* Washington, DC: Center for American Progress. https://www.americanprogress.org/wp-content/uploads/2013/10/StateOf WomenColor-1.pdf.

Alexander, Michelle. 2010. *The New Jim Crow: Mass Incarceration in the Age of Colorblindness.* New York: New Press.

Auerbach, Susan. 2002. "'Why Do They Give the Good Classes to Some and Not to the Others?' Latino Parent Narratives of Struggle in a College Access Program." *Teachers College Record* 104 (7): 1369–92.

Bok, Marcia. 2004. "Education and Training for Low-Income Women: An Elusive Goal." *Affilia* 19:39–52.

Castro, Erin L., and Edén Cortez. 2016. "Exploring the Lived Experiences and Intersectionalities of Mexican Community College Transfer Students: Qualitative Insights Toward Expanding a Transfer Receptive Culture." *Community College Journal of Research and Practice* 41 (2): 77–92.

Cherlin, Andrew J., Karen Bogen, James M. Quane, and Linda Burton. 2002. "Operating Within the Rules: Welfare Recipients' Experiences with Sanctions and Case Closings." *Social Service Review* 76 (3): 387–405.

Christopher, Karen. 2005. "Welfare Recipients Attending College: The Interplay of Oppression and Resistance." *Journal of Sociology and Social Welfare* 32 (3): 165–85.

Deparle, Jason. 2009. "The Safety Net for Victims of Recession, Patchwork State Aid." *New York Times*, May 10, 2009. http://www.nytimes.com/2009/05/10/us/10safetynet.html.

Foucault, Michel. 1991. *Discipline and Punish: The Birth of the Prison*. Translated by Alan Sheridan. London: Penguin Books.

Galván, Ruth Trinidad. 2006. "Campesina Epistemologies and Pedagogies of the Spirit: Examining Women's Sobrevivencia." In *Chicana/Latina Education in Everyday Life: Feminista Perspectives on Pedagogy and Epistemology*, edited by Dolores Delgado Bernal, C. Alejandra Elenes, Francisca E. Godinez, and Sofia Villenas, 161–80. Albany: SUNY Press.

Gándara, Patricia. 2015. *Fulfilling America's Future: Latinas in the U.S., 2015*. Washington, DC: White House Initiative on Educational Excellence for Hispanics. https://sites.ed.gov/hispanic-initiative/files/2015/09/Fulfilling-Americas-Future-Latinas-in-the-U.S.-2015-Final-Report.pdf.

Gaxiola Serrano, Tanya. 2016. "'Wait, What Do You Mean by College?': A Critical Race Analysis of Latina/o Students and Their Pathways to Community College." *Community College Journal of Research and Practice* 41 (4): 239–52.

Gonzalez, Roberto G. 2016. *Lives in Limbo: Undocumented and Coming of Age in America*. Oakland: University of California Press.

Hays, Sharon. 2003. *Flat Broke with Children: Women in the Age of Welfare Reform*. New York: Oxford University Press.

Hernández-Truyol, Berta E. 2008. "The Gender Bend: Culture, Sex, and Sexuality—A LatCritical Human Rights Map of Latina/o Border Crossings." *Indiana Law Journal* 83 (4): 1283–1331.

Jones-DeWeever, Avis, and Barbara Gault. 2008. *Resilient and Reaching for More: Challenges and Benefits of Higher Education for Welfare Participants and Their Children*. IWPR D466. Washington, DC: Institute for Women's Policy Research. https://iwpr.org/publications/resilient-and-reaching-for-more-challenges-and-benefits-of-higher-education-for-welfare-participants-and-their-children/.

Kohler-Hausmann, Jullily. 2017. *Getting Tough: Welfare and Imprisonment in 1970s America*. Princeton, NJ: Princeton University Press.

Krogstad, Jens Manuel. 2016. *5 Facts About Latinos and Education*. Washington, DC: Pew Research Center.

López, Gerardo R. 2001. "The Value of Hard Work: Lessons on Parent Involvement from an (Im)migrant Household." *Harvard Educational Review* 71 (3): 416–37.

Maréchal, Nathalie. 2015. "First They Came for the Poor: Surveillance of Welfare Recipients as an Uncontested Practice." *Media and Communication* 3 (3): 56–67.

Mathur, Anita, Judy Reichle, Julie Strawn, and Chuck Wiseley. 2002. *From Jobs to Careers: How California Community College Credentials Pay Off for Welfare Participants*. Washington, DC: Center for Law and Social Policy.

Oliva, Nereida, and Hortencia Jiménez. 2017. "*Nepantleras* in a Community College: Student Mothers Negotiating Mothering, School, and Work." In *Readings in Race, Ethnicity, and Immigration*, edited by Hortencia Jiménez, 285–99. San Diego, CA: Cognella.

Oliva, Nereida, Judith C. Pérez, and Laurence Parker. 2013. "Educational Policy Contradictions: A LatCrit Perspective on Undocumented Students." In *Handbook on Critical Race Theory in Education*, edited by Marvin Lynn and Adrienne D. Dixson, 140–52. New York: Routledge.

Pérez Huber, Lindsay, María C. Malagón, Brianna R. Ramirez, Lorena Camargo Gonzalez, Alberto Jimenez, and Verónica N. Vélez. 2015. *Still Falling Through the Cracks: Revisiting the Latina/o Education Pipeline*. CSRC Research Report 19. Los Angeles: UCLA Chicano Studies Research Center. http://www.chicano.ucla.edu/files/RR19.pdf.

Polakow, Valerie, Sandra S. Butler, Luisa S. Deprez, and Peggy Kahn. 2004. *Shut Out: Low Income Mothers and Higher Education in Post-Welfare America*. Albany: SUNY Press.

Reichlin Cruse, Lindsey. 2015. *Supporting Student Parent Success in Community Colleges*. Washington, DC: Institute for Women's Policy Research. https://iwpr.org/wp-content/uploads/2017/01/PowerPoint-Supporting -Student-Parent-Success-in-Community-Colleges.pdf.

Rodríguez, Louie F., and Leticia Oseguera. 2015. "Our Deliberate Success Recognizing What Works for Latina/o Students Across the Educational Pipeline." *Journal of Hispanic Higher Education* 14 (2): 128–50.

Romo, Laura, and Denise A. Segura. 2010. "Enhancing the Resilience of Young, Single Mothers of Color: A Review of Programs and Services." *Journal of Education for Students Placed At Risk (JESPAR)* 15 (1): 173–85.

Sidel, Ruth. 2006. *Unsung Heroes: Single Mothers and the American Dream*. Berkeley: University of California Press.

Thompson, Gail L., Susan Warren, and LaMesha Carter. 2004. "It's Not My Fault: Predicting High School Teachers Who Blame Parents and Students for Students' Low Achievement." *High School Journal* 87 (3): 5–14.

Valdés, Guadalupe. 1996. *Con Respeto: Bridging the Distances Between Culturally Diverse Families and Schools—An Ethnographic Portrait*. New York: Teachers College Press.

Valencia, Richard R. 2010. *Dismantling Contemporary Deficit Thinking: Educational Thought and Practice*. New York: Routledge.

Van Stone, Nadine, J. Ron Nelson, and Joan Niemann. 1994. "Poor Single-Mother College Students' Views on the Effect of Some Primary Sociological and Psychological Belief Factors on Their Academic Success." *Journal of Higher Education* 65 (5): 571–84.

Zarate, Maria Estela, and Rebeca Burciaga. 2010. "Latinos and College Access: Trends and Future Directions." *Journal of College Admissions*, no. 209, 24–29.

Zarate, Maria Estela, and Harry P. Pachon. 2006. "Perceptions of College Financial Aid Among California Latino Youth." *TRPI Policy Brief*, June 2006. http://files.eric.ed.gov/fulltext/ED502067.pdf.

Zavella, Pat. 2016. "Contesting Structural Vulnerability Through Reproductive Justice with Latina Immigrants in California." *North American Dialogue* 19 (1): 36–45.

Part II

Chicana/Latina/Women of Color Mother-Activists

6

Ain't I a Mama?

A Black Revolutionary Mother in the Women's Rights Movement

Trina Greene Brown

In 1851, former slave Sojourner Truth gave a moving speech at the Women's Rights Convention in Akron, Ohio (Truth 1851). Her speech reflected on the intersections of gender and racial inequality experienced by Black women. While white women were fighting for their right to be treated as equal to white men, Black slave women were fighting for their right to be treated as whole humans. While men used white women's fragility and gentleness as excuses to deny women equal rights, abolitionist Truth pointed out—over the cries of white women's rights activists—that as a Black former slave, she was expected to do the same work as men and received no such preferential treatment. She demands answers and clarity to a double standard of womanhood by repeatedly asking, "Ain't I a Woman?"

While years of progress have rippled in waves through the U.S. women's rights movement—from the Voting Rights Act, Pregnancy Discrimination Act, and Violence Against Women Act, to the Fair Labor Standards Act and Lilly Ledbetter Fair Pay Act, as well as cultural shifts around gender norms—Black feminists and other feminists of color have maintained a long-standing critique that the movement lacks, and has a limited application of, an intersectional analysis and frame inclusive of Black women and other Women of Color (Rampton 2008; Smith 2013–14). Sojourner (Truth 1851) exclaimed in her speech, "I have borne thirteen children, and seen most all sold off to slavery, and when I cried out with my mother's grief, none but Jesus heard me! And ain't I a woman?" Today, more than 150 years later, I echo Truth's words, as a long-term Black mother-activist in the women's rights movement, and question, *Ain't I a Mama?*

Through personal storytelling about my experiences birthing and caregiving while working in the women's rights movement, this chapter reflects on motherhood and the inequities and hypocrisies of the feminist movement in the United States. My experiences led to the creation of Parenting for Liberation, which was originally conceived because Black mothers, like myself, were receiving a critical lack of support and were suffering in silence. As Audre Lorde wrote, "My silences had not protected me. Your silence will not protect you. But for every real word spoken, for every attempt I had ever made to speak those truths for which I am still seeking, I had made contact with other women while we examined the words to fit a world in which we all believed, bridging our differences" (1984, 41). These words reflected my experiences and those of the Black mothers and women in my life. I took Lorde's statements to heart and used them to guide me to these writings. This is not meant as a recrimination of white women and mothers, but rather as a challenge to #WhiteFeminism to seek the intersections that bind and connect us more deeply and to support Mothers of Color. When the day-to-day work of a feminist is to ensure that women's voices are heard, this Black feminist Mama's personal experiences of being silenced and denied access to privileges embolden me to raise the question harkening back to the ancestral spirit of Sojourner Truth: *Ain't I a Mama?*

Ain't I a Mama?
Navigating Maternity Leave, Systemic Oppression, and the Birth of My Child

California was the first state to pass a paid family leave policy, in 2002. The U.S. feminist movement fights for paid family leave to foster gender equity between working women and men and to support greater balance between work and family lives (Peck 2015). As women disproportionately bear the brunt of the mothering and caregiving workload, in addition to working outside the home, paid leave makes taking time off for care work accessible and affordable. So when I became pregnant while working in the feminist movement, I knew I'd be taken care of. Luckily, my nonprofit employer had a paid family leave policy that offered to offset state disability pay. There was a stipulation to receive this privilege though: time served. Paid family leave was afforded only to folks who had worked at the organization for a year.

My son was born prematurely, as are lots of Black babies, which is a reproductive health crisis for Black mothers, who have the highest rate of premature births in the United States. This is a result of systemic oppression in reproductive healthcare (Ross and Solinger 2017). My son arrived two months shy of my one-year employment anniversary, and therefore I was denied access to employer-paid family leave; I instead found myself at the welfare office to supplement my income. Midway through my leave, I requested an extension from my employer in an effort to access the pay benefit, and I was informed that my position on staff *may not* be available that long. Worried that I would potentially be unemployed, on welfare, with an infant, I returned to work. This was the first of many times to come that I would seek access to a privilege and be rejected. I choked on my silent protest and whispered, *"Ain't I a Mama?"*

Ain't I a Mama?:
Back to Work, Back to Reality

Returning to work, I cried like a baby because my mind, body, and soul missed my baby. To add to the pain of leaving my beautiful three-month-old baby boy at home, I observed my white colleague's privileged arrangement to regularly bring her baby to the office. Beyond the emotional toil, the mere sound of her baby crying or the sight of her breastfeeding would make my breast milk let down uncontrollably. I did not begrudge my white coworker's ability to bring her child to work. I benefited from bringing my son to work with me for special occasions, as well as if I had a family emergency or no other childcare; but my arrangement was on a case-by-case basis, while my white colleague's was a permanent agreement. I wasn't the only one who had questions about this preferential, inequitable treatment. Other Mamas of Color who'd been at the organization for more than a decade didn't have this privilege with their small children. The U.S. feminist movement has advocated for women to get equal treatment at work, such as the Lilly Ledbetter Act to ensure equal pay for equal work, as well as for not penalizing women who parent and work, such as the Pregnancy Discrimination Act to protect pregnant women from losing their jobs. The ability to be both mother and staff was like a badge of honor. As women, we actually could have it *all*, right? Unfortunately, not *all* of us. *Ain't I a Mama?*

Beyond the disparity in my white colleague's privilege of bringing her child to work, another layer made the dynamics of mothering while white versus mothering while Black more nuanced and fucked up. She was able to bring her child and her Latinx caregiver. Picture a white woman with her child and a monolingual Spanish-speaking Latinx nanny sitting in her office with her, surrounded by colleagues who were nearly 75 percent Latinx women. I was taken aback to see a Woman of Color serving a white woman's baby and reminded of my grandmother, a domestic worker who traveled weekly by bus to clean and care for a white family. I respect the profession. The issue was not with having a caregiver but with not having a conversation about the repercussions of a Latinx woman serving a white woman in a predominantly Latinx office. The silence and the avoidance of the elephant in the room had a huge impact on folks. I was appalled, and some of my Latinx coworkers, who were also mothers with small children, were enraged, rightfully. They were brought to tears, and they shouted the question, *"Ain't I a Mama?"* but no one heard them either.

Ain't I a Mama?:
Lions, Gorillas, and Dogs, *Oh My!*

My identity is a Mama who is raising a Black boy. A Black boy is a baby who wasn't meant to survive, a boy who's cute until he's ten or so, and then he becomes a threat (Gumbs, Martens, and Williams 2016; Goff et al. 2014). While I see the beauty, innocence, pain, joy, challenges, and triumphs of raising a Black boy, I never receive the same level of compassion, concern, happiness, or support that my white colleagues receive from one another about their children. This was most apparent when my son needed additional support at school, and because of my commute, I didn't have time or space to help him. I put in a request to work remotely a couple days a week in an attempt to eliminate my daily three-hour drive. Instead of sitting in traffic, I planned to invest those three hours in my son. As before, I witnessed white colleagues working remotely and sought to access a similar privilege being offered to them. Again, however, that privilege was apparently not available to me, as my supervisor denied my request. She said she understood, but her actions demonstrated a lack of empathy and compassion. Instead, she recommended that I hire a nanny to support him, but I didn't want someone else to support my son through his trauma. I wanted to be there for him.

I spent months pleading the many reasons my son needed me; he had transitioned to a school lacking representation of Black children and began showing signs of self-hate, such as telling me he wanted white skin. Eventually I received a piecemeal offering of one day of telecommuting; however, the inequity and disregard for my son's plight became more apparent months later, when teammates shared stories about their traumatized pets and pets with special needs, and they received empathy, concern, and options to be home to support their "fur babies."

In the months to come, it became even more clear that an animal's life was more important than the life of my Black son—and the lives of Black people in general. My experience was triggered by the international uproar over the death of African animals. Folks called for punishment of the white man who had hunted Cecil the lion but denied and victim blamed Sandra Bland, who had been murdered within weeks of Cecil in July 2015 (Howard 2015). While both deaths created a stir, Cecil was mourned, and Sandra was blamed. Similarly, when Harambe, an African gorilla at the Cincinnati Zoo, was shot to save the life of a Black child, there was a huge outcry and victim blaming of the Black child's parents (Baker 2015; Savali 2016). Yet in Cincinnati, months prior to the Harambe incident, Samuel Dubose had been murdered during a traffic stop, and there had been absolutely no public shaming of the officer (Barajas 2017). My blood boils when people are more distraught over the death of African animals than the murder of African American children. So when my own son was also being devalued, I questioned whether his life or the lives of any Black children mattered to white people as much as the lives of a dog, a gorilla, or a lion. *Ain't I a Mama?*

Ain't I a Mama?:
Black Children Matter

How does a feminist movement with principles around equity and fair treatment for women miss the mark when it comes to race? Well, maybe that has to do with who holds the most positions of power—white women. According to research conducted by the Women of Color Network, for the last thirty years white women have maintained positions of leadership within U.S. feminist organizations, and thus "the analysis and framing of the issue of violence against women as a gender issue [only] has remained intact," without a strong intersectional analysis that looks at race (Mason 2014, 11).

Working in this movement as the mother of a Black boy, I couldn't stomach certain aspects of the status quo anymore. Specifically, working in schools where Black and Brown children filled the hallways and classrooms, I noticed the effects of racism and poverty on their interpersonal relationships. My job was to advise girls to call school police without acknowledging that those same school officers at times harassed the girls at school; according to my students, that advice was inviting more trauma and violence into their lives and not offering a real solution. The retraumatization and perpetuation of incarceration were at play. Raising my Black son under those same circumstances revealed the inconsistencies of my work in the feminist movement, which, along with my lived experience as a Black Mama, began taking a major toll on me until I felt like a grenade whose pin was about to be pulled.

And boom! I exploded, just as many other Black folks did in 2012, with the murder of Trayvon Martin and the rise of the Black Lives Matter movement.[1] While many Black feminists could see the interconnectedness of gender and race in the Trayvon Martin case, many white feminists stood silently. Sybrina Fulton, Trayvon Martin's mother, expressed major disappointment in the white woman judge, as well as with the jury, which was well populated with white mothers. Fulton felt that the not-guilty verdict for George Zimmerman in the trial for the murder of her son was a travesty, illustrating a complete lack of empathy toward her own pain and the loss of her son. She had believed that all mothers had a solidarity between them, but she now realized that she was wrong. *Ain't she a Mama?* Does her son's life matter to non-Black mothers? This was not new. As Sojourner Truth raised in her speech in 1851, the gentleness, fragility, and safety of white women had long been used to justify preferential treatment over Black women and in many cases to justify violence against Black bodies. President Barack Obama had connected to and empathized with Trayvon Martin's parents. Shedding tears while speaking about the matter on national television, he said that if he'd had a son, he would have looked like Trayvon. I waited for the white feminist movement I was part of to stand up in solidarity with Black Mamas not only for gender justice, but also against racism. Though some did, I sensed an overall lack of compassion from the feminist movement.[2] What Black Mamas want is to be treated as equal and for our children's lives to matter. As the late great organizer Ella Baker said in the 1960s, "Until the killing of black men, black mothers' sons, becomes as important to the rest of the country as the killing of a white mother's sons, we who believe in freedom cannot rest" (quoted in Grant 1981).

Like President Obama's hypothetical son, my son did look like Trayvon; thus I felt the pain and heartache Sybrina Fulton experienced. I saw my son's face in photos of Trayvon, Tamir Rice, Jordan Davis, Michael Brown, and Emmett Till on the nightly news and lit up on my Facebook newsfeed every time a young Black boy was murdered. With all these modern-day Emmett Tills, I fear that one day I'll be a modern-day Mamie Till, crying over the body of my Black son, born from my womb. I am not alone in this feeling of fear, as many Black parents feel the same. Mother and author Karsonya Wise Whitehead writes, "We are the parents of African American boys, and every day that we leave the house, we know that we could become Trayvon Martin's parents" (2015, 132). Is that what it will take for me to be seen as a Mama, and for my child's life to matter? Black Mothers of the Movement are only acknowledged after the loss of their children, as opposed to being celebrated for our mothering (Sebastian 2016). I'm not sure what's more critiqued, criminalized, surveilled, and punished, Black Mamas and motherhood or Black children? Why can't our mothering be seen? Why is it intentionally or accidentally ignored? When I ask for equitable treatment or access to "general policies," why do I have to plead my case and prove my worth? Why do I have to petition to be seen as a Mama? Why can't you see my children as you see your own? *Ain't I a Mama?*

Ain't I a Mama?: Parenting for Liberation

I wrote this piece because my silence will not protect me (Lorde 1984). Plus, white women's silence is not protecting me either. In fact, their silence has harmed me. I wrote this piece not to knock, judge, or critique white mothers. My challenge and invitation is for those white women who demand for their own mothering to be seen to not sit in silence when Mothers of Color make similar requests (Lorde 1984). White women who received special privileges watched me beg and plead, and they did nothing.

I request that feminists practice what they preach; for #White WomenSolidarity, if you are working and fighting for justice and equity in the world but allow injustice to occur, you are perpetuating systemic oppression. Justice doesn't begin in the streets; it begins in our homes, offices, and relationships. This is not an ask only for white women. As a Black feminist Mama, I commit to partnering and supporting other Mothers of Color, by navigating workplace and structural policies. Inequitable internal policies contribute to a fragmented movement, so we must bridge the gap and create more equitable systems for all of us. This is one of the many reasons I founded Parenting for Liberation, a space for Black parents who are freedom fighting for our collective liberation to engage with one another and share how we operationalize liberation in our homes.[3] In a world where Black boys and girls are set up to fail, parents can build up their children to do more than survive or thrive—they can live liberated. Parenting for Liberation is for the incredibly passionate parent warriors who are fighting for liberation and freedom on multiple fronts—on the front lines of the movement and on our front porches. I do this to avenge the Black Mama ancestors and to create openings for future generations of Black Mamas to come. I do this for Sojourner Truth, who'd "seen most all [of her children] sold off to slavery, and when [she] cried out with [her] mother's grief, none but Jesus heard" (Truth 1851). Until we have reconciliation around inequities within this fragmented movement, until we move toward eradicating racism within the feminist movement, we will always be held back, and the history and foundation our foremothers laid will not be honored. I will continue to do this until the day when any and every Black Mama no longer has to question, *Ain't I a Mama?*

Notes

1. Black Lives Matter website, accessed August 5, 2018, http://blacklives matter.com/.
2. Move to End Violence and Movement Makers, "Advancing An Inclusive Racial and Gender Justice Agenda," statement on Black Lives Matter, December 15, 2014. http://www.movetoendviolence.org/wp-content /uploads/2015/05/mev_blacklivesmatterstatement_12.15.2014_2.pdf.
3. Parenting for Liberation website, accessed August 5, 2018, https://www .parentingforliberation.org.

References

Baker, Courtney R. 2015. "Outrage Over the Death of a Lion, But Not Black Women and Men?" *Huffington Post*, July 30, 2015. https://www.huffington post.com/courtney-r-baker/outrage-over-the-death-of-a-lion-but-not -black-women-and-men_b_7903892.html.

Barajas, Joshua. 2017. "Second Mistrial Declared in Ohio Officer's Fatal Shooting of Sam DuBose." *PBS News Hour*, June 23, 2017. https://www .pbs.org/newshour/nation/second-mistrial-declared-ohio-officers-fatal -shooting-sam-dubose.

Goff, Phillip Atiba, Matthew Christian Jackson, Brooke Allison, Lewis Di Leone, Carmen Marie Culotta, and Natalie Ann DiTomasso. 2014. "The Essence of Innocence: Consequences of Dehumanizing Black Children." *Journal of Personality and Social Psychology* 106 (4): 526–45.

Grant, Joanne, dir. 1981. *Fundi: The Story of Ella Baker*. New York: Icarus Films. 16 mm film. 60 min.

Gumbs, Alexis Pauline, China Martens, and Ma'ia Williams, eds. 2016. *Revolutionary Mothering: Love on the Front Lines*. Oakland, CA: PM Press.

Howard, Brian Clark. 2015. "Killing of Cecil the Lion Sparks Debate Over Trophy Hunts." *National Geographic*, July 28, 2015. https://news.national geographic.com/2015/07/150728-cecil-lion-killing-trophy-hunting -conservation-animals/.

Lorde, Audre. 1984. *Sister Outsider: Essays and Speeches*. New York: Crossing Press.

Mason, C. Nicole. 2014. *Gaining Ground, Breaking Through: A Report on the Leadership Experiences of Women of Color, Lesbian, Gay, Bisexual, Transgender and Queer Individuals of Color, Individuals with Disabilities, Native Women, Aspiring Allies, Immigrant Women Working in the Anti-Violence Movement in Four States*. Vol. 1. Harrisburg, PA: Women of Color Network. http://www.wocninc.org/wp-content/uploads/2014/11/GainingGround.pdf.

Peck, Emily. 2015. "The Feminist Case for Paternity Leave." *Huffington Post*, July 9, 2015. https://www.huffingtonpost.com/2015/07/09/paternity-leave -policies_n_7762108.html.

Rampton, Martha. 2008. "Four Waves of Feminism." *Pacific Magazine*, Fall 2008. https://www.pacificu.edu/about/media/four-waves-feminism.

Ross, Loretta, and Rickie Solinger. 2017. *Reproductive Justice: An Introduction*. Oakland: University of California Press.

Savali, Kirsten West. 2016. "Racists Prove That They Care More About Gorillas than Black Children." *Root*, June 1, 2016. https://www.theroot.com/racists-prove-that-they-care-more-about-gorillas-than-b-1790855492.

Sebastian, Michael. 2016. "Who Are the 'Mothers of the Movement' Speaking at the Democratic National Convention?" *Elle*, July 26, 2016. https://www.elle.com/culture/career-politics/news/a38111/who-are-mothers-of-the-movement-dnc/.

Smith, Sharon. 2013–14. "Black Feminism and Intersectionality." *International Socialist Review*, no. 91. https://isreview.org/issue/91/black-feminism-and-intersectionality.

Truth, Sojourner. 1851. "Ain't I a Woman?" Speech at the Women's Rights Convention, Akron, Ohio, May 28–29, 1851. Transcript available in *Internet Modern History Sourcebook*, Fordham University, last updated August 1997, https://sourcebooks.fordham.edu/mod/sojtruth-woman.asp.

Whitehead, Karsonya Wise. 2015. *Letters to My Black Sons: Raising Boys in a Post-Racial America*. Baltimore, MD: Apprentice House.

Mothering
the Academy

An Intersectional Approach to Deconstruct and Expose the
Experiences of Mother-Scholars of Color in Higher Education

*Monica Hernández-Johnson, Shahla Fayazpour,
Sandra L. Candel, and Ravijot Singh*

This *testimonio* study deconstructs how we, as Mother-Scholars of
Color (MSOCs) in a highly diverse Southwest university, conavigate
our personal and professional worlds as we challenge the demarcations of these contending spheres. As colleagues in the same doctoral
program, who have known one another for three to four years, we
benefited from the close relationships that facilitated the interview
process. We analyzed our narratives using thematic analysis to amplify
our voices and life stories as four doctoral students of Guatemalan,
Indian, Iranian, and Mexican origins. Although our research exposes
our struggles, more importantly, it focuses on the strategies and the
empowerment we found in the Mother-Scholar overlap (MSO). We
use the term "Mother-Scholar overlap" as a way to challenge traditional narratives that emphasize the *balance* or juggling between
the mother and scholar identities, two separate and opposing forces;
instead we believe both those identities are conjoined, empowering
MSOCs and enriching academia and the spaces they inhabit. Last, we
permitted ourselves to share our vulnerabilities and strengths through
our lived experiences, which remain hidden in the personal and professional spheres—in doing so, we challenge the self-censorship that

upholds hegemony and patriarchy. For this study, we defined invisibility as a general failure of academic and familial spaces to fully recognize the dual identities of Women of Color as responsible mothers and competent scholars. Balance was analyzed in terms of striking the right chord between home life and academic work, spending adequate time attending to demanding motherly duties, producing valuable graduate-level research, exercising self-care, and fulfilling social engagements. Previous studies have centered on the experiences of being a mother and a scholar, with others later including a much-needed intersectional analysis incorporating race (Lapayese 2012). Nevertheless, we choose to use the term Mother-Scholar of Color, in that order, as we reposition the word "mother" at the forefront of our study. In doing so, we attempt to reveal the values and assets brought to academia and personal spheres as mothers, Women of Color, and scholars.

Literature Review

The number of Women of Color is increasing in U.S. society and institutions. The percentage of Women of Color in the United States is estimated to grow from 38.3 percent in 2015 to 52.5 percent in 2050 (Catalyst 2016). MSOCs are present in higher education, but the conflicts of their roles and responsibilities as mothers and as scholars are mostly invisible at home and in the academy (Catalyst 2016). According to the logic of the gendered modernity/traditional binary, Women of Color are considered subordinates because of the structurally and socially reproduced patriarchal patterns of hierarchy, domination, and oppression based on race, class, gender, and sexual orientation (Zinn and Dill 1994). Alongside, Yvette V. Lapayese explains, the "concept of motherhood is virtually invisible in the writings of female scholars within the field of education. . . . [S]ome feminist theorists feel that academia has ignored and misrepresented the reality of difference" (Lapayese 2012, ix–xi). Although a growing amount of research explores the experiences of women as faculty, graduate students, and administrative and higher-level personnel in academia, the study of MSOCs is largely neglected (Witkin Stuart 1997; Williams 2007; Ledford 2012; Schlehofer 2012; Craft and Maseberg-Tomlinson 2015; Isgro and Castañeda 2015). The intersectionalities of MSOCs in terms of race, gender, ethnicity, religion, and culture make their journeys much different from those of dominant groups in higher education, and they deserve a more nuanced lens to further the overall study of the experiences of Women of Color in academia.

Reyna Anaya also argues that traditionally, motherhood has been closely associated with guilt and "good mothering" habits, which are usually understood in terms of white, privileged parenting styles that include staying at home to care for children (Anaya 2011). According to the dominant cultural expectations, a "good mother" is a dedicated and self-sacrificing mother who is available to her children around the clock; however, this poses the dilemma of juggling between the dichotomous roles of being a graduate student and a mother simultaneously (Anaya 2011). Anaya also challenges this idea of the good mother, further complicating it by adding the dimension of scholar and what it means to be not only a good mother, but a good student at the same time. She concludes that Mother-Scholars need to create support systems to survive, particularly if they are Women of Color in higher education, who tend to be "overused, misunderstood, and unappreciated" (Anaya 2011, 22).

Theoretical Framework

Paulo Freire's methodology of problem posing, critical dialogue, and *concientización* to bring forth transformation is central to this work.

The use of testimonios is critical in creating a place where we can be heard, understanding that speaking and naming the world is what transforms it (Freire 2003). Through this process, we can begin to critique the societal and institutional structures that condition our understandings of what truth is, and who the possessors of knowledge and models of humanity are, to unpack the human experience (Freire 2003). As such, we use a Freirean feminist theoretical framework that challenges essentialist categorizations and commonalities of oppression, recognizing that oppression is experienced differently by different actors, and refuting the assumption of a universal experience of being a woman (Weiler 1991). Graduate students in institutions where academic knowledge and experience is valued, but the knowledge and capital that Mother-Scholars contribute in those spaces can be difficult to recognize and validate, "almost never do they realize that they, too, 'know things' they have learned in their relations with the world" (Freire 2003, 63).

Because of the need to recognize the multilayered dimensions of identity, which include gender, class, race, religion, education, and so forth, this study uses an intersectional lens to make the experiences of MSOCs visible. Intersectionality is utilized as both a theory and a form of analysis to reveal the interacting effects of multiple identities, which converge to render some as invisible by sociopolitical and economic structures (Crenshaw 1991). A good question to probe into this concept of intersectionality is: who is the system *not* working for? Interest in intersectionality arose out of a critique of gender-based and race-based research for failing to account for lived experiences at neglected points of intersection—ones that tended to reflect multiple subordinate locations as opposed to dominant or mixed locations.

Informed by our review of the literature and theoretical framework, this study seeks to answer the following research questions: How does intersectionality affect the lived experiences of four diverse Mother-Scholars in a doctoral program? To what extent does the use of collective testimonios allow for a construction and deconstruction of oppression for Mother-Scholars in a doctoral program? How do these four MSOCs enact their agency?

Methodology: Sample, Data Collection, Analysis, and Validation

We took part in this testimonio study as both researchers and participants by sharing our collective experiences as four MSOCs who attend a doctoral program at one of the most diverse universities in the Southwest United States. We identify as Women of Color, married, middle class, immigrants, heterosexual, and cisgender (see table 7.1). We are also mothers of children ranging from four to twenty-seven years of age. This study used convenience and criterion sampling, and the criteria included being doctoral students, from minority ethnic backgrounds, and mothers. In addition, we use the terms "data" and "testimonios" interchangeably to affirm the legitimacy and validation of these modes of knowledge, thereby challenging hegemonic methodologies, which usually ignore the stories, voices, and lived experiences of the marginalized.

Table 7.1 Participants' demographics

Pseudonym	Ethnic background	Age	Number of children	Spouse's ethnic background	Family structure
Sadaf	Iranian	48	2	Iranian	Nuclear
Jósi	Guatemalan	34	3	Black American	Nuclear
Avni	Indian	36	1	Indian	Joint and extended
Libertad	Mexican	49	3	Spaniard	Nuclear

We use nuclear family to describe a household that consists of parents and their dependent children. A joint and extended family system is a large undivided family in which more than one generation live together in the same household.

To share our experiences in challenging cross-cultural environments while balancing our roles as mothers and scholars, we used testimonios, "an approach that incorporates political, historical, social, and cultural histories that accompany one's life experiences to bring about change through consciousness-raising" (Delgado, Burciaga, and Carmona 2012, 364). In-depth interviews were used to engage in meaningful discussions about a topic of mutual interest (Marshall and Rossman 2016). To collect our data, we held weekly audio-recorded meetings, lasting from one to two hours, during the fall 2016 and spring 2017 semesters. We chose to conduct testimonios to share our words and to name our worlds; our stories and counter-narratives offer an opportunity to contest hegemonic discourse and to rewrite our stories in our own voices as a form of liberation (Alarcón et al. 2011, 369). The use of testimonios was imperative to this project because in this tradition, the *testimonialista* is considered "the holder of knowledge" (Delgado, Burciaga, and Carmona 2012, 365). Finally, in the spring 2017 semester, we conducted one-hour audio-taped in-depth interviews with one another to allow for a deeper understanding of the meanings each of us attaches to our lived experiences. Our close relationships facilitated sharing intimate details about our lives during our testimonio sessions and in-depth interviews.

We used thematic analysis to analyze our testimonios. In the step-by-step guide developed by Virginia Braun and Victoria Clarke (2006), thematic analysis patterns are identified through a rigorous process that begins with data familiarization, continues with the development of initial codes, and is followed by the development, revision, and definition of analytical themes. The process ends with a narrative that contextualizes the themes and connects them to research questions, literature review, and a theoretical framework. We first performed a free coding of the data individually. Then, we met weekly during the data-analysis phase to organize these free codes into descriptive themes, and, finally, we generated analytical themes (Thomas and Harden 2008). We continued the coding process until we achieved full reliability by coming to full consensus.

Major themes that arose included (1) struggles experienced by MSOCs, represented by the pressures of academic, cultural, and familial expectations; guilt; and invisibility/nonrecognition in familial and academic spaces; (2) strategies used by MSOCs, represented by how we navigate between being a scholar and a mother through validation and support networks; and (3) the Mother-Scholar overlap, demonstrating MSOC capital and debunking deficit perspectives by finding empowerment in education.

We actively participated in the coding process and in the development of themes in the data-analysis process until consensus among the four of us was reached. We used a dialogic process from the beginning of the project by engaging in deep formal and informal conversations to collectively disseminate our experiences. This dialogue continued throughout our data-analysis phase, as we met several times to summarize one another's interviews, ensuring that our interpretations of data, the codes, and the theme chosen were approved by all participants, a process known as "member checking." This dialogic exchange allowed for a deeper construction of meaning, as it included our perspectives as both researchers and participants. Last, we used two data-collection methods to enable data triangulation.

Collective Struggles Theme

To answer our first question—how does intersectionality affect the lived experiences of four diverse MSOCs in a doctoral program?—we found that intersectionality shows up in different ways: in the gendered expectations placed on us by our families; in the guilt we experience when fulfilling academic demands at the expense of family time; and in the invisibility of our scholarly side in familial spaces and the nonrecognition of our motherly side in academic spaces.

Gendered expectations were prevalent among us; however, our postcolonial lens allowed us to challenge hegemonic assumptions (Bhabha 1994). Libertad shared, "I was told by my mother at the beginning of my marriage: '75 percent of the success of your marriage depends on you.' So she basically put everything on me, right? 'If this marriage fails, it's going to be because of you.' So there were many, many things that I didn't voice because of this burden that had been put on me, and . . . this program was like a veil had been lifted off of me. I was like, 'I've been lied to all my life! This is not how it was supposed to be.' And I started being more vocal. I started being more assertive. So, on the one hand, going for my doctoral degree makes my husband proud, but having this new partner that is assertive and that says what she wants now, and that kind of demands what she wants now, it's been hard for him, but he has been able to keep up, and I could also tell you that he is starting to think in feminist ways."

Guilt was a recurring theme. We all struggled with the academic demands that take time away from our families, and we all expressed difficulty striking a healthy balance.

Libertad said, "Motherly challenges [include] the time that I have dedicated to this program and that somehow has taken me away from my family. I am a perfectionist, and at times I have allowed my program to take precedence over my family. . . . My oldest has told me, 'You have not been a present mother,' and those words eat you up. Since then, I have tried to strike a balance. It won't matter what a successful professional or scholar woman I am if my motherly side suffers; it won't matter my accomplishments as a scholar if my family suffers."

Similarly, Avni expressed, "I have been a victim of self-pity. I have been angry at my little one, and I feel guilty . . . because he doesn't understand. I brought him in [so] I should understand, and he is just being a child. I feel guilty, and I can never get rid of it. I have never as a mother, since the time he joined school, since the last two and a half years, allowed him to have a spring break. I get him into his optional weeks, pay extra, and he is at school. I feel guilty of not spending enough quality time."

Libertad's and Avni's feelings were consistent with Anaya's argument on guilt and the social construction of a "good mother" (Anaya 2011, 16). Culturally, as women, we have been socialized under the politics of "devotion of care and self-sacrifice," that is, to feel guilty if we don't put the needs of others before ours; therefore, if we seek self-fulfillment to the detriment of our children, we are made to believe that we must be bad mothers (Anaya 2011, 17). This shared notion of guilt is important because we can expose it for what it is (problem posing), a byproduct of the failures to meet and maintain the expectations (gendered, cultural, societal, etc.) constructed by external systems of oppression, and be empowered (through critical dialogue) to challenge them, which brings forth transformation (Freire 2003).

Another theme that arose was invisibility and nonrecognition. Sadaf believed her academic side was invisible in her house, while her motherhood was invisible in school. As she explained, "I never take stuff from home to academic [spaces] and from academic [spaces] to home. . . . I tried to keep [to] myself, and it was very, very hard. . . . You have to have two masks at home and school to be a mother over there and be a scholar here [at school], with all challenges. . . . I feel that people judge differently, [assuming] that I can't do something or [that] I am [facing] challenges. They say, 'She has lots of problems.' That's why I tried to keep many times to myself, and it wasn't easy to do that." Similarly, Jósi stated, "There is no space for motherhood in my academic side." Consistent with Freirean thought, we believe that the knowledge, skills, and experiences that we bring as mothers do not have a place in academia's epistemological reservoir (Freire 2003).

Avni, living in a joint family that shares the household with her in-laws, experienced nonrecognition in her familial spaces: "At some point my [extended family] saw that what I am trying to do was for my own fulfillment, and no one is going to benefit from it. This is something I am doing for myself. . . . I would go to someone and try to tell them that I am struggling at this point, and I need more time, I need more peace of mind, or I want someone to take my responsibilities for family and help me out so that I can focus more academically—getting that kind of attention was very tough for me because it was considered as my personal endeavor, and I am the one who is solely responsible for it. . . . I was also told that I need to take a break."

MSOCs experience invisibility and nonrecognition in both familial and academic spheres, which creates a deeper division between both spaces. This demarcation prevents others from valuing the work and effort performed by MSOCs in both spheres.

Reflections

To answer our second question—To what extent does the use of collective testimonios allow for a construction and deconstruction of oppression for MSOCs in a doctoral program?—we found that hearing the different testimonios among us encouraged us to unpack our lived experiences at a deeper level, engaging in topics of validation and support from a cultural and social perspective.

Avni searched for self-validation while experiencing a dilemma in prioritizing her various familial roles and scholarly endeavors, as she confessed: "I had a lot of mental struggle trying to weigh out what is important. Is my personal life [important]? Or, because I live with my in-laws, is that whole family setting [and] their needs more important? [Or] should I suffice them at some point and look at my academic requirements to validate what I am doing academically? Should it matter in my personal life?"

Libertad sought validation by entering the doctoral program after being a stay-at-home mom for ten years: "For some reason that I'm still trying to explore, being a mother I didn't see as being validating enough, being a mother was not enough, so when I came here I saw myself as not having much to offer to the program, or with not as many qualifications as my colleagues because I had, quote unquote, 'only been a mother' for ten years, right? That was all that I did, which was really not because I did a lot more, but in my mind it was like, 'Oh, what do I have to offer?' and being a scholar to me has always been the more valued of the Mother-Scholar equation, and I was sharing with you that it is problematic, but to me it's like, 'Oh, I finally have the scholarly side to validate the motherly side. And I really need to unpack that: Was it cultural? Was it family? Was it my own insecurities? Why did I not see myself as worthy of these scholarly spaces only being a mother? So I need to problematize that." Her ability to stay home, on the one hand, evidenced her class privilege, while her decision to go back to graduate school, on the other hand, reflected the need to maintain her sense of self-worth in response to the lack of value society places on motherhood (Anaya 2011).

Consistent with Anaya, we found that forging support networks was imperative for our success. As MSOCs, we derived support, guidance, and encouragement from partners, family, and mentors (Anaya 2011). Libertad's decision to attend graduate school was a form of validation and came with the full support of her partner and children. For others, however, that same decision isolated them and prevented them from receiving support from their nuclear and/or extended family.

For example, Jósi shared, "My education is my education." Her pursuit of a doctorate was seen as her own professional endeavor, which severed the connection between the academic and personal spheres.

As Avni shared above, "At some point my [extended family] saw that what I am trying to do was for my own fulfillment, and no one is going to benefit from it. This is something I am doing for myself." As a result, Jósi and Avni felt isolated in both academic and personal spaces, unable to cross over and be understood or supported in either.

Sadaf expressed receiving indirect support from her partner: "I always wanted to be more and to do more, and after that, my husband, I can't say he was really supportive, but he didn't stop me. . . . I think encouragement is the best support that a person can have at home, but my husband maybe didn't encourage me in the word [verbally], but it is a kind of cultural thing. . . . When I saw him very proud, telling everybody, 'My wife [is] doing [her] doctoral degree,' I could say, even if he doesn't mention it to me, he is proud, and he likes what I do." The pursuit of a terminal degree was perceived as a personal endeavor separate from the collective aims and growth in familial circles, which further demarcates the professional and personal spheres, placing them at odds with each other.

Important to disclose, as much as we were invested in this study and wanted to contribute to in-depth testimonios, we also had to be cognizant of our own positionality as doctoral students seeking a terminal degree in an institution of higher education, as wives in households where gendered and cultural expectations are ever present, and as women in a patriarchal society. Unfortunately, the silencing effects of power dynamics became apparent in areas of this study, which challenged us to critically but carefully navigate through them while prioritizing the authenticity and reality of our experiences as both mothers and scholars. The study of gender-based censorship is insufficient and is in dire need of further exploration. One organization tackling this need is Women's World (Tax 1995), which describes itself as an international network of free-speech feminist writers, who work to identify and fight self-censorship based on gender and to expose institutional violence directed at women.

A Source of Empowerment:
The Mother-Scholar Overlap

To answer our third question—How do these four MSOCs enact their agency?—we all agreed that being both mothers and scholars has given us a sense of agency and assertiveness, which counters traditional narratives that view the coexistence of personal and academic spaces as always being in competition, with rigid demarcations separating both spheres. Yet, this study first required that we examine our own perceptions regarding motherhood and its place in academia. In doing so, there was a need to use problem posing, to reach *concientización*, and to reclaim our identities as mothers and scholars who viewed the MSO as a source of empowerment (Freire 2003).

As Women of Color in familial and academic spaces, we challenged the dichotomous relationship between motherhood and higher education, unearthing the strengths and capital of the MSO, and countering traditional hegemonic narratives of cultural and gender norms, which value the role of a mother only in the domestic sphere, or vice versa, and that perceive motherhood as an impediment and a detriment to a woman's career.

Avni mentioned the empowerment she found in being a scholar, which also strongly influenced her identity as a mother: "That culmination [of being a mother and a scholar] became my spirit, that also became my struggle, that has also [became] my success. . . . I feel more accomplished." Additionally, she stated, "Being a first-time mother, one, I am open to taking the academic challenge; two, the side of a mother that is automatically associated to being a nurturer and a caregiver comes to me anytime I see any of my friends or colleagues in need of any kind of help. . . . That soft corner turns on automatically as a mother. As an academic mother, when it comes to my students, I have seen that side surface a lot more because I taught multicultural education courses. . . . If they share any personal matter, I think that I have a personal understanding, and I can relate. . . . Motherhood has trained me to be more compassionate towards my students."

Jósi stated, "The way I teach my children is heavily influenced by my role as both a Mother and Scholar of Color. There are no filters, and so the answers they get from me are . . . based on my work, so I believe that they're more critically conscious as individuals. . . . They are able to see neoliberalism, they are able to see capitalism and [its] influences, and they are so young, but yet they can see it because I don't put any filters in what I teach them. . . . They challenge me, and I welcome it. They question me, and I welcome it because I don't want to make little minions; I want them to be thinking individuals, so I think that has definitely been influenced by my academic side."

Sadaf believed that education helped her have better communication with her kids: "I always wanted to be more. Here, my kids were kind of the reason that I wanted to be educated because I wanted them to have an educated mother. . . . I wanted to know everything. . . . I didn't want to be a mother that in the future, they would tell me, 'You know, we are educated; you are not educated as much to understand us,' and I wanted to use education as a tool to have more communication with my kids."

Libertad explained that her sense of empowerment from the scholarly arena had a trickle-down effect on her motherly and personal facets: "The best experiences [from this program] were having those female mentors. All the people that come to mind that really have had an impact on me are females, and the best experience for me has been to finally come to terms and find my own voice as a female, and in the process I also became a feminist, or muxerista, and I finally found the courage to find my worth as a female [and mother]. Also, my children have told me that me getting a doctoral degree has inspired them, it has made them proud, and for me, academically, it means preaching with my actions what I'm asking of them." In addition, Libertad felt a sense of empowerment not only in her role as a scholar, and through collective reflection, as a mother, but particularly as a Person of Color: "Being a Person of Color to me is a source of pride. That is one of the terms that I do not look at from a deficit perspective. It has always been a reason for me to be proud. . . . Ever since I migrated to this country, being a Mexican has always been a great source of pride, and I cling to that."

These are the stories that are missing, which demonstrate that the merging of the academic and personal/familial spaces is a source of empowerment and a venue for power and transformative change in both domestic and professional spaces.

Conclusion

Based on our testimonios and current literature, while recognizing that no lived experience is homogeneous, we advocate for more inclusive practices that focus on eradicating the marginalization of MSOCs in higher education, which affects the physical, emotional, and cognitive aspects of Mother-Scholars, by eliminating role assumptions and celebrating motherhood in academia and vice versa. Our purpose for using counter-narratives in this study was to demonstrate MSOCs' capital and to debunk deficit perspectives and highlight value-added perspectives. At the same time, the use of testimonios to counter hegemonic and patriarchal narratives challenges self-censorship, which contributes to women's oppression and nonrecognition, and could help eliminate role assumptions as women, as mothers, and as scholars. Most importantly, the highly dialogic and self-reflective nature of this project led to a deconstruction and reconstruction of our collective and individual realities, resulting in an ongoing process of healing, reintegration, and transformation of the self.

References

Alarcón, Wanda, Cindy Cruz, Linda Guardia Jackson, Linda Prieto, and Sandra Rodriguez-Arroyo. 2011. "Compartiendo Nuestras Historias: Five Testimonios of Schooling and Survival." *Journal of Latinos and Education* 10 (4): 369–81.

Anaya, Reyna. 2011. "Graduate Student Mothers of Color: The Intersectionality Between Graduate Student, Motherhood and Women of Color in Higher Education." *Intersections: Gender and Social Justice*, no. 9, 13–31.

Bhabha, Homi K. 1994. *The Location of Culture*. New York: Routledge.

Braun, Virginia, and Victoria Clarke. 2006. "Using Thematic Analysis in Psychology." *Qualitative Research in Psychology* 3 (2): 77–101.

Castañeda, Mari, and Kirsten Lynn Isgro, eds. 2013. *Mothers in Academia*. New York: Columbia University Press.

Catalyst. 2016. *Quick Take: Women of Color in the United States*. New York: Catalyst.

Craft, Christy Moran, and Jo Maseberg-Tomlinson. 2015. "Challenges Experienced by One Academic Mother Transitioning from Maternity Leave Back to Academia." *NASPA Journal about Women in Higher Education* 8 (1): 66–81.

Crenshaw, Kimberlé Williams. 1991. "Mapping the Margins: Intersectionality, Identity Politics, and Violence Against Women of Color." *Stanford Law Review* 43 (6): 1241–99.

Delgado Bernal, Dolores, Rebeca Burciaga, and Judith Flores Carmona. 2012. "Chicana/Latina Testimonios: Mapping the Methodological, Pedagogical, and Political." *Equity and Excellence in Education* 45 (3): 363–72.

Freire, Paulo. 2003. *Pedagogy of the Oppressed*. New York: Bloomsbury.

Isgro, Kirsten, and Mari Castañeda. 2015. "Mothers in U.S. Academia: Insights from Lived Experiences." *Women's Studies International Forum* 53:174–81.

Lapayese, Yvette V. 2012. *Mother-Scholar: (Re)imagining K-12 Education*. Transgressions, Cultural Studies and Education 85. Rotterdam: Sense Publishers.

Ledford, Kathryn Fair. 2012. "Navigating the World of Academia as a Other and a Contingent Faculty Member: A Narrative Inquiry." PhD diss., Clemson University, South Carolina.

Marshall, Catherine, and Gretchen B. Rossman. 2016. *Designing Qualitative Research*. 6th ed. Thousand Oaks, CA: Sage.

Schlehofer, Michele. 2012. "Practicing What We Teach? An Autobiographical Reflection on Navigating Academia as a Single Mother." *Journal of Community Psychology* 40 (1): 112–28.

Tax, Meredith. 1995. "The Power of the Word: Culture, Censorship, and Voice." Women's World, August 1995. http://www.wworld.org/publications/powerword1.htm.

Thomas, James, and Angela Harden. 2008. "Methods for the Thematic Synthesis of Qualitative Research in Systematic Reviews." *BMC Medical Research Methodology* 8 (1): 1–10.

Weiler, Kathleen. 1991. "Freire and a Feminist Pedagogy of Difference." *Harvard Educational Review* 61 (4): 449–74.

Williams, Shirlan A. 2007. "Graduate Students / Mothers Negotiating Academia and Family Life: Discourses, Experiences, and Alternatives." PhD diss., University of South Florida, Tampa.

Witkin Stuart, Bonnie Joyce. 1997. "Balancing Between Worlds: A Qualitative Study of Mothers in Academia." PhD diss., University of Oregon, Eugene.

Zinn, Maxine Baca, and Bonnie Thornton Dill. 1994. "Difference and Domination." In *Women of Color in U.S. Society*, edited by Maxine Baca Zinn and Bonnie Thornton Dill, 3–12. Philadelphia: Temple University Press.

8

MALA

Mama Academic Liberadora Activista

Victoria Isabel Durán

My homemade theory is the promise of a utopia, rooted in the sac-rifices and hopes of my ancestors, with dedication to fighting for my children and generations of grandchildren to come. My theory is grounded in radical revolutionary mothering and the raising of Black and Brown babies. It is tied to the collective education of youth from East San Jose to dismantle the systems that reproduce the sta-tus quo. It is the process of reimagining a collective vision of utopia. My theoretical framework centers the experience of MALA MADRE and activates critical consciousness, self-determination, and collective action to resist neoliberalism, hegemony, and all forms of oppression. It is prompted by two guiding questions: "What do I hope for?" and "How will I use my agency to bring this hope to flourish?"

Mamas of Color (MOCs) across the globe have raised and con-tinue to raise children in times of repression and economic depres-sion, where structures of power have operated in denial of funda-mental human rights. During these times, mamas have committed to organizing resistance collectives and activating social movements for justice, in the name of hope for future generations. Social inequities, economic dispossession, racism, sexism, and homophobia explicitly affect the mothering of children, particularly for Families of Color, who have been subjected to centuries of colonization, capitalism, and white supremacy, across the United States and internationally. Neoliberal policies in education, such as privatization, meritocracy, and competition, are normalized and reinforce social constructs, including racism, sexism, and various forms of oppressions, for children and families to internalize (Kumashiro 2012, 2015). Here I pose the question, How do MOCs develop homemade theories (Latina Feminist Group 2001) of revolutionary mothering (Gumbs, Martens, and Williams 2016), rooted in liberation, to raise children grounded in critical consciousness, self-determination, and critical hope?

Drawing from Indigenous knowledge (Smith 2012), Black feminist thought (Collins 1990), U.S. third-world feminism (Sandoval 2004), and critical race theory (CRT) (Crenshaw et al. 1995; Ladson-Billings 2013), I offer my homemade theory, mama academic *liberadora activista* (MALA). This theory is dedicated to the MOCs who are educators, students, activists, and freedom fighters working to transform our society. This framework includes five tenets: modeled hope, audacious love, determination, relentless resilience, and emancipation (MADRE).

MALA MADRE emerged from honoring epistemologies of Indigenous knowledge (Smith 2012) and building from the intersectionality (Crenshaw et al. 1995) of revolutionary Mothers of Color in the United States as a theoretical foundation. I am a Xicana MALA MADRE, daughter, partner, educator, and doctoral student. Home, familia, comunidad, music, activism, and education have been my foundation to politically engage in the world for social justice. My positionality informs how I developed and cultivate MALA MADRE while raising my babies, situated in times of state-sanctioned violence against women, Black lives, and queer and trans communities, along with the dehumanization of Native peoples and immigrant communities, the dispossession of People of Color, and the collective trauma of oppression.

MALA MADRE is what I extend to my babies and to other MOCs to transform and create an equitable world of justice. It is rooted in matriarchal lineage, which manifests itself with the birthing and raising of children who hold the promise of creating utopias of hope. MALA MADRE is in solidarity with Mamas of Color who have birthed children vaginally or via cesarean, who are unable to birth, who have lost a child, who were sterilized, who are trans, who are queer, who are raising children across borders, who are mothering children they did not physically birth—this is in solidarity with mamas raising children through love and hope.

I offer this homemade theory to invoke a beautiful utopia and to raise babies in a world of justice and freedom. Aurora Morales testifies the power and authenticity of homemade theory:

> The intellectual traditions I come from create theory out of shared lives instead of sending away for it. My thinking grew directly out of listening to my own discomforts, finding out who shared them[,] who validated them[,] and in exchanging stories about common experiences, finding patterns, systems, explanations of how and why things happened. This is the central process of consciousness raising of collective *testimonio*. This is how homemade theory happens. (Latina Feminist Group 2001, 67)

The capacity for homemade theory reveals an intersection of critical consciousness, the ability to read the word and the world (Freire 1970); self-determination, the power of dispossessed people to independently and collectively develop (Newton 1980); and critical hope, an important and active struggle against oppression (Duncan-Andrade 2009).

Critical hope and utopias are central for MALA MADRE to express the abundance of mama power activated in interwoven identities, which comes with raising children through revolutionary mothering while pursuing educational dreams, navigating institutions, and activating change for a more just world.

Revolutionary Mothering and Indigenous Knowledge

MOCs who fight for justice, to liberate themselves and children from internalized centuries of oppression in the United States, are the embodiment of revolutionary mothering to dismantle social injustice. Nurturing our children with essential care means preparing mamas to call out and critique various forms of oppression, to model and prepare children to do the same as they enter schools, and to learn how to navigate for liberation in various institutions. Alexis Pauline Gumbs, China Martens, and Mai'a Williams present a narrative of mothering to love oneself, as resilience in a system of capitalism that calls for the extermination of deviant, queer, othered-bodied individuals.

> We say that mothering, especially the mothering of children in oppressed groups, and especially mothering to end war, to end capitalism, to end homophobia and to end patriarchy is a queer thing. And that is a good thing. That is a necessary thing. That is a crucial and dangerous thing to do. Those of us who nurture the lives of those children who are not supposed to exist, who are not supposed to grow up, who are revolutionary in their very beings are doing some of the most subversive work in the world. If we don't know it, the establishment does. (Gumbs, Martens, and Williams 2016, 20)

Mothers are the something else; mothers are the other. The infinite possibilities of what comes after the *m* in mother strikes transformation against institutions. These systems are essentially what disempowers mothers to act on their radical revolutionary mothering.

MOCs are holders of Indigenous knowledge and of space to activate, claim, and decolonize what it means to be a mother. Mothering is revolutionary and is tied to Indigenous knowledge, as it has been attacked and purged from the memories of Native bodies, from Africa and the diaspora, across Asia, Latin America, and the Caribbean, the Indigenous bodies from island nations that have been co-opted for the politics of power, oppression, colonization, and neoliberalism. Indigenous knowledge is informed by ways of being in the world and with the world. MALA MADRE recognizes that the bodies who hold Indigenous knowledge are complex and diverse, and that the individual relation to this way of knowing is personal, political, and fluid in the claiming, unknowing, and sacredness in what it carries spiritually, epistemologically, and culturally.

Cindy Cruz emphasizes the role of mothers as central to the development of learning, positing that "the production of knowledge begins in the bodies of our mothers, and grandmothers, in the acknowledgement of the critical practices of women of color before us" (2001, 658). In essence, the maternal lineage and histories guide and inform knowledges and epistemologies that are central to the development of children in utero and as they are raised. Cruz symbolically emphasizes the body as physical and historically central to knowledge production: "The body prompts memory and language, building community and coalition. The body is a pedagogical device, a location of re-centering and recontextualizing the self and the stories that emanate from that self" (658). MOCs carry their children and pass on their historical wisdom, emotions, traumas, hope, and cultural ways of knowing, informing the growth and development of their children.

Patricia Hill Collins captures the essence of Black feminist thought and the significance in centering Black mothering and womanhood:

As mothers, othermothers, teachers, and churchwomen in essentially all-Black rural communities and urban neighborhoods, U.S. Black

women participated in constructing and reconstructing these oppositional knowledges. Through the lived experiences gained within their
extended families and communities, individual African-American
women fashioned their own ideas about the meaning of Black womanhood. When these ideas found collective expression, Black women's
self-definitions enabled them to refashion African-influenced concep-
tions of self and community. (1990, 10)

Examining this connection can unearth the lived realities of race as
a social construct that is internalized at a young age, as race is rooted
in social, cultural, economic, and historical legacies of racism. Black
feminism according to Collins is also one that captures the duality of
experience and consciousness and the pervasive shaping of everyday
life (1990, 668). Gumbs, Martens, and Williams position Black women
and children as the "generators of an alternative destiny," who possess the capacity to dream of utopian societies rooted in "a forward-
dreaming diasporic accountability" to confront white supremacy and
systems of oppression (2016, 21). Black mothering channels the power
to reimagine, reconstruct, and thrive in utopias of hope.

Cruz (2001), Collins (1990), and Gumbs, Martens, and Williams
(2016) emphasize that Black and Brown mothers' bodies function as
pedagogical structures, where maternal histories are passed on and
inform mothering. This yields a powerful praxis of mamas raising
children in the name of hope to transform the world.

The Cauca Indigenous activists of Colombia believe that utopias
are attainable and will flourish, as there are intentional objectives in
life to achieving and forming the utopia (Suárez 2017). That is to say,
holding and acting on your vision and the promise of utopia makes
it possible to achieve. This is Indigenous knowledge and decolonized
thinking. This ability to hold a permanent commitment and obligation to forming justice in society for future generations falls in line
with the connection of activism as tied to future generations (Eber

2012). Mamas are an incredible force in the fight for justice in fostering, inspiring, loving, and raising children in a utopian world for future grandchildren. The act of dreaming and engaging in activism disrupts hegemony and shatters the colonized mind's preservation of neoliberalism.

Feminist Foundations

Cruz (2001), Collins (1990), and Gumbs, Martens, and Williams (2016) present the radical feminism of the female body and mind. The physical body and consciousness inform the duality of a quintessential feminist resistance. The notion of revolutionary mothering is rooted in this feminist tradition as the embodiment of praxis by simultaneously manifesting the theory of feminist consciousness and the pedagogy of honoring history and constructing the future. Similarly, bell hooks (1994) describes the progressive female resistance to theory, as it has been historically inaccessible and often overlooked in the urgency of action. She emphasizes that for theory to function as revolutionary, it must be purposeful and accessible. Mamas are the first teachers, the ones to help children decode life lessons and prepare to explore freely in the world, to fall and get up again and again.

Chela Sandoval provides context to international feminist solidarity with historically dispossessed nations: "U.S. third world feminism provided access to a different way of conceptualizing not just feminist consciousness but oppositional activity in general: it comprised a formulation capable of aligning U.S. movements for social justice not only with each other, but with global movements toward decolonization" (2004, 41). This context provides a foundation to recognize the shared social structures and institutions rooted in U.S. colonization and imperialism, which manifest as white supremacy in nations that have often been historically dispossessed by political and economic policies. This theoretical platform facilitates an opportunity for MOCs across nations to communicate shared racialized experiences of mothering Children of Color through an anti-neoliberal, liberatory, racial justice framework of critical hope.

Mothering Through Critical Race Theory

The situation of MOCs raising Children of Color in a society that protects whiteness is dire, and a theoretical analysis of race is essential to offer support. CRT was developed by Derrick Bell, Kimberlé Williams Crenshaw, and Richard Delgado in the 1970s as a theory to explore the intersections of race and racism through daily aggressions with a critique of the systems that reproduce and profit from racism (Crenshaw et al. 1995, 1363–74). According to Gloria Ladson-Billings (2013), CRT is the deconstruction of racism and racist policies in institutions that benefit the elite through a focused approach to race as a means to reproduce hegemony. CRT includes five tenets: counter storytelling, the permanence of racism, whiteness as property, interest convergence, and the critique of liberalism. CRT guides by challenging the notions of race as a social construct in a world where systems of oppression and violations of fundamental freedoms are pervasive, especially for Communities of Color who have been historically dispossessed in society.

CRT offers mamas a theory to inform what advocacy and organizing look like, while raising children and Families of Color and having to navigate neoliberal policies, hegemony, and oppressions replicated in education. Tara J. Yosso describes CRT as "challenging the way race and racism impact educational structures, practices and discourse—towards liberatory potential of schooling" (2005, 74). Furthermore, CRT presents a theoretical analysis of structural racism to reimagine and counter the construct of race in society. The theory offers a foundational basis for mamas constructing homemade theories in that it provides language to name, dismantle, and formulate narratives and counter hegemony as race remains pervasive in the United States and internationally.

MALA MADRE

MALA is rooted in the aforementioned theories and identifies the role of CRT in mothering, envisioning new theories to inform praxis and activism in revolutionary mothering. This homemade theory is an extension of the love and resilience of my maternal grandmother, who raised eleven children and supported her family with a foundation of homemade inventions to survive. I name this project MALA in the spirit of my paternal grandmother, who has adopted the nickname Mala as a term that recognizes her strength as a mama and an *abuela* through her resistance to American traditional values as well as her inventions and homemade hustles to provide her familia with *remedios*. MADRE, the framework, honors my grandfather, the *corazón* of Mala. It is the reminder to "échale ganas, mija, todo va estar bien," the affirmations from my *tata* to give it my all and know that it will be fine. My grandfather would always offer me encouragement to hold onto my *coraje* when the weight of the world would bring down my spirits; to always stay *trucha, mija*, stay vigilant. MADRE honors his longing for his estranged mama, who was banished from the family for birthing him out of wedlock. Together MALA MADRE is a tribute to honoring my grandparents and their commitment to love, familia, and comunidad.

The mala madre spider plant symbolizes this framework. It is an air-filtering plant that reduces indoor air pollution. The mother plant cultivates and extends baby clusters to grow externally from itself. Baby clusters grow adjacent to the mother plant and are capable of being transplanted, to grow and multiply with the capacity to decontaminate the air. Mala madre plants are revolutionary and radical in their ability to exist and extend powers that purify the climate. This plant offers a powerful lesson in surrendering and releasing the baby clusters into independence. The powers and capacities of this plant represent a foundation to the power of MALA MADRE and the capacity to mother in this current political climate.

MALA is the homemade theory to honor the multifaceted responsibilities of mamas who are actively engaged in the praxis of preserving social justice as mama, academic, liberadora, activista. This theory is an embodiment of carrying my babies each for ten months into doctoral classes, actively marching in protests with my babies, teaching and engaging high school students, all the while dreaming and striving for utopia. MALA embodies the journey of making space within my body (literally), heart, and soul, and sharing spaces with my babies where our ancestors have historically been excluded. It is transforming these spaces into reflections of our historical truths and cultivating futures rooted in social justice and collective action for liberation. MOCs are the manifestation of homemade theory turned praxis, rooted in liberation to raise children with a foundation in consciousness, self-determination, and critical hope to create utopias.

MADRE is the framework with five tenets: modeled hope, audacious love, determination, relentless resilience, and emancipation. MADRE comprises the little heartfelt reminders to MALA MADREs that everything will be fine. It is for those moments when the weight of the world tries to knock the glorious crown from our heads; when tears of anguish flood our hearts from attacks of state violence on Indigenous, Black, and Brown babies across the globe; and when our throats tighten and our mouths can barely muster the truth of the world to our babies because so badly we want to protect their innocence.

Modeled hope is the constant act of engaging our children with our hearts and our consciousness, to activate our third eye and envision a different world. It is the praxis. It is the truth we honor and model to inspire children who observe what we do. It is the constant reminder to release and surrender fear and affirm in hope. *Audacious love* is to be bold, brilliant, unapologetic, and determined in achieving that vision for the babies of our world. To be audacious is to hold accountability in transforming systems and institutions in the name of love, progress, and freedom. It is the courage to speak our truth honestly and boldly even when our voices shake. It is to elevate our babies to do the same. *Determination*, the knowledge of self, to hold our self-determination high, to inspire our children to be knowledgeable, wise, confident, and determined in their utopias, then to dream and work toward their vision. Determination to give all that we can also means being mindful of the rest, recharge, and reflection that are needed to fight the long fight. *Relentless resilience* is the armor we wear that is essential to survive in this work, and the purpose that inspires us to get up time and time again is what will always carry us through to liberation. In the spirit of resilience, our ancestors fought for our freedom. *Emancipation* refers to freeing ourselves from colonized standards of mothering, Western standards of education, European standards of beauty, and white supremacy. Emancipation is to use knowledge and wisdom from family and community, along with education about and research into how to critique institutions and policies, to create new ways of being in the world informed by ancestral and Indigenous knowledge. It is also to emancipate our children from ourselves. As children grow, they are emancipated from mamas to go into the world and purify the world of toxins, to use their clarity, wisdom, and agency to transform the climate and restore justice.

MALA is an ownership of not having it all together, not having all the answers, not having all the hope in the exact moment; it is the will and determination to make things happen in the name of our children and their children. MALA is learning to be purposeful and intentional with time. MALA is honoring the physical, spiritual, and authentic connections of love with our partners, children, and village, because nothing is permanent, yet everything is infinite. It is seizing each moment while forgiving ourselves when we lose sight of these values. MALA MADRE is constantly negotiating the following questions while engaged in the praxis:

What does it mean for me, my children, and my comunidad to be a Mama-Scholar in academia?

To what extent does my role as a mama influence my career as an educator?

How am I intentional with my corazón, time, and familia in my role as activista?

How do I embody liberatory critical hope during these trying times?

Conclusion

The utopia I envision for the future is one in which neoliberalism and hegemony can be abolished by cultivating critical consciousness, self-determination, and critical hope. Cultivation through MALA MADRE is centered in antiracism, honoring Indigenous knowledge, and elevating counter-narratives. Fighting dispossession through cultivation creates spaces of tension. Within these spaces of tension, liberation resides. More specifically, engaging in these spaces through radical and revolutionary acts of love is precisely the intention of revolutionary mothering. It is to move away from the isolation of the individual and in the direction of collective activism. Through communal dialogues, support circles, and activism, mamas and families equip themselves to dismantle division through solidarity.

The interconnection of generations, identities, relationships, and differing positionalities of MOCs informs the details in the fabrics of mamas' lives. In doing so, it creates and informs the intertwined fibers of MALA MADRE. The academic and political identities of MOCs are tied together and cannot be classified as independent or different, because all identities are negotiated, contradicted, experienced, and informed by one another. This introspective position informs the process of revolutionary mothering, consciousness raising, and politics of memory, where history informs the present. Babies and future generations are shaped and guided through the knowledges passed through mamas, for our future warriors of racial justice and critical hope, who are rooted in liberatory praxis.

References

Collins, Patricia Hill. 1990. *Black Feminist Thought: Knowledge, Consciousness, and the Politics of Empowerment.* Boston: Unwin Hyman.

Crenshaw, Kimberlé Williams, Neil Gotanda, Gary Peller, and Kendall Thomas, eds. 1995. *Critical Race Theory: The Key Writings That Formed the Movement.* New York: New Press.

Cruz, Cindy. 2001. "Toward an Epistemology of a Brown Body." *International Journal of Qualitative Studies in Education* 14 (5): 657–69.

Duncan-Andrade, Jeff. 2009. "Note to Educators: Hope Required When Growing Roses in Concrete." *Harvard Educational Review* 79 (2): 181–94.

Eber, Christine. 2012. *The Journey of a Tzotzil-Maya Woman of Chiapas, Mexico: Pass Well over the Earth.* Austin: University of Texas Press.

Freire, Paulo. 1970. *Pedagogy of the Oppressed.* New York: Herder and Herder.

Grande, Sandy. 2004. *Red Pedagogy: Native American Social and Political Thought.* Lanham, MD: Rowman and Littlefield.

Gumbs, Alexis Pauline, China Martens, and Mai'a Williams, eds. 2016. *Revolutionary Mothering: Love on the Front Lines.* Oakland, CA: PM Press.

hooks, bell. 1994. "Theory as Liberatory Practice." In *Teaching to Transgress: Education as the Practice of Freedom,* 59–76. New York: Routledge.

Kumashiro, Kevin. 2012. *Bad Teacher! How Blaming Teachers Distorts the Bigger Picture.* New York: Teachers College Press.

Kumashiro, Kevin. 2015. *Against Common Sense: Teaching and Learning Toward Social Justice.* New York: Routledge.

Ladson-Billings, Gloria. 2013. "Critical Race Theory—What It Is Not!" In *Handbook of Critical Race Theory in Education*, edited by Marvin Lynn and Adrienne D. Dixson, 34–47. New York: Routledge.

Latina Feminist Group. 2001. *Telling to Live: Latina Feminist Testimonios*. Durham, NC: Duke University Press.

Newton, Huey P. 1980. "The Ten Point Program." In "War Against the Panthers: A Study of Repression in America," 83–85. PhD diss., University of California, Santa Cruz.

Sandoval, Chela. 2004. *Methodology of the Oppressed*. Minneapolis: University of Minnesota Press.

Smith, Linda Tuhiwai. 2012. *Decolonizing Methodologies: Research and Indigenous Peoples*. London: Zed Books.

Suárez, Leonor Lozano. 2017. "Participate, Make Visible, Propose: The Wager of Indigenous Women in the Organizational Process of the Regional Indigenous Council of Cauca (CRIC)." In *Demanding Justice and Security: Indigenous Women and Legal Pluralities in Latin America*, edited by Rachel Sieder, 173–94. New Brunswick, NJ: Rutgers University Press.

Yosso, Tara J. 2005. "Whose Culture Has Capital? A Critical Race Theory Discussion of Community Cultural Wealth." *Race, Ethnicity and Education* 8 (1): 74.

Chicana M/other Alliances

Making Alianzas from Scratch

Cristina Herrera and Larissa M. Mercado-López

Cristina's Testimonio: Being an Othermother Is an Act of Love

In a few short months, I'll turn thirty-nine years old, a fact that I accept with no small amount of pride. As I age, I find myself growing more comfortable in my skin, more confident, more *chingona*, if you will. And with this wisdom and chingona pride, which accompany age, I have also embraced a more maternal and nurturing identity, which comes from being an "othermother," what the brilliant Black motherhood scholar Patricia Hill Collins calls women engaged in the political act of mothering children not "biologically" theirs. This pride in my othermother identity, my insistence on visibility as a Chicana feminist academic who supports, loves, and cares for children, my students, and other Chicana mothers, is my fierce commitment to cultivating an environment that recognizes the work we, as othermothers, do, all in the name of love.

As a Chicana scholar without children, I am constantly reminded that my decision to remain child-free must be a sign of my acquiescence to academe's harsh treatment of mothers, particularly Mothers of Color. I'm doing the work of racist patriarchy, it would seem. But these accusations and false assumptions could not be further from the truth, and my claiming an othermother identity as a radical and political act of love works alongside my refusal to be categorized so simply and incorrectly. My words here also free me and potentially other Women of Color academics from racist and heteropatriarchal academic norms that work to silence our experiences and lived realities. In writing this testimonio, I am daring to speak openly and honestly about my body, my life, and my experiences as a child-free Chicana feminist academic who lives daily with the realities of infertility, multiple health concerns, and stigmas associated with these challenges.

In July 2005, just a month shy of my twenty-seventh birthday, I learned from my endocrinologist, a doctor who specializes in the body's complicated system of hormones, that I suffered from several endocrine issues: hypothyroidism, a small pituitary adenoma (tumor), and, most important, premature ovarian failure (POF), a devastating diagnosis that put me at increased risk of heart disease, not to mention that this meant an early menopause, a dangerous scenario for such a young woman. "Did you want to have children?" my doctor asked, with a slight tremble in his voice. "I ... I ... uh, I don't know?" I responded, my own questioning tremble. How could I respond? I was newly married, had just completed my PhD-qualifying exams, was set to begin drafting a dissertation proposal, and was otherwise trying to keep up with the endless stress of graduate school. Children were not a consideration at this time, but my doctor's choice to use the past tense—"Did you want to have children?"—told me in no uncertain terms that whether I wanted children or not, that was now a thing of the past. Poof, it's over.

More than ten years later, my body remains in constant battle with itself. Rheumatoid arthritis keeps my joints stiff, psoriasis inflames my skin, and monthly "fake" periods, brought on by the hormonal birth control I use to supply my body with much-needed estrogen that it cannot produce on its own, are a cruel irony, a humorless joke I can't laugh at. Recently, I asked my endocrinologist how long I had to continue using the pill to supply hormones. "When will I be allowed to enter normal menopause?" "When you're fifty. That's the average age of menopause. For you, it's important we supply you with enough estrogen until then." A certain powerlessness overcame me, but the harsh truth is that if I choose to forego this medical advice, I put my health in real danger.

I speak of these bodily themes to unearth the silences surrounding infertility and health, taboo subjects that also place my body against the all-too-common stereotype of the hyperfertile Chicana. Although I know these are, after all, stereotypes, I have been pitied, seen as inferior, as "antichild," and even shamed by family members who have announced my inability to have children, without my permission to share this knowledge. In my immediate family, I am seldom acknowledged as anything other than a *madrina* or *tía* to my nieces. Although I have taken great part in raising one of my nieces, who has just completed her first year of college, I have had to endure an erasure of the mothering I have contributed, a refusal to see my actions as mothering. Mother's Day celebrations are melancholic; while I honor my mother and the love I have for her, my family has never recognized me on this occasion.

Yet among my Chicana and Latina colleagues, including my coauthor, I have found a space of radical acceptance as an othermother. I advocate for them in their work as mothers and academics, and in return, they have stood alongside me as allies, engaging in their own acts of othermothering. Supporting, uplifting, and caring for my *colegas* and amigas *is* an act of mothering, a political commitment based on *alianzas*, solidarity, visibility, and the empowering possibilities of love. Until we recognize the multiple forms that mothering takes on, biologically rooted or not, we risk maintaining and reinforcing

hierarchies that divide women/womyn/muxeres. With this testimonio, I seek not only my inclusion in mothering practices and identities but advocate for the visibility of othermothers, who nurture and
empower in the name of love.

Larissa's Testimonio:
On Transforming a Resistance to
Motherhood into Mothering as Resistance

I am a mother who actively avoided becoming a mother. Growing
up in my tiny town of Gregory, Texas, I had few models to show me
what it could look like to be a mother and a professional, so I prob-
lematically discerned from the women around me that motherhood
and a fulfilling career were incompatible. The oldest of five children, I
wanted to escape my town and live the life of a solitary yet somewhat
famed author, and resisting motherhood was, I convinced myself,
essential. I even have memories of sweeping the kitchen floor and
being told that if I swept over my feet, I would never find a husband
and get married; in quiet (and misguided) defiance, I swept the broom
across my feet anyway, hoping to avoid a life of marriage and children
and to preserve my ambition and identity. I would never have guessed
that not many years later, my life and scholarship would be dedicated
to lifting the stigma of an identity that I so strongly resisted.

In 2003, I was newly engaged and in my last year of my undergraduate degree, set to finish a semester early, when I discovered that I was
pregnant. Until that moment, by all accounts, I had "done everything
right," with the exception of living with my boyfriend before marriage—a clear violation of my Catholic upbringing. After half a dozen
pregnancy tests, I was still heavily in denial, so I put my ego aside to
visit my university student health center for a more accurate blood
test. What I experienced as I sat scared on that crinkly exam-table

paper was nothing short of pregnancy shaming by a white physician's assistant, whose rapid-fire questions were accompanied by strong head shakes, sighing, and judgmental stares (only to tell me that blood tests were not administered in their office). I left the center with an embodied experience of shame and woundedness that I would carry with me, draw from, and eventually transform into the foundational base of my social justice politics.

I continued with graduate school at that same institution, and while I felt somewhat empowered as a graduate student, I had few peers with children. I mourned my dreams of what I had imagined the grad student life to be like—living in my PJs, studying late into the night at the library, and going on the occasional road trip with friends to check out the archives at libraries across the state. Instead, I stayed up late into the night writing and nursing infants and toddlers, spent much of my time managing and cooking for a household of five (I had three children by the time I became ABD), and struggled to make "mom friends." I was a highly motivated scholar but grew frustrated with the time and energy walls that I encountered as a mother of toddlers. I wondered if I'd be able to sustain the level of productivity that I aspired to in my work and service.

The energy depletion was worsened by the messages continuing to haunt me about my out-of-placeness as a young Brown mother in academia and what I perceived to be my failure to mother in "acceptable" ways. Ana Castillo's concept of the Llorona complex captures my feelings of guilt as I "sacrificed" time with my children for my own desires. I was further reminded of how nontraditional my work was when, after telling my mother-in-law that I was leaving for a few days to attend a conference, she told me, "And don't forget to come back!"

All these experiences led to my dissertation project, in which I constructed a theory of maternal *facultad*. Drawing from Gloria Anzaldúa's facultad, I developed the concept of maternal facultad to theorize the critical knowledges that are honed from Chicana mothers' experiences of oppression and marginalization. My maternal facultad has continued to inform how I experience and make sense of the world as a Mother of Color in academia. I drew from those feelings of shame and out-of-placeness in my research and my teaching as a graduate student. In the classroom, I found my body to be a useful pedagogical tool to help my first-generation students draw from their own bodies and experiences to critique mainstream narratives of "traditional" college students. My pregnant and mothering body became a way for those students to identify their own facultades and to see their marginalization as an impetus for knowledge. Pregnancy and motherhood situated me in a space of epistemic richness, but I had to dig through the messages that I continued to battle within my own psyche and in my social world to find those knowledges. Ironically, it was the academy and its theories that helped me insist on my right to occupy it.

Thanks to excellent feminist Chicana mentors, I was a successful graduate student, and as a result of their training and opportunities to develop my professional faculties, I was hired as an assistant professor of women's studies at California State University, Fresno. When I announced my fourth pregnancy at the end of my first year, my feminist colleagues happily celebrated the news in a way that I had never experienced before. The joy was short lived, however, when other colleagues inquired whether my pregnancy was "on purpose or an accident" and suggested that because I was Mexican, I could "pop out" another baby during my maternity leave.

When my son was born, I knew that isolation and hiding the realities of my maternal identity—both forms of self-erasure—were not only antithetical to my scholarly and personal beliefs, but spiritually destructive. For me to continue thriving, I had to forge spaces for my mothering on campus. As faculty here at Fresno State, I learned to leverage the inevitable intertwining of my maternal and scholarly identities, turning those experiences into opportunities for connection, mentorship, collaboration, and research. Because of the isolation

I feel many times as a mother of four children living states away from family, this integration of my whole self into my campus has proved to be vital to my sense of home and belonging in Fresno. This work is hard and messy but necessary, not only for me, but for other mothers at my institution.

But this act of intertwining is not possible without the support of colleagues, both mothers and nonmothers, who recognize and value the synergistic intersections of my maternal identity, scholarship, and personal politics—who understand that the challenges I face in enacting these messy identities in ways that reflect the fullness of my humanity are the result of years of exclusion and erasure by an androcentric, patriarchal university culture, which continues to enact its violences on the bodies of Women of Color to this day. When we collaborate, we see it as an act of resistance to an institutional structure designed to reward men for being fathers but punish women for being mothers. We forge these alliances in defiance of patriarchal ideologies about motherhood, which perpetuate the stigma of motherhood that keeps women in the academy from collaborating with, supporting, nurturing, and endorsing one another.

This year, just two years after having my fourth child, I achieved early tenure. When I received my official letter of notification, I insisted to my fellow Chicana colleagues that we celebrate my promotion as a collective win because, from joint publications to babysitting to the constant reminders that, indeed, "Chicana mothers are chingonas!" my success has not been without the support of this Chicana alianza, one that we made, with loving hands, from scratch.

Toward a Radical Chicana Alianza

We (Cristina and Larissa) met in early 2013 when Larissa arrived at Fresno State for her campus interview. Cristina was invited to her talk because of their shared research interests in Chicana motherhood; she also happened to be the only Chicana faculty member in the College of Social Sciences, and she was very excited about the prospect of having Larissa, another Chicana, as her colleague. Upon Larissa's hire, we soon developed a close collegial relationship, as we organized a symposium and worked on joint publications emerging from the synergies of our research interests. Through our collaborative work, we forged a strong friendship and care for each other's well-being, grounded in a politics of radical sisterhood and our shared recognition of our outsider status in a college largely responsible for most of the social justice education on our campus.

We share our testimonios to call for a radical Chicana alianza based on our reimagined notions of mothering in ways that sustain one another, promote meaningful productivity, and nurture emotional empowerment. We recognize that many Women of Color in academia perform acts of mothering in various ways, and we insist that while many have a conflicted relationship with the title of "mother," part of our work as feminists should be to dispel these notions and return power to those who claim a maternal identity. We also recognize that Women of Color are implicated in many types of labor within the university, including the emotional labor they provide for one another and their students, and the antiracist education they provide for their white colleagues. Thus, we are not issuing a mandate but are calling for consideration of how we have arranged the labor we perform and for whom we perform this labor. We hope that this critical introspection will then lead to more mindful practices of collegiality that are radically inclusive.

The Chicana alianza we call for is grounded in a commitment to justice for Mothers of Color in an academy rooted in white supremacy. As mothers who, within mainstream anti-immigrant ideology, are constructed as symbolic "threats" to the hegemony of whiteness and the sovereignty of the nation, their bodies have been medically

controlled through reproductive measures and ideologically surveilled through political discourse and within the academic community. We recognize that, as the title of this collection insists, there is
no revolution without mothers.

As a mother and an othermother, we have spent the past four years
negotiating the complexities of our lives to sustain our scholarship,
our places in the academy, and, importantly, our friendship. Over
the years, we have brought other Chicana colleagues into the fold,
helping one another through first years on the tenure track, single
motherhood, pregnancy, tenure, promotion to full professor, and first
year as department chair. In the face of an absence of formal support
for Chicanx and mothering faculty at our university, we have culled
our knowledge and resources to create our own.

Based on our experiences, these are our recommendations for
building the foundation of a Chicana alianza from scratch within
institutions of higher education:

1. Find research synergies to create meaningful publication opportunities by building relationships across disciplines and colleges,
   using existing infrastructure or developing your own through
   creative and accessible means, such as social media networks.
   This is especially helpful for mothers who are returning from
   maternity leave or are in the throes of toddlerhood, who may
   find it especially difficult to sustain their writing.

2. Don't hold back from inviting mothers to be part of collaborative
   projects, even if they don't seem "meaningful." Mothers sometimes
   struggle to remain visible in service and through projects because
   of the assumptions made about their availability and interest.

3. Create "breathable" time lines for publications. That is, set "soft"
   deadlines for one another, send reminders, and leave room for
   extensions.

4. When appropriate, express that children are welcome in your homes or in meetings, and secure larger conference rooms for those meetings.

5. Propose various alternatives to traditional face-to-face meetings, such as Skype, phone conversations, and even email.

6. Offer to take care of children. For children to feel a sense of belonging within the university community is just as important.

7. Be attentive to intersectionality and how it complicates our assumptions about mothers. Our alianzas cannot be liberatory if we don't recognize our queer, trans, single, gender nonconforming, and disabled Mothers of Color.

8. Empower one another to assert your needs and share your times of availability. Consider reframing the language around time, so that discussions center on times of availability rather than time conflicts.

9. Avoid scheduling meetings too close to drop-off or pick-up times at schools and daycares, or propose meetings closer to a mother's home or her child's school for late meetings.

10. Mothers need to socialize, too! If possible, propose times to socialize *during* the traditional "work" day. This is often when children are in daycare or school. Depending on the situation, arranging schedules to socialize in the evening can be complicated and stressful. This is especially important for mothers who have limited opportunities to network.

11. Nominate one another for awards and exchange letters of support for promotion files. In spaces where we lack support, we need to be our best champions.

12. Celebrate children, pregnancy, and diverse representations of family. Sharing in our joy is affirming.

13. Challenge your institution to recognize parents and to promote a positive caretaking culture.

We challenge all Chicanx mothers and othermothers to create their own alianzas and, importantly, to pressure their institutions to provide support to sustain them. Our alianzas, much like the alianzas forged by our mothers and Chicana academic foremothers, have the potential to transform the academy—to be liberatory. But there is no true liberation if it does not include mothers.

Madres en Lucha

Forging Motherhood as Political Movement Building Across Borders

Verónica N. Vélez

Arrieros somos y en el camino andamos.
—MEXICAN SAYING

We were all nervous on our drive back from New Orleans. I still could not believe so many ALIANZA mothers decided courageously to organize the forty-hour drive to the educational conference.[1] So, when ten mothers signed up to go, I felt a mix of excitement and awe as well as fear and apprehension. They understood the risk as im/migrant mothers, many of whom were undocumented, but felt it necessary to go.[2] With the blessings and prayers of family, ALIANZA made it to New Orleans, successfully and powerfully delivered their presentation, and were now making the drive back home. We were getting close but had one last obstacle to cross: the agricultural checkpoint coming into California. Although we had taken Highway 40 to avoid the additional risks of driving along the U.S.-Mexico border, we could not avoid the checkpoint. We approached the officer. I showed him my conference badge and explained the purpose of our trip. He motioned us through. Before we started picking up speed again, a wave of applause and laughter immediately broke the silence. One by one the mothers began sharing their stories of migrating to the United States, celebrating each other's courage and laughing at the mishaps along the way. The mood had changed, and I looked over to Justo, one of ALIANZA's founding members, who smiled with relief.[3] We were only a few hours from home. "La hicimos, Justo," I shouted.[4] Justo smiled and shouted back, "Si Vero, arrieros somos y en el camino andamos."[5]

Although I grew up hearing *dichos* at home, the saying shared with me on that road trip from New Orleans, by a member of ALIANZA, a Los Angeles–based im/migrant mother group, was new to me. When I probed further, the mothers explained that the *arrieros* (muleteers) were a marginalized group whose everyday lives were likely similar to those of Latina/o im/migrants today.[6] In their travels, they must have felt the same apprehension ALIANZA experienced traveling to New Orleans. But the explanation for the second part of the dicho caught my attention the most. For the mothers, it reflected a deep-rooted sense of *esperanza* (hope), a belief that it shouldn't matter whether you are an arriero, or an im/migrant for that matter, our journeys in life are inevitably intertwined and will eventually depend on recipro-cal acts of aid. Although ALIANZA mothers deeply understood the insurmountable challenges to this vision, they believed that the dicho embodied a hope that one day, they would drive fear-free to confer-ences and continue supporting efforts for social change.

For the remaining drive home, I kept thinking about the dicho. ALIANZA members' willingness to risk so much, including their safety, kept me wondering—*is it worth it?* What informs their deter-mination? Why undertake this eighty-hour round trip to speak to educational researchers about the importance of Latina/o im/migrant mothers' organizing, despite the many potential dangers along the way?

I had begun asking similar questions seven years prior, when I joined ALIANZA as an organizer and adult literacy popular edu-cator and started witnessing the mothers' boundless drive to seek educational justice for their children and those of others. I joined ALIANZA after organizing with similar mother groups in Northern California, largely informed by my experience growing up as a child of an im/migrant mother from México and an im/migrant father from Panamá. My entry into ALIANZA was motivated by a desire to support parents like my own, in creating spaces, both inside and outside schools, that facilitated their participation in local politics and school decision making. I was frustrated that schools, and other institutions, could marginalize the very communities they blamed for not being more involved in education. My organizing work was initially aimed at exposing and dismantling this contradiction. It later evolved into a community-based participatory-action research project with ALIANZA, at the request and direction of the mothers. Collectively, we sought to document the formation of ALIANZA, in an effort to recognize and theorize about Latina/o im/migrant mothers as powerful agents of change in schools and in society at large.

We were deep into the research project when we traveled to New Orleans and decided to document our experiences, the aftermath, and what it ultimately meant for ALIANZA's future organizing. We discovered that the political agency behind this risk-filled expedition was the product of the mothers' journeys, across time and borders, which rested on an ever-evolving and mutually informing relationship between their sense of belonging to a political community and their ability to enact change. Throughout their lives, the mothers had been rendered outsiders, as im/migrants, Mexicans, women, and non-English-speaking individuals. Through ALIANZA, they fought to recreate a sense of belonging and, in the process, to claim a political place, centered in *motherhood*, from where to exert their agency as activists.[7] But migrating to el norte—to the United States—was key in shaping their identities as political actors. For the mothers, migration disrupted their sense of belonging, extended their threshold of hope, and developed their consciousness as agents of change. In this chapter, I capture the dynamic nature of this process and argue that the mothers' political formation resulted largely from crossing borders, which led to forging motherhood as political movement building through

ALIANZA. Specifically, migrating *as mothers* shaped the urgency and purpose of work later in life as mother-activists, by linking their drive to immigrate with their drive to improve schools. Border crossing, thus, became their everyday life in the United States (Anzaldúa 1987, 1990), positioning their migration experience as core to their identities as political actors and to their campaign for social change. Their shared experiences as im/migrant mothers produced skills, knowledges, and networks that linked each mother's coming to consciousness with their collective enactment of their agency publicly and unapologetically as *madres en lucha* (mothers in struggle).

To situate this analysis, I first provide an overview of ALIANZA, summarizing its work and purpose, particularly its aims to disrupt deficit characterizations of Latina/o families. Next, I briefly provide a methodological description of the community-based participatory-action research project, rooted in Chicana feminist epistemology, which guided our collective inquiry. I then highlight findings that link the mothers' migration experiences to their development as madres en lucha. Finally, I conclude with a few thoughts about what ALIANZA, as a critical case, reveals for theorizing the necessity of motherhood in movements for social change.

ALIANZA

Although ALIANZA has existed in its current form since the late 1990s, its history traces back to the early 1980s, when its umbrella organization, Centro para Inmigrantes (CI), was formed.[8] CI was initially an organization that worked with families to address racism and the lack of educational opportunities and affordable housing for the working poor in a racially segregated area of Los Angeles County. In 1987, a group of local popular educators joined the group, introducing the concepts of popular literacy and popular education.[9] ALIANZA grew out of this process, developing into a mother-led group that sought to train, organize, and facilitate the participation of Latina/o families in school reform and local city politics.

Broadly, ALIANZA aims to reconfigure the terms of parent involvement in schools. While members recognize the importance of parent involvement for student achievement, particularly among Latina/o families (Cotton and Wikelund 1989; Delgado-Gaitan 1990, 1996, 2001; Jasis and Ordoñez-Jasis 2004; McCaleb 1997; Moll and González 1997; Olivos 2006; Valdés 1996), they also acknowledge crucial contradictions in how "parent involvement" is operationalized, arguing that "the concept of parent involvement is a social construct whose boundaries and expectations are impacted by culture, race, class and gender issues" (Jasis and Ordoñez-Jasis 2004, 32). ALIANZA mothers have consistently challenged the unrelenting search in the home for the problem of low Latina/o parent participation in schools, refusing arguments that brand Mothers of Color in particular as the primary culprits for their children's academic failure (Moreno and Valencia 2002; Valencia and Black 2002).

Participatory Action Research Rooted in Chicana Feminist Epistemology

In 2007, ALIANZA determined that it was important to engage in critical inquiry of its own process, documenting its organizational history and assessing the role of popular education in its work. A graduate student at the time and a *comadre* in ALIANZA's efforts, I shared with group members what I had learned about research methodologies.[10] They immediately gravitated to community-based participatory-action research. They felt it held the most promise for employing inquiry toward transformative ends, not just in the outcome of a project but throughout its process.

As a research paradigm, community-based participatory-action research (PAR) facilitates a space for research and community collaborators to construct knowledge, transform their experiences, and work to change those conditions that affect their lives (Lather 1986; Maguire 1987; Finn 2008). The democratic character of PAR is supported and furthered by feminist critiques of traditional, positivist research paradigms. Among these critiques is Chicana feminist epistemology (CFE), which challenges how traditional research approaches are deployed to inappropriately characterize the experiences of Chicanas/os specifically and Latinas/os generally (Delgado Bernal 1998; Calderón et al. 2012). It calls on researchers to center the lived experiences of communities within research in a deliberate attempt to create social change (Hurtado 2003). By recognizing the fundamental value of lived experience, not just within the content of knowledge produced but in the very process of creating that knowledge, PAR aligns with CFE. Guided by a Chicana feminist standpoint, PAR provided the tools to help capture the experiences of ALIANZA mothers and to situate my positionality as a Chicana researcher, which informed my subjectivity throughout the study.

Migrating to el Norte: Motherhood, Borders, and Movement Building

While I wasn't fully aware of it then, the event captured in the opening vignette of this chapter symbolizes the importance of the mothers' migration experience in their development as political actors. What made the moment so telling was how it transitioned from an anxiety-filled van of passengers to a seemingly celebratory recalling of memories crossing the U.S.-Mexico border. Beyond the laughter and relief, there was a deeper sentiment, a more profound *rootedness* that explains why that checkpoint was so significant. I returned to that moment when I looked through the rearview mirror right before crossing. The anxious glances, the uncontrollable foot tappings, the nervous handling of rosaries, and the stiff upright postures made clear that something had been triggered in each of the mothers. Once the officer motioned us through, the joyous singing and storytelling about migration experiences erupted, embracing us with a sense of accomplishment and happiness that can only fully be understood by those of us who experienced it. As I reflected further, it became apparent that what was triggered at the checkpoint were precisely the memories, both physiological and psychological, of migrating to the United States.

Once triggered, the immediacy of those memories crossing the U.S.-Mexico border manifested in two ways: (1) the corporal changes in the mothers as we approached the officer, reflecting an almost instinctive response of their bodies to what that agricultural checkpoint signified within the repertoire of their migration experiences; and (2) the instant and spontaneous sharing of migration stories right after we crossed, an indication that these memories were, indeed, painfully near. The bodily changes I witnessed brought to life the experiences each of the mothers had shared with me on several occasions, either through interviews or informally at ALIANZA events, about migrating to el norte. While each journey was unique, all shared the theme of an *embodied* experience, one that foregrounds the physicality of that moment and evokes all too well just how life defying crossing the U.S.-Mexico border was.

One of the first narratives that stood out was from an ALIANZA mother who meticulously detailed the treacherous moments of crossing the border.[11] When I asked how those experiences of migrating to the United States affect her today, she responded:

Estaba perdida dos días sin agua y comida. Llegó un momento que dije, "o luchas o te mueres." Me acuerdo bien después que crucé el río, el dolor en mis piernas. Estaban llenas de cortadas de las ramas de árbol y las espinas del cacto. Mira, todavía tengo las cicatrices. Pero las ganas de vivir fueron más fuertes. De repente escucho que alguien muy lejano gritaba, "cuidado, viene la migra!" Creo que corrí más de treinta minutos sin parar. No sé de donde saqué tanta fuerzas pero el deseo tan grande por vivir y para ayudar a mi familia fue más grande que mi propio ser. Y es lo que me sigue impulsando. La lucha que hoy hago [con ALIANZA] es la misma lucha que cargaba sobre mi cuerpo cuando crucé la frontera—para un mejor futuro no solo para mí pero también para mis seres queridos, que ahora incluye todos los niños del distrito escolar. La experiencia cuando crucé sigue siendo como una fuente de fuerza, de haberme visto con la muerte y haberla retado. Esa lucha para sobrevivir todavía sigue.[12]

As this ALIANZA mother narrated her experience, I couldn't help but notice how she kept touching and rubbing the scars gained from crossing the border. Whether it was her intent to soothe the remnants of any bodily pain she still felt or her way of exposing and making evident the visible markers of that journey, it was clear that recalling these memories was physical *just as much as* it was verbal. Maybe, in part, she rubbed her scars to remind herself that she truly is human, even though getting through that experience required extraordinary strength, a type of "sixth sense of survival" (Espinoza-Herold 2007, 261). She later connected the experience of crossing the border to her efforts with ALIANZA today, identifying her current efforts as an activist mother as *rooted* in her migration. For this mother, the goal remains the same: to address unjust obstacles that have relegated her to a marginal place in society, from where she continues to fight, in her words, for a better future. And while the tactics have changed, and those dreams have extended to include other people's children as an "other" mother, the linking of these experiences demonstrates the impact of border crossing on her development of political agency.[13]

Remembering this experience was so powerful that it produced a mechanical response to brush over her scars as a reminder of its lasting effects.

For another ALIANZA mother, reliving her border crossing was like riding a bike: "A tu cuerpo jamás se le olvida lo que viviste al cruzar. Aunque tu mente ya no acuerda cada detallito, a tu cuerpo nunca se le olvida. Es igual cuando aprendemos a manejar una bicicleta. Pueden pasar años, pero cuando te vuelves a montar es casi inconsciente como uno se recuerda cómo conducirla."[14] Her comparison stresses the extent to which a migration experience like hers is fundamentally *embodied*, similar to the narrative from the first mother, in which the memories of that event are physically stored and the flesh becomes the source of narrative when recalling what happened. She also mentioned that since making the treacherous crossing twenty years ago, she had never retold the moment-to-moment encounters of that experience until my request. But like riding a bike, she argued, one's body immediately remembers what occurred and what one learned from it, even if at first the story may lack a bit of cohesiveness, structure, and specificity.

What struck me most about this mother's story was the connection she made between her embodied memories and how they challenged her threshold of hope. This mother knew firsthand what it meant to have gendered norms weigh heavily against her aspirations to become a doctor. She had grown up with a socialized understanding that hope, at least for her, had a limit. But when she made the decision to leave for the United States against the will of her family, she began to extend the scope of her esperanza, with its most radical expansion occurring during the actual migration and triumph of reaching *el otro lado* (the other side).[15] She recalled,

Salir al norte fue un momento de rebeldía, y también de liberación. Quise irme, y estuve dispuesta a arriesgar mi vida. Pero el momento que retas la muerte y llegas al otro lado, te sientes fortalecida aunque tu cuerpo esta totalmente rendido. En mi misma carne encontré otro sentido de lo que es la esperanza. Es difícil ponerlo en palabras. Para mí, aprendí en ese desierto que la esperanza es algo que experimentas al ver tu triunfo al lograr cruzar la frontera. Sientes que no hay nada que no puedes hacer. Por eso ahora cuando me siento que me quieren volver a apachurrar en mi lucha como madre, me acuerdo del sacrificio que hice y lo que logre al cruzar. Es lo que me hace sentirme fuerte.[16]

When this mother realized she had accomplished the life-defying act of crossing the desert, she gained a new perspective on her agency. Experiencing firsthand the sacrifice, will, and triumph of border crossing removed any limit she had previously held on her definition of hope. Alluding to her work with ALIANZA, she directly connected her efforts to challenge unjust practices in schools to crossing the border. The source of hope that informed and linked both acts now gives her strength to continue *luchando* (fighting). Thus, her political agency today is profoundly *rooted* in her experience of migration, which triggered an extended and *embodied* awareness of hope from which her actions as a political actor are rendered possible.

To extend this notion to the development of political agency in ALIANZA, an exploration of the role of motherhood *during* migration is needed. The majority of ALIANZA mothers were already mothers when they made the decision to journey to el norte. One mother's story stands out as emblematic of a shared experience in ALIANZA of what it meant to cross the border *as mothers*. Holding back tears during our interview, she remembered,

Mandamos a mis hijas primero. La grande tenía casi seis años, y mi chiquita solo diez meses. Pudieron cruzar con las actas de nacimientos de las hijas de mi hermano. El día que cruzaron yo hice el intento de pasar por la noche. . . . Me lastime mucho al cruzar, pero el dolor que mas acuerdo era el de mis senos porque todavía le estaba dando pecho a mi hija. Ya habían pasado varias horas de la última vez que le di de comer, y pues a una madre le duele mucho cuando pasa tanto tiempo. Pero el dolor aun era más fuerte porque necesitaba ver a mis hijas. No sabía al cruzar si ellas llegaron bien. Eran mi motivación y mi urgencia por llegar. Cuando finalmente cruzamos y ví a mi hermano abrazando a mi chiquita sentí un alivio que solo una madre puede sentir.[17]

Once again, this mother, like the others highlighted in this chapter, foregrounded the corporeal element of her experience crossing the border. Though she remembered being injured, she centered on the physical and emotional pain of being separated from her daughters, particularly on what it meant to be a nursing mother when she migrated. Unable to breastfeed for almost twenty-four hours, she experienced grueling pain unique to a lactating mother. It directly shaped her agency and became her central drive to cross the border and reunite with her child. Later in our conversation, she mentioned that every now and then she would sense the same pain when she felt challenged to become more politically active. Arguing it was most likely the psychological aftermath of border crossing, she sees her pain today as a reminder of the urgency of her actions. To stress this point, she added, "Igual como cuando crucé la frontera, no hay vuelta atrás, tengo que vencer los obstáculos porque al final están los niños de este distrito igual como estaban mis niñas en los brazos de mi hermano."[18] In other words, the embodied urgency she felt as a mother when she crossed the border is the same one that gives haste to her efforts as a political actor today.

Although several ALIANZA mothers didn't cross while nursing a child, the same sense of urgency was present in their stories. One mother, for example, recalled the pain she felt from the blisters that had developed on her feet from walking so many hours without rest. When the pain became unbearable, she would pull out a small picture of her son and immediately feel as if she was being carried across the treacherous terrain. Another mother described what it felt to be three months pregnant when she crossed: "Cargaba en mi vientre la mas grande razón por llegar a mi destino. Mi hijo nunca era una carga en esos momentos. Al contrario era la fuerza que necesitaba para poder cruzar. Y por cuidarlo a él y asegurar que nada me pasara, hice la cruzada con más prisa."[19] For this mother, pregnancy fueled her drive to cross, which underscores how intimately tied her identity as a migrant mother is to her sense of agency. And still another mother described how her sister, who had left to the United States about two years before she crossed, needed her help as she was about to become a mother for the first time. The necessity to help her sister was just as urgent in driving her efforts to cross the border as the motivations other mothers have described here.

For these and other ALIANZA members who crossed *as mothers*, their maternal identity was foregrounded as a source of support and strength as they migrated. This was powerfully evident in the story of an ALIANZA mother who described what it felt to confront the possibility of never being able to return home to México and the unknown reality of whether she would be accepted as part of U.S. society:

Cuando estas cruzando, te pones a pensar que a lo mejor ya no volverás a regresar a tu tierra natal, y que solo te quedan los recuerdos de los rostros de tus familiares, de tus papás, tus hermanos. Y luego te pones a reflexionar si verdaderamente vas a encontrar un hogar autentico en los Estados Unidos. Ahora con diez años de estar aquí, puedo decir con seguridad que los obstáculos son grandes para que te acepten. Pero en los momentos cruzando la frontera, lo único en que te pones a pensar son tus hijos. Ellos son tu motivación y son lo único con que te identificas. Ser madre es donde te ubicas, donde te agarras cuando enfrentas la realidad que ya no eres de allá pero tampoco eres de acá.[20]

For this mother, her sense of belonging was disrupted the moment she embarked on her journey. Forced by migration to reclaim a place of belonging, she found her figurative home in her role as a mother, which she identified as permanently tied to the desert she crossed. She highlights, "Cuando decidí enfrentarme a la muerte por mis hijos, es cuando yo verdaderamente me hice madre."[21] For her, being a mother and an im/migrant are deeply intertwined, and she noted that while giving birth entered her into motherhood, migrating, and all the sacrifices it entails, made her worthy of such a title.

Conclusion: (Re)imagining Motherhood for Social Change

Taken as a whole, the stories of ALIANZA mothers demonstrate how motherhood and migration are fundamentally interconnected in the development of political agency. Though the range and degree to which mothering played a role in each of their stories varied, it was nonetheless central to understanding how migration was simultaneously one of the most traumatic and transformative moments of their lives. The collective impact of these experiences on ALIANZA's organizing was visible in multiple forms. One of those was in the way the mothers challenged an understanding of motherhood as solely defined by the biological or adoptive act of having children, and especially by the more restrictive requirements of the local school district to have a child enrolled in public school to be eligible to participate in educational decision making. As noted above, several ALIANZA mothers were unable to bring their children from their home countries, while others had committed to caring for children whose mothers were unable to migrate with them.

During an ALIANZA meeting I attended, the mothers discussed the importance of redefining the concept of motherhood *as a political identity*, as a movement committed to challenging educational and civic institutions that marginalize families like those in ALIANZA. The mothers stressed that reconceiving motherhood must continue to honor mothers and their relentless struggle for their children and families in a patriarchal society, but that it must simultaneously extend its reach to include others who, despite falling outside motherhood's traditional definition, stood in solidarity with and worked alongside ALIANZA for the same goals, *para los mismos sueños* (for the same dreams). During the conversation that evening, the mothers returned to their migration experiences, citing what Kathleen Coll has described as the "complexity of their position as local mothers, long-distance mothers, sisters, daughters, and as paid care providers for the children of other working women . . . [that influenced] how they understood their position and rights in the United States" (2010, 74). Risking their lives to cross borders, dealing with the daily lucha against institutional efforts that seek to render them silent, and stepping in to mother other people's children as a result of anti-im/migrant policies provided ALIANZA mothers the *embodied* insight to (re)imagine motherhood as a political platform.

ALIANZA continues to engage in various public campaigns for educational change. Their collective experience makes them a critical case for theorizing how motherhood shapes social movements, particularly for im/migrants. By centering the experiences of border-crossing mothers, ALIANZA deprivatizes motherhood, reappropriating domesticity as a way of staking claim to U.S. society, despite continued efforts by the state to keep them out. In other words, by publicly mobilizing and seeking rights *as mothers*, ALIANZA shifts the boundaries of belonging for im/migrants who would otherwise be kept at the margins. As one ALIANZA mother reminded me, "Seguiremos luchando hasta que reconozcan que tenemos derechos simplemente por ser madres."[22] For ALIANZA, motherhood *is* movement building. Interconnected with their identities as im/migrants, motherhood was *how* they built collectives, resisted in the name of justice, and nurtured futures.

Notes

Epigraph: Closely translated as "Muleteers we are and on the road we travel."

Acknowledgment: I want to acknowledge and honor the work of the Chicana M(other)work collective (https://www.chicanamotherwork.com/), who, among other inspirations and guidance, have pushed me to consider "motherwork" over "motherhood" to foreground the everyday labor of mothering, particularly for Mothers of Color. Rather than appropriate the term in this chapter, I acknowledge the critical shift using "motherwork" provides and intend to adapt it in future writing and theorizing after consultation with the collective.

1. ALIANZA is a pseudonym for the group.
2. I place a "/" between "im" and "migrant" to challenge the notion that all im/migrants move to the United States in pursuit of the "American dream," which often masks the underlying sociopolitical and economic factors for their migration, or that transnational migration is always unidirectional. Im/migrants may migrate back and forth from the United States and their home countries, send remittances to family members outside the United States, and/or disidentify with citizenship structures and efforts to assimilate (Morrissey 2013). To more accurately represent these varied and complex realities, and as a grammatical move toward justice, I use "im/migrant" in lieu of "immigrant" in this study.

    I use "undocumented" to refer to im/migrants who come to the United States without "proper" documentation that would otherwise permit them legal authority to reside within U.S. borders. This label is highly contested. I use the term cautiously, recognizing that it is problematic to define or frame U.S. im/migrants from a nation-state position without adequately recognizing global conditions that have led many to risk their lives crossing the border without this documentation. I have chosen to use this term in lieu of others currently used in public discourse that inhumanely criminalize and demonize im/migrant populations, particularly Latina/o im/migrants in U.S. society today.

3. Justo is a pseudonym.

4. "We made it, Justo."

5. "Yes, Vero, muleteers we are and on the road we travel." This vignette is an excerpt from my personal journal documenting my experiences working with ALIANZA. Dated April 2011, the journal entry reflects only my recollections of and reflections on the event it describes.

6. I acknowledge that this chapter comes at a time when the label "Latina/o" is being challenged to better reflect intersectional identities, particularly gender-fluid and gender-nonconforming individuals. I have seen various iterations of the term, including Latinx and Latinx/a/o. I recognize and applaud these efforts, often engaging in conversations about the meaning of rejecting grammatical norms as we seek social justice. These conversations have also revealed the concern that the evolution of labels can often be taken up uncritically, with symbols and rhetoric frequently the first to be co-opted in struggles for inclusivity. Amid these debates, I recognize the need to reimagine language to reflect intersectional experiences while making sure I do so in a way that centers those that will be most affected by the change in representative labels. Thus, I have decided to use Latina/o for now as I continue to wrestle with how best to represent the complexity of experiences among Latinas/os in my writing and teaching.

7. I'm using the terms "mother," "mothering," and "motherhood" intentionally, while recognizing that not all ALIANZA mothers are women who have children in U.S. public schools, or at all. As I explain later, I'm challenging the boundaries of these terms to refer to all ALIANZA mothers included in this study, whether or not they had biological or adoptive children of their own, and theorizing around the concept of motherhood in ways that extend its scope and understanding.

8. Centro para Inmigrantes is a pseudonym for the organization.

9. During its first methodological workshop in 1997, CI defined popular education as "a process of analysis, critical and participative reflection through economic, political, and socio-cultural realities that arise from impoverished organized groups" (organizational website, concealed to protect anonymity).

10. My use of the term "comadre" is similar to how Aurora Chang uses it to define her relationship with women colleagues in a research and writing collective (Martinez et al. 2015). She defines comadres "as those sister

friends whom with you share *confianza* (trust). They are non-blood family who have your back every step of the way. They share, listen, gossip, cry, laugh, fall apart and come together at life's cruxes. Perhaps most importantly they embody a sort of joy that can only be had by friendship bound by a common goal, mutual suffering and a collective sense of goodness" (Martinez et al. 2015, 85).

11. I have taken a silent evidentiary position when discussing data that highlight or make reference to the undocumented status of any of the mothers in this study. This means, but is not limited to, refusing to use any type of identifier, including pseudonyms, when providing quotations that refer to crossing the U.S.-Mexico border without proper documents as deemed by U.S. immigration laws.

12. "I was lost for two days without food and water. There came a moment when I said, 'either you fight or you die.' I remember well the pain in my legs after I crossed the river. They were full of cuts from tree branches and cactus thorns. Look, I still have the scars. But my desire to live was stronger. All of a sudden I hear a distance voice scream, 'watch out, the border patrol is coming!' I started running and running. I think I ran for more than thirty minutes without stopping. I have no idea where I got the strength but the desire to live and to help my family were greater than my being. And it is what keeps me going today. My struggle I embrace [alongside ALIANZA] is the same struggle I carried on my shoulders when I crossed the border—for a better future not only for me but for all my loved ones, that today includes all the children in the school district. The experience when I crossed continues to be a fountain of strength, of having seen death in the face and overcome it. That struggle for survival still continues today."

13. See Patricia Hills Collins (1990), who uses the term "othermothers" to capture the shared mothering practices common in African American communities, where women support one another in the care of other people's children. I would argue that a similar practice occurs in Latina/o communities, and particularly among Latina/o im/migrants locally and transnationally, as the separation of families becomes more and more common under U.S. anti-immigrant policies.

14. "Your body never forgets what you lived when you crossed. Even though your mind may not remember every little detail, your body never forgets. It's like when you learned to ride a bike. Years can go by,

but when you get back on it, it's almost unconscious how one's body remembers how to ride it."

15. The phrase "el otro lado" refers to the United States.

16. "Leaving to the United States was a moment of rebellion, and, well, liberation too. I wanted to leave, and I was willing to risk my life. But the moment you challenge death and get to the other side, you feel strengthened even though your body is totally vanquished. In my own flesh, I found another sense of hope. It's difficult to put it in words. For me, I learned in that desert that hope is something you experience when you see yourself triumph at crossing the border. You feel that there isn't anything you can't do. That's why now when I feel that others are trying to squash me again in my fight as a mother, I remember the sacrifice I made and what I accomplished when I crossed. It is what makes me feel strong."

17. "We sent my daughters first. The oldest was almost six years old, and my little one was only ten months. They were able to cross using the birth certificates of my brother's daughters. The day they crossed I attempted to cross at night. . . . I was very hurt when I crossed, but the pain that I remember the most was the one I felt in my breasts because I was still breastfeeding my daughter. Several hours had passed since the last time I had fed her, and for a mother it hurts when so much time passes. But the pain I feel was even greater because I needed to see my daughters. I didn't know when I crossed whether they had gotten there okay. They were my motivation and my urgency to get to the other side. When I finally crossed and I saw my brother holding my youngest, I felt a relief that only a mother could feel."

18. "In the same manner of when I crossed the border, there is no turning back. I have to overcome obstacles because at the end are the children of this district in the same way my daughters were in my brother's arms."

19. "I carried in my womb the greatest reason for reaching my destination. My son was never a burden in those moments. On the contrary, he was the strength I needed to cross. And in an effort to care for him and ensure that nothing would happen to me, I made haste in my crossing."

20. "When you're crossing, you begin to think about the possibility of never being able to see your home country, and that all you have left are the memories of the faces of your loved ones, your parents, your brothers. And then you begin to reflect if truly you will find an authentic home

in the United States. After being here ten years, I can tell you with confidence that the obstacles are great in having others accept you. But in the moments you are crossing the border, the only thing you can think about are your children. They are your motivation and the only thing you can identify with. Being a mother is how you orient yourself, what you grab on to when you confront the reality that you're neither from here nor from there."

21. "When I decided I was willing to die for my children is when I truly became a mother."

22. "We will continue fighting until they recognize that we have rights simply because we are mothers."

References

Anzaldúa, Gloria. 1987. *Borderlands / La Frontera: The New Mestiza*. San Francisco: Aunt Lute Books.

Anzaldúa, Gloria. 1990. "Haciendo Caras, una Entrada." In *Making Face, Making Soul / Haciendo Caras: Creative and Critical Perspectives by Feminists of Color*, edited by Gloria Anzaldúa, xv–xxviii. San Francisco: Aunt Lute Books.

Calderón, Dolores, Lindsay Pérez Huber, María C. Malagón, and Verónica N. Vélez. 2012. "A Chicana Feminist Epistemology Revisited: Cultivating Ideas a Generation Later." *Harvard Educational Review* 82 (4): 513–39.

Coll, Kathleen. 2010. *Remaking Citizenship: Latina Immigrants and the New American Politics*. Stanford, CA: Stanford University Press.

Collins, Patricia Hill. 1990. *Black Feminist Thought: Knowledge, Consciousness, and the Politics of Empowerment*. New York: Routledge.

Cotton, Kathleen, and Karen Reed Wikelund. 1989. "Parent Involvement in Education." Education Northwest (formerly Northwest Regional Education Laboratory), School Improvement Research Series, May 1989. https://educationnorthwest.org/sites/default/files/ParentInvolvementin Education.pdf.

Delgado Bernal, Dolores. 1998. "Using a Chicana Feminist Epistemology in Educational Research." *Harvard Educational Review* 68 (4): 555–79.

Delgado-Gaitan, Concha. 1990. *Literacy for Empowerment: The Role of Parents in Children's Education*. New York: Falmer Press.

Delgado-Gaitan, Concha. 1996. *Protean Literacy: Extending the Discourse on Empowerment.* London: Falmer Press.

Delgado-Gaitan, Concha. 2001. *The Power of Community: Mobilizing for Family and Schooling.* Lanham, MD: Rowman and Littlefield.

Espinoza-Herold, Mariella. 2007. "Stepping Beyond *Sí Se Puede: Dichos* as a Cultural Resource in Mother-Daughter Interaction in a Latino Family." *Anthropology and Education Quarterly* 38:260–77.

Finn, Janet. 2008. "The Promise of Participatory Research." *Journal of Progressive Human Services* 5 (2): 25–42.

Hurtado, Aida. 2003. "Theory in the Flesh: Toward an Endarkened Epistemology." *Qualitative Studies in Education* 16 (2): 215–25.

Jasis, Pablo, and Rosario Ordoñez-Jasis. 2004. "Convivencia to Empowerment: Latino Parent Organizing at La Familia." *High School Journal* 88 (2): 32–42.

Lather, Patti. 1986. "Research as Praxis." *Harvard Education Review* 56 (3): 257–77.

Maguire, Patricia. 1987. *Doing Participatory Research: A Feminist Approach.* Amherst: Center for International Education, University of Massachusetts.

Martinez, Melissa A., Danielle J. Alsandor, Laura J. Cortez, Anjale D. Welton, and Aurora Chang. 2015. "We Are Stronger Together: Reflective Testimonios of Female Scholars of Color in a Research and Writing Collective." *Reflective Practice* 16 (1): 85–95.

McCaleb, Sudia Paloma. 1997. *Building Communities of Learners: A Collaboration Among Teachers, Students, Families, and Community.* Mahwah, NJ: Erlbaum.

Moll, Luis, and Norma González. 1997. "Teachers as Social Scientists: Learning About Culture in Household Research." In *Race, Ethnicity, and Multiculturalism: Policy and Practice,* edited by Peter Hall, 89–114. New York: Garland.

Moreno, Robert P., and Richard R. Valencia. 2002. "Chicano Families and Schools: Myths, Knowledge, and Future Directions for Understanding." In *Chicano School Failure and Success: Past, Present, and Future,* edited by Richard R. Valencia, 227–49. New York: Routledge.

Morrissey, Megan. 2013. "A DREAM Disrupted: Undocumented Migrant Youth Disidentifications with U.S. Citizenship." *Journal of International and Intercultural Communication* 6 (2): 145–62.

Olivos, Edward M. 2006. *The Power of Parents: A Critical Perspective of Bicultural Parent Involvement in Public Schools.* New York: Peter Lang.

Valdés, Guadalupe. 1996. *Con Respeto: Bridging the Distances Between Culturally Diverse Families and Schools—An Ethnographic Portrait.* New York: Teachers College Press.

Valencia, Richard R., and Mary S. Black. 2002. "'Mexican Americans Don't Value Education!'—On the Basis of the Myth, Mythmaking, and Debunking." *Journal of Latinos and Education* 1 (2): 81–103.

Part III

Intergenerational Mothering

11

A Chicana Mother-Daughter Spiritual Praxis

Alma Itzé Flores

When I started my dissertation work on Chicana mother-daughter pedagogies, I was looking for Chicana first-generation college students who considered their mothers to be integral to their educational success.[1] I was interested in documenting the teaching and learning practices of immigrant mothers who had little formal education but had raised high-achieving daughters who were now professors or in doctoral programs. I wanted to disrupt the narrative that Chicana immigrant mothers do not care about their children's education by showing how these mothers envisioned higher education for their daughters, despite never being part of that world themselves. This was my story after all; my mother did not attend college, yet I know that without her, I would not have gone on to pursue higher education.

The daughters in my research were all raised in predominantly Latinx working-class communities in Los Angeles, and the mothers were all immigrants from Mexico.[2] They immigrated to escape poverty or abusive relationships, or to support their families financially. When I sat down with the mothers, they all spoke about the substantial role religion played in raising their daughters. Many attributed their daughters' educational success to Dios.[3] The daughters ranged in terms of how they identified, some holding tight to religion, whereas others saw themselves as more spiritual. Although they had all grown up in Christian, often Catholic, homes, some had begun to practice other religions, like Buddhism, or saw their ties to religion as cultural.

Because of these varying identities between the mothers and daughters, discussions around religion often led to disagreements. I struggled with mothers' strong assertions that Dios had paved the path for their daughters' educational achievements, because I felt that this diminished their own effort and their daughters'. While I grew up in a Catholic home, I never fully embraced Catholicism; however, it is still a big part of who I am. For me, being Catholic is a reminder of my immigrant journey; my first language, Spanish; and the family that still lives al otro lado. Yet, I recognize that Catholicism has also been a tool of colonization for our communities, especially for Women of Color and LGBTQ people.

This feeling of being in between (Anzaldúa 1987) is nothing new to me. I grew up never fully fitting in—whether it was growing up poor in a predominantly rich white community like Santa Barbara, not speaking English, or being the only Latina in Advanced Placement courses, I have always navigated this in-between state. When it comes to religion, I have found stability in what I refer to as a Chicana mother-daughter spiritual praxis. This is a continuously shifting space of exploration, pain, and love, where the spiritual and religious often collide, connect, and transform each other. It is an intergenerational space where Chicana mothers and daughters challenge, maintain, and transform spiritual and religious practices. The word "praxis" is important because through action and reflection on the religious and the spiritual, mothers and daughters embody and enact an ethic of love, justice, and interconnectivity with each other, their communities, and their work.

In this chapter I share the muxerista portraits of two mother-daughter pairs to further illustrate what I mean by a Chicana mother-daughter spiritual praxis.[4] This is my own analysis of a spiritual praxis based on thirty pláticas with ten mother-daughter pairs.[5] To begin, I briefly discuss the literature that informed my theorization of a Chicana mother-daughter spiritual praxis. My goal is to show how religion or spirituality is one of the many ways in which Chicana immigrant mothers support their daughters' educational achievements. Although this praxis can at times be opposing, in this space, daughters like me learn how to craft their own sense of religion or spirituality.

Religion, Spirituality, and Education

Situating the terms "religion" and "spirituality" is important because the two are not the same. I use both words to honor the language the mothers and daughters used. Like Theresa Delgadillo, I use the term "religion" to refer to "organized, institutionalized, traditional religions in Western thought" (2011, 3). As Elisa Facio and Irene Lara explain, "Being 'religious' connotes participating in a religious institutional structure and following specific religious tenets and canonical practices, even if in popular or hybrid cultural forms" (2014, 4). Most of the mothers described religious practices that aligned with this understanding. When referring to spirituality, Lara Medina's definition as "the multiple ways in which persons maintain and nurture balanced relationships with themselves, others, the world, and their creator or creation" (2006, 257) fits with how the daughters made sense of their religious or spiritual identities. Being spiritual certainly can go hand in hand with being religious. The two are similar in that both are based on the practice of an ideology; whether that practice is organized and institutionalized or more relational or fluid is what makes them different.

A Chicana mother-daughter spiritual praxis is continuously shifting between these two definitions. At times this praxis can align more with traditional religious practices, and at other times, it can be more in between, where there is a mixing of the Indigenous and

Christian. The Chicana mother-daughter relationship is central to this praxis because it speaks to the intergenerational muxerista wisdom that emerges through this spirituality.[6] This is what makes it different from Gloria Anzaldúa's conceptualization of spiritual activism, which is "spirituality that recognizes the many differences among us yet insists on our commonalities and using these commonalities as catalysts for transformation" (Keating 2009, 323). A Chicana mother-daughter spiritual praxis is grounded in Anzaldúa's idea that we are all connected to one another and as such should work together to improve the world. Anzaldúa insisted that spirituality was centered in an interconnectedness of all aspects of life, that spirituality connected us with the world, our ancestors, and contemporary relations.

A Chicana mother-daughter spiritual praxis adds to Anzaldúa's spiritual activism by centering the Chicana mother-daughter relationship not only in spirituality, but also in the teaching and learning that emerge from this space. Often, ideas of how religion and spirituality should be expressed collide or transform each other. Chicana mothers and daughters become subjects in deciding how to practice their religion or spirituality. This praxis becomes a site of transformation for mothers and daughters to explore how religion or spirituality can coexist, at times in contradiction with each other and at other times connecting.

Little work centralizes religion or spirituality in Chicana mother-daughter pedagogies, especially through a mother-daughter perspective. Dolores Delgado Bernal (2006) and Lindsay Pérez Huber (2009) did find that for Chicana college students, spirituality helped them persist and maintain their educational goals. The women saw spirituality as a tool of resistance and a source of community cultural wealth maintained by the women in their families. Moreover, Jeanett Castellanos and Alberta M. Gloria (2008) found that Latinx undergraduate students call on their sense of spiritualty or religious practices as a coping mechanism for their educational challenges and experiences. Thus, religion or spirituality has played an important role in the educational success of Latinx students; as a way to resist, to cope, or to maintain connections to their families or communities, it helps them persevere through often hostile institutions. Through the muxerista portraits of Nati and Cecilia as well as Rosario and Maria, I expand on this work by highlighting the maternal in Chicana students' expressions of spirituality or religion and how this affects their educational success.

Nati and Cecilia: Prayer, Faith, and Miracles

Nati and Cecilia are one of the mother-daughter pairs I knew prior to the study. At the time, Cecilia and I were working on our PhDs together. Since I met Cecilia, she has given birth to two beautiful babies. Prior to sitting down with Cecilia and Nati for their mother-daughter plática, I had several individual pláticas with each of them. Cecilia's mother, Nati, reminds me of my grandmother because of her unwavering faith and devotion to Dios and especially to La Virgencita. She is what people in Mexico often call a Guadalupana, to express the feminine and matriarchal spirit of La Virgen de Guadalupe.

Every time I left Nati's house, she said she would pray for me and ask Dios to watch over me. She knew about the challenges and loneliness of being the first in the family to go to college from Cecilia's experiences. I would smile and thank her, often feeling tears begin to form in my eyes. Cecilia and the other daughters in this study described university and college campuses as different worlds, where they did not always feel welcomed or supported. These feelings of isolation are often a result of how schooling disconnects the mind from the body and spirit; objectivity is associated with the mind and is thus prioritized, while emotion and intuition are linked with the body and spirit, and as such are marginalized. This separation is understood as integral to student success. I realize now that I approached my explo-ration of achievement through this lens and therefore struggled to see the significance of spirituality.

Nati pushed me to understand the connections between spiri-tuality, education, and mothers and daughters. When I first asked her about Cecilia's educational success, she explained that it was a reflection of Cecilia's own hard work and familial support, but most importantly, God's love and guidance. The quotations that follow are from Nati, in which she is explaining the role of religion in Cecilia's education. Note that in the first quotation, when Cecilia is faced with a challenge, Nati turns to her own belief in milagros.[7] The last two quotations show how centrally Nati sees God in Cecilia's education.

Mira mi participación fue que cuando ella no pensó que fuera ir a la universidad, cuando me comento que eran tres mil aplicaciones y que era demasiado que a lo mejor no podía entrar, yo confié en Dios. Yo siempre he tenido fe en Dios, y yo sé que Dios puede hacer un milagro, y el milagro se hizo de que podía ser aceptada, porque para mí fue un milagro, después de tanta gente si le dieron la oportunidad, eso sola-mente Dios. Dios mueve las cosas.

Look, my participation was that when she [referring to her daughter] didn't think she was going to get into the university, when she told me that there are three thousand applications and that it was a lot and that maybe she wouldn't get in, I confided in God. I've always had faith in God, and I know that God can make miracles happen, and the miracle happened when she was accepted, because for me it was a miracle that after so many people they gave her the opportunity. That is only God's doing. God makes things happen.[8]

Como te digo Dios esta con ella, pero Dios hace su parte, y ella hace su parte.

Like I told you, God is with her, but God does his part, and she does her part.

Bueno que con todos sus planes, proyectos, y deseos que pongan a Dios por adelante, es así como se realizan las cosas, Dios por adelante y con los esfuerzos de ella.

Well, that with all her plans, projects, and wishes that she put God first, that is how things get accomplished, God first and with her hard work.

When Cecilia was applying to transfer from community college to a prestigious university in Los Angeles, she told her mother how competitive it was and that there was a possibility she would not be admitted. Because Cecilia lived at home, Nati had witnessed how hard she had worked in community college and knew how much she wanted to attend this university. She felt guilty that she was not able to help with her daughter's college applications, and the only thing she felt she could contribute was her prayer, her faith in God that things would work out. She shared with me how much she prayed during this time. Cecilia was admitted, and Nati sees this as the miracle she prayed for. Throughout our plática, Nati explained that God, Cecilia's work ethic, and the support that Nati was able to provide were the reasons Cecilia had done so well. Together, these three things helped Cecilia successfully navigate, resist, and transform challenges she faced in her education.

I recognize that I was originally looking for more "objective" or "concrete" actions that Nati had done to support Cecilia. My initial understanding of achievement was based on the separation of the mind and the spirit. Yet, Nati's strong faith led me to acknowledge how important the spiritual is in the educational achievements of Chicana first-generation college students and how central it is to Chicana mother-daughter pedagogies. Nati's quotations show how Chicana mothers maintain the spiritual in education through prayer, faith, and the belief in miracles. At the core of these practices is love. Despite lacking the knowledge of how higher education functions (Nati has a second-grade education), immigrant working-class mothers provide spiritual capital (Pérez Huber 2009) to help their daughters navigate their education. In this way, la oración, la fe, y los milagros are used to leverage the educational barriers that their daughters face.

While Pérez Huber does not center the role of mothers in her discussion of spiritual capital, all the women in her study explained their connection to religion or spirituality as something they inherited from their mothers. This is important because it speaks to the centrality of the mother-daughter relationship and the muxerista sensibility in spirituality. Although the daughters did not agree on just how major these religious practices were for their educational achievements, in the sense that not all of them practiced Catholicism, they did not reject the practices. Instead, they transformed them into deeper connections with their mothers, as we see in Cecilia's quotation below.

Cecilia described her faith through her connection with her mother. She shared that her mother's faith in her gave her the self-confidence that school did not always provide her with. While Cecilia grew up Catholic, she sees herself as more culturally Catholic, participating in some religious practices, like baptizing her daughter, but also being critical of how women are framed in Catholicism. Cecilia has especially relied on her mother's faith during her doctoral program:

I was telling her [referring to her mother] about the lack of funding, . . . and she's like, you have to act like algo va salir, va salir, something will happen. You have to have that faith that it will happen, and she's never been wrong. She's never been wrong so I don't question it. . . . So in that way she's always physically here, like, in my mind she's here with me now. She continues to guide me and provide me with the strength I need to get through this place.

Funding is one of the biggest stressors that Students of Color from working-class backgrounds face. In graduate school, funding can often change from term to term. This unpredictability causes a lot of anxiety in students. The daughters all spoke about this stressor and how they turned to their mothers for support. Yet, they did not seek support in the financial sense but in a spiritual one. As Cecilia explained above, whenever she encountered financial hardships, her mom would remind her to have faith that things would work out. In the last part of the quotation, when Cecilia expresses how her mom is always with her, it shows how her spiritualty is grounded in her relationship with her mother. Whether in physical or spiritual form, Cecilia's mother guides her and provides her with the courage to continue navigating what she described as a doctoral program that can be hostile to her identity as a Mother of Color in academia. Her mother's religiosity is a reminder to never lose trust in herself and in the power of having faith, de que algo va salir.

The mothers, in discussing their daughters' educations, talked about the importance of prayer, faith, and miracles. Because the mothers on average had an elementary education, they felt that often, they could not help when their daughters faced academic challenges. Many spoke about not always being able to help with homework, because of the language barrier, or provide support during college applications, never mind the stress of navigating financial aid. They did their best; if they could not help, they would turn to what allowed them to get through their own tribulations—religion. Religion had helped them during difficult times in their own lives, such as experiences of poverty, worker exploitation, and domestic abuse.

Therefore, when the mothers witnessed the stress, sleep deprivation, and anxiety that their daughters were experiencing, they prayed, turned to their church groups, tended their home altars, and asked for milagros. While Cecilia's faith in God was perhaps not as strong as her mother's, her faith in her mother got her through many difficult moments in her education. In this mother-daughter dyad, Nati's prayer, faith, and milagros were her way of connecting with Cecilia or offering support. Although Cecilia's religious practices did not align perfectly with her mother's, and often collided, she transformed them into a spiritual connection with her mother, rather than one with a god. This exemplifies a Chicana mother-daughter spiritual praxis, where the religious and spiritual often collide, connect, and transform.

Rosario and Maria: A Social Justice Praxis

Rosario described her daughter Maria as someone always willing to help others. When I was recruiting women to participate in my dissertation, Maria was one of the first to express interest. In my intake survey, I asked her why she was interested, and she responded that it was important to support other Chicana doctoral students since there are so few of us. I had never met Maria or her mother before the study, so it touched me that she was so willing to support me despite knowing very little about me.

Rosario, Maria's mother, had been a teacher's aide for most of Maria's life, at one point working in Maria's class. Maria chuckled as she recalled this and told me that she had to promise not to call her "Mom" while in school. Rosario and Maria struck me as more than just mother and daughter; the way they spoke to each other and their playful mannerisms gave me the impression almost of sisters or longtime girlfriends. This speaks to their close and honest relationship; they shared a lot with each other and have supported each other through many challenges.

Maria is a pastor's kid, who grew up in church. Her mother and father were both very involved in their local church, yet Rosario shared that she was more concerned about her children following

Catholic morals than she was about their church attendance or participation. When I asked Rosario about her faith and where it came from, she began to describe her family. Rosario lost her mother at a young age and experienced a lot of poverty before making it to the United States. She explained that faith got her through those difficult times.

Similar to Nati, she believes that her biggest contribution to Maria's educational success is her faith: "I felt that whatever little I can give them [referring to her children], if I gave them faith, they would have everything, because I know that faith carried me through all the obstacles I had to overcome." Beyond faith, Rosario talked about religion as something you lived. Because of this, she instilled in Maria the significance of actively working to improve the conditions of the people around her. When I asked Rosario about where this came from, she shared the following:

> My dad used to say all the time that whenever somebody came to him asking him for food or money, he would always say, when he was giving, "Lord, may my children one day, when they need the help, find that generous help." You know somebody that is willing to help them, and I always have that in mind, you give now, but who knows when you need, somebody will be there for you. Like when they helped Maria go to Stanford during the summer, I said right now is your time to ask. There will come a day where you will give, and the same way you felt that happiness and that joy when you received, have it when you give, because we're all at both ends at different times.

A Chicana mother-daughter spiritual praxis is guided by a deep commitment to social justice. It draws on moral principles like justice, solidarity, and service to actively work toward a better world. Beyond the critiques of Catholicism, or religion as an institution, the daughters always came back to these ideas and often said that their introduction to social justice began in church. Rosario did not teach Maria about religion; instead she embodied it through her actions. In the quotation above, she is speaking to an ethic of service, which is a substantial part of a Chicana mother-daughter spiritual praxis. As I spoke to earlier, a Chicana mother-daughter spiritual praxis is informed by Anzaldúa's spiritual activism, which means that for Chicana mothers and daughters, spirituality is about service to each other, their families, and their communities. Rosario and Maria embody this principle with each other. Maria often took on the mother role to help with her sister with special needs, and Rosario frequently made the drive from South Gate to Claremont to visit her daughter as she struggled at a predominantly white, affluent college.

Another example of this service to each other is how Rosario helped Maria raise money so she could go to a summer camp at Stanford University (as Rosario mentions above). Maria was admitted to a competitive science camp, but unfortunately Rosario could not afford to send her. Together they raised the funds so Maria could attend. They picked up cans; sold food; wrote letters to politicians, former teachers, and church members asking for donations, and in time, they had raised the money. Maria was ecstatic. Through this experience, Rosario taught Maria how as a community, we need to support each other, because there will always be a time when you are in need and a time when you can give.

Maria learned from her mother that spirituality was lived, not defined or restricted to a place—it was a way of being. Her religious upbringing informed how she saw herself, her community, and her work as an academic. Her mother inculcated in her a strong self-awareness of the world around her, teaching her about oppression but also about the power she had to change these injustices. From a young age, Maria volunteered at local schools as a tutor. During high school, she volunteered at a clinic, and currently she dedicates her time to community environmental justice work. Thus, from early on Maria witnessed just how much of an impact one person could have on improving the lives of others. This lesson continues to guide her graduate school journey. In the quotation that follows, Maria explains what religion means to her now:

> Those ideas, like social justice, love, compassion, which I think I've actually drawn a lot more away from the church because at a certain point I felt like people were speaking of those things but not necessarily living them, and I think it became more important to me to understand that church or that religiosity or spirituality was not a place but a practice, and even my mom would always say that about our abuelito. He didn't ever read the Bible, but he was a very religious man, in that if he saw someone hungry, he would give them a taco, and I think to me that's the driving force . . . how I try to treat people . . . the role I see myself playing in students' lives in the future, like I don't want to just go up and lecture and be done. . . . I hope my biggest intervention isn't just a book. I hope it's being able to be there and be a source of love and justice and compassion in an institution that does not offer any of those things for historically marginalized communities.

Maria is speaking to how a Chicana mother-daughter spiritual praxis is lived. It is based on the premise that we all can change the world, that we all have the will to improve the lives of others. For Maria, who is currently in graduate school, the morals her mother taught her inform how she treats people, as well as her teaching. Her pedagogy is informed by a Chicana mother-daughter spiritual praxis, in that she practices justice, love, and compassion with her students. She recognizes how higher education can be a hostile place for historically marginalized communities. As a graduate student, she uses her classroom as a site of resistance by practicing pedagogy that is based on students' bodymindspirit. This shows how Maria's conception of spirituality is not a place but a practice, a lesson she learned from her mother. For Chicana first-generation college students, spirituality informs their work as academics. Their research, teaching, and service are all spiritual acts of justice and transformation. This is why a Chicana mother-daughter spiritual praxis is important, because it becomes a tool of resistance in the face of oppression.

Conclusion

In this chapter I share a glimpse of Nati and Cecilia's and Rosario and Maria's muxerista portraits to illustrate a Chicana mother-daughter spiritual praxis. My aim is to show how this praxis can be messy yet empowering for Chicana mothers and daughters, and how the mother-daughter relationship, and its muxerista sensibility, is central to spirituality. Nati and Cecilia showed that mothers and daughters may not agree in their faith in one god, but that their faith in each other is often more than enough to sustain them. Rosario and Maria remind us that spirituality should be lived, not contained to a place. This is why I use the word "praxis," to remind us that while the theoretical can be influential, actions speak louder.

As a Professor of Color who started her career at a Catholic institution, I often reflect on my spirituality, and I always return to the women in my family. I realize that we are daughters of women who relied on their spirituality to survive and resist. As our mothers witness our trepidation in traversing academia, a space they always envisioned for us but never experienced themselves, they pass down their tool of survival and resistance—spirituality. So even if we refuse to pray to their god, we never lose faith in our mothers. They become our spiritual guides, nuestros angeles de la guarda, in our survival as Brown women.

Notes

1. I use Chicana to refer to women of Mexican ancestry. All the women in my dissertation research were Chicana.

2. I use Latinx to refer to people of Latin American ancestry, to disrupt the gender binary and hierarchy in the Spanish language, and to account for varying gender identities, such as transgender and gender-nonconforming people.

3. I purposefully do not italicize words in Spanish or translate them (with the exception of quotes) as a way to honor my bilingualism and to disrupt the hegemony of the English language.

4. Muxerista portraiture is the methodology I used in my dissertation research. For more on this methodology, see Flores (2017).

5. According to Francisca E. Gonzalez, pláticas are conversations that take place in one-on-one or group spaces, and that are a "way to gather family and cultural knowledge through communication of thoughts, memories, ambiguities, and new interpretations" (2001, 647). For more on pláticas as a methodology, please see Fierros and Delgado Bernal (2016).

6. Muxerista translates to "womanist," referring to someone who is deeply committed to the struggle and liberation of Women of Color. Anita Tijerina Revilla (2004) first used the concept to describe a theoretical and pedagogical framework based on critical race theory and Chicana/Latina feminisms.

7. Milagros are miracles, events or actions that cannot be explained by natural or scientific causes, so instead they are considered the work of God.

8. When translating quotations from Spanish, I choose to italicize the English translation as a way to disrupt the hegemony of the English language and bring attention to the conflicting process of translation that Chicana scholars often face. I translate conceptually rather than literally to avoid language marginalization.

References

Anzaldúa, Gloria. 1987. *Borderlands / La Frontera: The New Mestiza*. San Francisco: Aunt Lute Books.

Castellanos, Jeanett, and Alberta M. Gloria. 2008. "Resé un Ave María y Encendí una Velita: The Use of Spirituality and Religion as a Means of Coping with Educational Experiences for Latina/o College Students." In *Latina/o Healing Practices: Mestizo and Indigenous Practices*, edited by Brian W. McNeill and Joseph M. Cervantes, 195–219. New York: Routledge.

Delgadillo, Theresa. 2011. *Spiritual Mestizaje*. Durham, NC: Duke University Press.

Delgado Bernal, Dolores. 2006. "Learning and Living Pedagogies of the Home: The Mestiza Consciousness of Chicana Students." In *Chicana/Latina Education in Everyday Life: Feminista Perspectives on Pedagogy and Epistemology*, edited by Dolores Delgado Bernal, C. Alejandra Elenes, Francisca E. Godinez, and Sofia Villenas, 113–32. New York: SUNY Press.

Facio, Elisa, and Irene Lara. 2014. *Fleshing the Spirit: Spirituality and Activism in Chicana, Latina, and Indigenous Women's Lives*. Tucson: University of Arizona Press.

Fierros, Cindy O., and Dolores Delgado Bernal. 2016. "Vamos a Platicar: The Contours of Pláticas as Chicana/Latina Feminist Methodology." *Chicana/Latina Studies* 15 (2): 98–121.

Flores, Alma Itzé. 2017. "Muxerista Portraiture: Portraiture with a Chicana/Latina Feminist Sensibility." *Center for Critical Race Studies Research Brief* (7): 1–4.

Gonzalez, Francisca E. 2001. "Haciendo Que Hacer—Cultivating a Mestiza Worldview and Academic Achievement: Braiding Cultural Knowledge into Educational Research, Policy, and Practice." *International Journal of Qualitative Studies in Education* 14 (5): 641–56.

Keating, AnaLouise, ed. 2009. *The Gloria Anzaldúa Reader*. Durham, NC: Duke University Press.

Medina, Lara. 2006. "Nepantla Spirituality: Negotiating Multiple Religious Identities Among U.S. Latinas." In *Rethinking Latino(a) Religion and Identity*, edited by Miguel A. De La Torre and Gaston Espinosa, 248–66. Cleveland, OH: Pilgrim Press.

Pérez Huber, Lindsay. 2009. "Challenging Racist Nativist Framing: Acknowledging the Community Cultural Wealth of Undocumented Chicana

College Students to Reframe the Immigration Debate." *Harvard Educational Review* 79 (4): 704–29.

Tijerina Revilla, Anita. 2004. "Muxerista Pedagogy: Raza Womyn Teaching Social Justice Through Student Activism." *High School Journal* 87 (4): 80–94.

12

Enseñanzas de Mi Madre

Chicana Mother-Daughter Digital Conexiones

Andrea Garavito Martínez

Ring, ring, ring.

"Aloo . . . ," I hear my mother say.

"Mami, ¿como se hace el caldo de pollo?" I ask.

"Déjame me siento." I hear her turn off the TV.

My mother lists the ingredients and explains the process.

We talk about the latest *Teresa* episode and family *chisme*.

Ring, ring, ring.

"Aloo . . . ," I hear my mother say.

"Mami, se me olvido que le pongo primero," I say.

"¡Hay, Andrea! ¿Como está el frio?" my mother asks.

She explains the process again.

We talk about the cold and long winter days.

Ring, ring, ring.

"Aloo . . . ," I hear my mother say.

"Mami, creo que, si me salió," I say.

"Tómale una pic-churr y ponla en el face," my mother says.

I laugh and hang up.

—ANDREA GARAVITO MARTÍNEZ, "TECH SUPPORT"

As my identities have shifted from a Chicana graduate student in a doctoral program at the University of Utah to a Chicana Mother-Scholar, I feel an urgent need to bear witness to how I reconceptualized mothering practices as a graduate student in a predominantly white institution (PWI) and to the influence of my mother's *enseñanzas* in shaping them. In this chapter, I describe the process of a *testimonio co-creado* with my mother to reflect on our *enseñanzas de madres* (Prieto and Villenas 2012, 411; Urrieta and Villenas 2013, 516). A testimonio co-creado is "a *testimonio* created in dialogue," based on mutually testifying (Prieto and Villenas 2012, 412). Linda Prieto and Sofia A. Villenas (2012) describe the process of testimonial co-creation between two teacher-educators to examine who they are, how they "know," and how they teach as Chicana/Latina educators of prospective teachers in PWIs. They recorded their testimonios in dialogue and reflected on them together, creating individual transcriptions and writings. Luis Urrieta Jr. and Sofia A. Villenas (2013) use testimonio as a Latina/o critical theory (LatCrit) methodology positioned within a Chicana feminist epistemology framework (Pérez Huber 2010, 77) to explore how race and racism have influenced their lives, from graduate students to teacher-educators and engaged scholars. In a session of three testimonios co-creado over telephone conversations and continuous email correspondence, they bore witness to each other's lived experiences.

Similarly, I had six testimonio co-creado sessions with my mother between September 2016 and March 2017, over the telephone and video chat, and once in person. Before our first conversation, I had listed a series of questions I wanted to ask her about what it meant to have a daughter in graduate school who is a mother and a future professor. I wanted our conversations to come naturally, however, instead of feeling prefabricated, so I decided to approach our digital talks as *pláticas* (Fierros and Delgado Bernal 2016; Huante-Tzintzun 2016, 51; Flores 2016, 71). Cindy O. Fierros and Dolores Delgado Bernal describe pláticas "as conversations that take place in one-on-one or group spaces, and which are a way to gather family and cultural knowledge through communication of thoughts, memories, ambiguities and new interpretations" (2016, 11–12). Pláticas happen "over the phone, at home, in community spaces, and even over lunch" (Morales 2016, 115). They are collectively the process of tapping into specific types of cultural knowledge using a culturally familiar way of conversing (115). Rather than scripted interview protocols, the use of pláticas as a method enables the researcher to have a dialogue with study participants in a more natural and bidirectional way (117). Similarly, I wanted to approach the conversations with my mother as an everyday dialogue.

Pláticas have been used in recent educational research as both method and methodology to examine teaching and learning practices between Mexicana/Chicana immigrant working-class mothers and their first-generation college daughters (Flores 2016, ii); the experiences of fifth-grade Latina/o students and their participation in an afterschool Chicana/o studies college class (34); and the co-construction of a Chicana feminist *rasquache* pedagogy (Mendoza Aviña 2016, 474). Growing up, my aunts and mother would sit around a kitchen table to drink coffee, eat pan dulce, and *platicar*. In this informal setting and format, my mother and her siblings created space for one another, shared their thoughts and ideas, and connected. I wanted to re-create this with my mother. My spoken-word poem "Tech Support" captures our digital tellings, or *conexiones*, the daily practices of communication (phone calls, video chats, and text messages) that connect us. Because of distance—I live in Utah, and she's in California—we used these media to share the personal narratives that encompass our testimonio co-creado on mother-daughter pedagogies, "the teaching and learning that occurs between mothers and daughters of color that are wrought with tensions and contradictions yet open with spaces of possibilities" (Villenas and Moreno 2001, 673).

Within the contours of testimonio co-creado is the element of *reflexión*, the analysis of similarities and differences in our personal narratives. In March 2017, my mother came to visit me in Salt Lake City. During her visit, at my kitchen table over *cafecito y pan*, I shared my thoughts, emotions, and partial writings (Villenas 1996, 712–13). Even though she did not want to write her testimonio, I wanted to make sure I had captured what she had shared over our phone conversations. The analysis of our testimonio co-creado centered on (1) migrations and transitions and (2) reconceptualizations of *el sacrificio de madre*. I wanted to start with our lived experiences migrating back and forth between the United States and México and across various neighborhoods in the East Los Angeles metropolitan area. We have both experienced various migrations and transitions—moving in between and among borders and having to restart our lives in new places—yet we've been propelled by different economic factors.

Migrations and Transitions

By remembering and reflecting on our experiences of migration in our first plática, I realized that in peculiar ways, we are transnational mothers (Villenas 2005, 273–74; Hondagneu-Sotelo and Avila 1997, 552), as our "resistance . . . occurs in direct and subtle ways in the intimacy of the home" (Villenas 2001, 10). In 2009, when I migrated from Los Angeles to Salt Lake City for graduate school, I had never imagined living, birthing, and studying in this place. It was different to move "away" for college from Los Angeles to Santa Barbara, California. In Utah, I was a minority, not only at the university campus but also in the city. Similar to my childhood transnational migrations, this migration was necessary, to obtain new academic and future opportunities. I had to transition to a new city, school, and life. Soon after completing the master's program, I stayed for the doctoral program, and before I knew it, I was married and pregnant.

After becoming a mother in 2014, I struggled with my decision to continue with the doctoral program. Learning to balance the daily tasks of motherhood and writing a dissertation was taking a physical, mental, and spiritual toll on me. One day, I called my mother and shared my feelings of guilt—not being able to spend enough time with my son. My mother replied, "Las madres son fuertes. Tienes que seguir, es para el beneficio de ti y tu hijo. Como yo lo hice contigo y tus hermanas."

In this moment, my mother's *consejo* reassured me that I was not alone in the process of obtaining a doctoral degree. I come from a legacy of transnational mothers. Women in my family were led and driven to el norte by economic and immigration policies (Hondagneu-Sotelo and Avila 1997, 552). My great-grandmother and grandmother had to leave their children behind in México for manual labor employment. My maternal grandmother was thirteen when my great-grandmother migrated north to Tijuana, México, in the 1950s, leaving behind her children in the care of their father and extended family. Throughout the years, my great-grandmother worked various manual labor jobs in factories, remarried, and had more children. She never returned to her hometown. Similarly, my mother was nine years old when her mother migrated with my grandfather to Los Angeles, California, in the 1970s. They left their five children under the care of my grandfather's sisters. First, my grandmother worked as a caregiver in a senior center in Los Angeles and later as a seamstress until her retirement. My mother was a child of their remittances, raised by extended family members. "¡Éramos muchos!" my mother said of the children who lived in México while their parents were living in the United States.

During our second plática, we talked about my transition from college to graduate school and toward motherhood. In the process of figuring out the type of mother I wanted to be for my son, I realized that I had to talk about my father and our constant migrations. I had lingering and pressing questions. "¿Porque mi papá nos dejo en México?" I asked my mother during our initial interview. She said, "Esas cosas no se platican," and quickly changed the subject. The next week, I asked again: "¿Porque nosotros vivíamos en México y mi papá estaba aquí en Los Angeles?" After a long pause, she replied, "No hay que hablar de cosas tristes." I wanted to respect her silence and ambivalence about answering the question. A third time, I gently said, "Necesito saber, porque nos movíamos mucho cuando estaba pequeña." This time my mother replied, "Tu eres madre y ahora entiendes que a veces tenemos que tomar ciertas decisiones para el futuro de nuestros hijos."

A peculiar detail of my birth accentuates the complexity of my constant migration during my childhood. I was born in Boyle Heights, in East Los Angeles. My father and siblings were living in México. I was only three months old when we moved back to México to join the rest of my family. My mother explained that they were worried about the immigration policies changing because of the political climate in the 1980s, with Ronald Reagan's presidency. When the economy began to change in the late 1980s, my parents migrated multiple times to El Norte. It was always temporary. My father would work enough to get back "on his feet," but when it became too difficult to support a family of seven all living in the United States, he would send my mother and siblings back to México, while he stayed and worked, saving up for us to be reunited. I have tried to remember the number of times my siblings and I moved between countries with my mother. My school records are evidence of the multiple transitions between school systems and cultures. I attended elementary school every other year in a different country and schooling system. Shifting from English-only curriculum in a large urban public school to a small rural private Catholic school with a Spanish-only religious curriculum was difficult. As the cities and schools changed, I had to shift too, very much like a chameleon.

It is painful, emotional, and upsetting for my mother to talk about her childhood as the oldest caring for her siblings, which shaped her mothering practices. Even though she had aspirations to complete high school and become a teacher, she did not have the economic resources or support to go to school. She was seventeen when she had her first child, and she married at eighteen. When I asked her about her desire to become a teacher, she replied, "Yo fui tu maestra." She never wanted to leave her children but understood that this decision meant our family income would be limited. My mother decided to stay home to care for her five children in México while my father worked in the restaurant industry. Every time I moved, it was with my mother and siblings. I was eleven when we finally settled in Los Angeles. Soon my mother started working in a textile factory in downtown Los Angeles, and later, to keep a close eye on her children, she began to care for young children in our home.

Shifting Away from el Sacrificio de Madre and New Migrations

Our mother-daughter testimonio co-creado is a narrative of mothering and an attempt to problematize the role of mothers as sacrificial. In Cristina Herrera's (2008) reading of Cherríe Moraga's *In Loving in the War Years*, Herrera argues that the mother-daughter bond, the alliance between these two generations of women, is at the core of Chicana/mestiza feminism. An analysis of mother-daughter relationships in Chicana/Latina literature points to the tension of not wanting to "sacrifice the unique self." In the process of our telling about (*testimoniando*) and reflexión on our migrations and transitions (DeNicolo and Gónzalez 2015), I noticed differences and commonalities in how we talked about a mother's sacrificio (Hondagneu-Sotelo and Avila 1997, 552). My mother talked about the difficult decision mothers make when they decide to leave their family and community to settle in a new city or country. She describes "breaking" *la cadenita*—the chain that forces women to leave their children behind in search of better work and life opportunities.

As a doctoral candidate and mother, I view el sacrificio de madre in academia as sacrificing our time, space, health, and bodies to achieve home, school, and work balance. This causes a splitting of the body, mind, and spirit (Lara 2005; Calderón et al. 2012, 514). I also actively wanted to avoid sacrificing my unique self. This was our point of tension.

Ring, ring, ring.

"Aloo . . . ," my mother answers.

"Todavía estoy esperando que me hablen sobre el trabajo [in the
    Midwest]," I say.

"¿Pero que va a pasar con tu esposo e hijo?" my mother quickly asks.

    "Pues, ellos se van conmigo," I reply.

"¿Cómo? ¿Porque los vas a mover? ¿Porque no puedes estar satisfe-
    cha con lo que tienes; una casa, un hijo, y matrimonio? ¿Qué más
    quieres? No puedes ser egoísta," my mother says.

"¿Y mi carrera? La trayectoria de un estudiante del doctorado es
    graduarse y comenzar una carrera como profesora," I answer.

"Pero ahora eres madre," my mother replies.

This vignette captures the contradictions in how we view decisions to leave, or migrate. In my mother's perspective and experience, the idea of leaving is solely based on economic and political need. I viewed the process of relocating as a career and professional need. In her view, my decision to relocate for a new job was a selfish act since I did not have the economic "need" to leave. After our pláticas on motherhood and balancing familial and work commitments, I did not expect this response from her. It was a reminder of el sacrificio de madre, which tosses my desires aside and places the needs of my family first. In that simple phrase "ahora eres madre," I was reminded that at the end of the day, I had to set my own desires aside.

My mother did not fully understand the demands of graduate school, and negotiating motherhood created a tension between us. As difficult as our final pláticas were, it was important to engage in reflexión. Together, we talked about the mother as always being the one who sacrifices. I expressed wanting to end the perception of la madre as *sufrida*, la madre as *chingada*, and la madre as self-sacrificing. In Catholic teachings and iconography, a mother's sacrifice is the ultimate act of love (El sacrificio de María, or El Sacrificio de Madre; Herrera 2008, 22). It is conceived as "pure love" when a mother is giving her body, mind, and spirit for the future of her children. Irene Lara (2005) has discussed the binary of virgin/whore being perpetrated by the Catholic Church in an attempt to enforce patriarchal authority on women (Villenas 2006, 661). The realities of motherhood are contrasted with the Mexican culture's tendency to elevate the self-sacrificing, self-abnegating mother. These discourses are entrenched in our familial practices. With tears in her eyes, my mother said, "Yo también estoy aprendiendo de ti. Lo que es ser Madre y mujer profesional. Es que las cosas cambian."

My mother was right: she has been and continues to be *mi maestra*, and together, we are learning to be mothers given the circumstances (e.g., economic/political migrations and education transitions). A *maestra* is someone who teaches but also learns from children and families. In moving forward, I want to shift away from being a mother who self-sacrifices and suffers to one who is empowered, starting with my own mother's story and highlighting how she loves to sit around the kitchen table or outside the house to platicar on her cell phone while she waters her plants. As I embark on new transitions, life post-PhD, our mother-daughter digital conexiones have allowed us to bring our relationship closer despite the distance and to continue the enseñanzas de madre that I will then share with my children.

Note

Epigraph: Andrea Garavito Martínez, "Tech Support," spoken word performance at *Ethnography of Love / Amor and Convivio*, Mestizo Institute of Culture and Arts, Salt Lake City, Utah, September 16, 2011.

References

Calderón, Dolores, Dolores Delgado Bernal, Lindsay Pérez Huber, María Malagón, and Verónica Nelly Vélez. 2012. "A Chicana Feminist Epistemology Revisited: Cultivating Ideas a Generation Later." *Harvard Educational Review* 82 (4): 513–39.

DeNicolo, Christina Passos, and Mónica Gónzalez. 2015. "*Testimoniando en Nepantla*: Using *Testimonio* as a Pedagogical Tool for Exploring Embodied Literacies and Bilingualism." *Journal of Language and Literacy Education* 11 (1): 109–26.

Fierros, Cindy O., and Dolores Delgado Bernal. 2016. "Vamos a Platicar: The Contours of Pláticas as Chicana/Latina Feminist Methodology." *Chicana/ Latina Studies: The Journal of MALCS* 15 (2): 98–121.

Flores, Alma Itzé. 2016. "*De tal Palo tal Astilla*: Exploring Mexicana/Chicana Mother-Daughter Pedagogies." PhD diss., University of California, Los Angeles.

Herrera, Cristina. 2008. "Mothers and Daughters in Contemporary Chicana Literature." PhD diss., Claremont Graduate University, California.

Hondagneu-Sotelo, Pierrette, and Ernestine Avila. 1997. "'I'm Here, but I'm There': The Meanings of Latina Transnational Motherhood." *Gender and Society* 11 (5): 548–71.

Huante-Tzintzun, Nancy. 2016. "The Problematics of Method: Decolonial Strategies in Education and Chicana/Latina *Testimonio/Plática*." PhD diss., University of Utah, Salt Lake City.

Lara, Irene. 2005. "*Bruja* Positionalities: Toward a Chicana/Latina Spiritual Activism." *Chicana/Latina Studies* 4 (2): 10–45.

Mendoza Aviña, Sylvia. 2016. "'That's Ratchet': A Chicana Feminist *Rasquache* Pedagogy as Entryway to Understanding the Material Realities of Contemporary Latinx Elementary-Aged Youth." *Equity and Excellence in Education* 49 (4): 468–79.

Morales, Socorro. 2016. "Fostering Critical Counterspaces in the Borderlands: Engaging Latin@ Elementary Youth in Chican@ Studies." PhD diss., University of Utah, Salt Lake City.

Pérez Huber, Lindsay. 2010. "Using Latina/o Critical Race Theory (LatCrit) and Racist Nativism to Explore Intersectionality in the Educational Experiences of Undocumented Chicana College Students." *Journal of Educational Foundations* 24 (1/2): 77–96.

Prieto, Linda, and Sofia A. Villenas. 2012. "Pedagogies from *Nepantla: Testimonio*, Chicana/Latina Feminisms and Teacher Education Classrooms." *Equity and Excellence in Education* 45 (3): 411–29.

Urrieta, Luis, Jr., and Sofia A. Villenas. 2013. "The Legacy of Derrick Bell and Latino/a Education: A Critical Race *Testimonio*." *Race Ethnicity and Education* 16 (4): 514–35.

Villenas, Sofia A. 1996. "The Colonizer/Colonized Chicana Ethnographer: Identity, Marginalization, and Co-optation in the Field." *Harvard Educational Review* 66 (4): 711–32.

Villenas, Sofia A. 2001. "Latina Mothers and Small-Town Racisms: Creating Narratives of Dignity and Moral Education in North Carolina." *Anthropology and Education Quarterly* 32 (1): 3–28.

Villenas, Sofia A. 2005. "Commentary: Latina Literacies in Convivencia." *Anthropology and Education Quarterly* 36 (3): 273–77.

Villenas, Sofia A. 2006. "Latina/Chicana Feminist Postcolonialities: Un/tracking Educational Actors' Interventions." *International Journal of Qualitative Studies in Education* 19 (5): 659–72.

Villenas, Sofia A., and Melissa Moreno. 2001. "To *Valerse por Sí Misma* Between Race, Capitalism, and Patriarchy: Latina Mother-Daughter Pedagogies in North Carolina." *International Journal of Qualitative Studies in Education* 14 (5): 671–87.

13

Abrazos de Conocimiento Across the Generations

Chicana Mothering and Daughtering in the Borderlands

Irene Lara

The Borderlands are physically present . . . where the space between two [or more] individuals shrinks with intimacy.

—GLORIA ANZALDÚA, *BORDERLANDS / LA FRONTERA*

This contribution to furthering our understanding of intergenerational Chicana M(other)work (Téllez 2011; Caballero et al. 2017) is based on a series of sacred *pláticas* with my mother, grandmother, and two daughters, interweaved with my own *autohistoria/testimonio* (Anzaldúa 2015; Delgado Bernal, Burciaga, and Flores Carmona 2012; Latina Feminist Group 2001) as a Chicana mother-daughter-granddaughter.[1] Complicating the dominant south-to-north, one-time immigration narrative, the women in my largely matriarchal genealogy have made familia back and forth across all kinds of borders, out of love and out of necessity, for "sobrevivencia" (Galván 2006). Indeed, going back at least six generations on my daughters' matrilineal line, we have survived and thrived in both Californias and, from the 1950s on, primarily in the broader Tijuana–San Diego metropolis.[2] As I teach my daughters, we have roots and are guests in these lands, the original tribal homelands of the Kumeyaay, within what many Indigenous peoples know as Turtle Island, or Abya Yala, before there ever were national borders. This place, within what became "las Américas" and what many of us now call "the Borderlands" (Anzaldúa [1987] 2012), is the context of our histories, lives, and *conocimientos*.[3] In addition to being a geopolitical place that embodies uneven border and border-crossing material histories, as Gloria Anzaldúa—a key theorist in our household—also gloriously offered, these are fertile spiritual, ecological, sexual, linguistic, and psychological borderlands, where systems of oppositional binaries are critically questioned and the third in-between generative space of *nepantla* reigns (2002, [1987] 2012, 2015).[4] This chapter explores how through engaging in sacred plática, where the spaces between our bodies, minds, and spirits "shrink with intimacy" (Anzaldúa [1987] 2012, i), we can create a "bodymindspirit" Borderlands that strengthens our mothering-daughtering relationships with ourselves and one another, birthing *curandera-guerrera* decolonial feminist conocimientos along the way (Lara 2002, 2014; Guzmán 2012).[5]

Disrupting the middle-class heteronormative nuclear family narrative of U.S. individualism, my family and I have directly survived and thrived because of the "motherwork" of many kin, be they kin by blood or by circumstance (Collins 1994; Udel 2001; Marrun 2016; Caballero et al. 2017). Indeed, my maternal grandmother, great-grandmother, and great-great-grandmother left, or were left by, their husbands or *compañeros* and were all involved—along with several *comadres*—in raising my mother and her seven siblings. My mother and mother-in-law have been instrumental in taking care of my daughters and me, in addition to caring for several other biological and extended family members. While men have also certainly worked to ensure that we individually and culturally survive and thrive, this chapter tracks women-centered intimate labor as part of our Indigenous and Women of Color history. As a Chicana Mother-Scholar engaged in my own "transformational care" (Ochoa 2011) work, committed to furthering the holistic wellness of our families and communities in and out of the university, I situate myself within this legacy.

With this context in heartmind, I developed ten guiding questions about mothering and daughtering that will be discussed in a panel of pláticas between (1) my daughters and me; (2) my mom, my grandma, and me; and (3) collectively, the four generations born between 1921 and 2008. This chapter is the first in a series of essays addressing initial conocimientos that emerged from my use of sacred plática methodology, which comes from generations of Indigenous knowledge, largely passed on via the oral tradition, and is informed by and aligned with work such as Angelita Borbón's "consciencia dialogue" (2007) and other ceremonial approaches to research (Wilson 2009; Chavez Arteaga 2012); the National Latina Health Organization's intergenerational peer-counseling talking circles (Lara 2008); curandera plática praxis (Ávila 1999); Mesoamerican-based healing and mental health praxis (Carrillo et al. 2017); and Chicana/Latina feminist storytelling and listening methodologies (Latina Feminist Group 2001; Fierros and Delgado Bernal 2016; Chabram-Dernersesian and de la Torre 2008). This chapter is based on a two-and-a-half-hour plática among Grandma Linda (age ninety-five), Mother Lola (age sixty-seven), and me (Irene, age forty-three), as well as three thirty-minute to one-hour pláticas between my daughters, Belén (age thirteen) and Xóchitl (age nine), and me, in summer 2017.

Ceremony of Return: Plantita Plática

It is a Friday about noon when Grandma Linda, Mom Lola, and I gather. As part of the ceremonial groundwork for our sacred plática, I have set up an *altarcito* on the table, which includes flowers, a Virgen de Guadalupe candle, my *sahumerio* with copal, and photographs of my grandma and mom with my daughters and me. My mom is still getting some *botanas* ready (of course—can it be a real plática without food?). Before I have a chance to turn on a recorder or officially introduce the plática, Grandma Linda and I start talking. I share how my daughters and I picked flowers with *permiso* for our plática altar a few days prior, and we admire the summer bouquet of white-, yellow-, and blue-hued flowers I brought for our altar that day, which flows into my grandma remembering how her grandmother used to "talk with *las plantitas,*" boil *saúco* "para un tecito . . . para la tos," and dig for "yerba del manso."[6] And ¡Zas! We are off!

While discussing the core beliefs I bring to my teaching and research to further establish our sacred brave space a little while later, with the video and audio recorders on this time, I make sure to bring it up again:

I (Irene): We are related to everything that lives.[7]

GL (Grandma Linda): That's right, uh-huh, that's right.

I: So, what were you saying[,] Grandma? About [Abuelita] Rosa that she would talk to the plantitas?

GL: Yeaaaah, she would talk to them. I used to go outside [to find her], "¿Qué pasó Abuelita?"

[Leaning into me, locking eyes, with a change in intonation, my grandma recounts what her abuelita would say:]

GL: "No, estaba hablando con las plantas. Tienes que hablarles," dice [Abuelita]. "Ellas les gusta que uno les hable. Y se van a poner bonitas. Se ponen bonitas, las plantas." She would always talk to them, always. . . . And I will never forget that. Nunca se me olvida.

Listening to my grandmother's story and my mom enthusiastically chiming in reminded me that I needed to do a better job of never forgetting myself and always acknowledging my sources, the material and spiritual footprints paving the way before any of my scholarly citations. The roots of my conocimientos are in these medicinal plantitas, in what Patrisia Gonzales, in *Red Medicine: Traditional Indigenous Rites of Birthing and Healing*, describes as the "Indigenous paradigm of the body-land or the body-spirit-land," our interrelatedness (2012, 216). This paradigm is always present, "but in encoded ways" (216).

So, as part of my "Ceremony of Return" (Gonzales 2012, 211) to recognizing living Indigenous knowledges within mestizo/detribalized families and the related commitment to bringing these knowledges to the university and to all my "classrooms," I am acknowledging my sources in these plantitas and in the pedagogical actions of my own plantita-talking grandmother and mother. In particular, I grew up with "my mother's performative narratives," as theorized by Sofia Villenas in her own research on Latina mothers teaching and learning (2006, 150).[8] My mother may not have directly pulled me aside to say, "You know we exchange energy with plantitas right? We are relatives?" But I grew up seeing her treating them with *cariño* always, which I now understand she learned from her *bisabuelita* Rosa, who was a key maternal figure, while her mom, my grandma Linda, worked. My serpentine path to recognizing the validity of spiritual epistemology and its role in healing my fragmented body-mindspirit in a patriarchal colonized education system and society in general, via writers, scholars, curanderas, and holistic health activists, has spiraled back to my mom, Lola Lara. Of course, *she* was the first to teach me through her own "pedagogies of the home" (Delgado Bernal 2006), cultural knowledge passed on to her, which I now pass on to my own children.

Indeed, "It is in the private sphere of the home, the patio, the garden, the bedroom that IK [Indigenous knowledge] survives," Gonzales writes (2012, 213). She elaborates: "Place is inherent in much of curanderismo's healing systems," and "the power of and relationship to place are inherent in the use of plants or how the plant is picked with prayers, talkings-to, and certain lunar cycles" (216). For Gonzales, such speaking with las plantitas and maintenance of altars are "hidden texts" that serve as evidence of the persistence of Indigenous knowledge despite colonialism's and secular modernity's attempts at destroying our identities, cultures, and power, not to mention capitalism's insistence on profiting over valuing all life as sacred (216). As a Chicana Mother-Scholar, I am engaging this aspect of m(other)work through enacting a sacred plática methodology with my family: plant picking and altar building as part of the ceremonial groundwork for our research that becomes the research itself. As Shawn Wilson discusses, such "setting [of] the stage properly" is essential for clearing space for everyone collaborating in the inquiry to "step beyond the everyday and to accept a raised state of consciousness" and thus be "ready to receive" conocimientos (2009, 69).

When Grandma Linda reminisced about medicinal *resetas caseras*, Mom Lola's excited rememberings also helped transport us to Abuelita Rosa's great *jardín* full of *claveles* and the herbal pharmacy growing around the lagoon in La Salina, Baja California. She lived on and off in an adobe house in this place with her siblings, grandmother, great-grandmother, and mother, from age three until she got married, at twenty-three.[9] She recalled her bisabuelita frequently asking her to harvest yerba del manso, with which, Grandma Linda claimed, she would make a tonic good for blood circulation and purification:

> **GL (Grandma Linda):** Ustedes convivian mucho con ella porque yo trabajaba pues.
> **ML (Mom Lola):** Sí, ella me mandaba al . . . ¿cómo se dice?
> **GL:** Yerba del manso, you had to dig it.
> **ML:** Yerba del manso . . . Estaba abajo de la tierra, sí. Pero salian unas ojas verdes, nacian bajitas. Nacian muchas allá cerca de la laguna.

She also fondly shared how Abuelita Rosa would cure her own headaches by placing *las ojas verdes* de la yerba del manso lengthwise underneath the *pañoleta* that she would always wear around her forehead. As part of the medicine las plantitas provide, and as what I interpret as evidence of the persistence of Indigenous knowledge, Lola later highlighted the relationship of reciprocity between living things and her own sense of responsibility for maintaining that balance: "Tengo una plantita cerca de la entrada. Y cada vez que la paso, le digo, con cariño, 'Come on, ¿cuando me vas a dar más flores?'" After a slight pause, as if Lola were listening with the ears of her heart to a response, she replies to the plantita, "Okay, te voy a dar más agua."[10]

With these and many other embodied examples throughout our lives, my mom shows me and others she cares for that she desires for las plantitas / us to not merely survive but to thrive, to "grow vigorously," and to be well and beautiful as part of the greater ecological circle of wellness and beauty.[11] Lola is doing her part to support the process by cultivating conocimiento through deep listening and speaking. Grandma Linda and Mom Lola have not overtly said that the plantitas are our mothers, but through their descriptions and everyday life interactions that "actively stage relationality" (Holmes 2016, 10), they embody and teach this conocimiento. In fact, plants are known as our "grandmothers" (and our second-oldest ancestors after stones) by Indigenous peoples the world over.[12] Moreover, this "Ceremony of Return" (Gonzales 2012, 211) to acknowledging Indigenous knowledge includes the conocimiento that we too need to mother the plantitas. Our m(other)work recognizes that we need one another to survive and thrive. These plantita pláticas held in the Borderlands, passed on from generation to generation, are among the "hidden texts" (Gonzales 2012, 216) ensuring the *sobrevivencia* of Indigenous knowledge and thus of ourselves and our families (Udel 2001).

Mothering Ourselves and More Interspecies Mothering

As Ana Castillo boldly reminds us, "Survival should not be our main objective. Our presence shows our will to survive, to overcome every form of repression known to humankind. Our goal should be to achieve joy" (1994, 146). In the context of colonial, patriarchal, heterosexist, racist, classist, ageist, and ableist histories of domination, to strive for joy is to insist on our right to not only exist, but to thrive, and is thus revolutionary. To thrive, *Merriam-Webster* documents, is to "progress toward or realize a goal despite or because of circumstances."[13] To strive for joy is not denying the reality of systems of inequality. On the contrary, it is lovingly working to break the spells of oppression. To strive for joy is to do our best not to allow systems of domination to rule over our lives, including by healing internalized oppression and domination so that our mothering-daughtering relationships can be infused with love toward self and other. Drawing on Castillo, Ruth Trinidad Galván, in her research on Mexican origin campesina mothers and what she calls their "pedagogies of the spirit," which she associates with "spiritual epistemologies of ancestral knowledge, dreams, and intuition" (2006, 170), powerfully articulates this aspiration as sobrevivencia: "*La sobrevivencia* is what lies ahead and beneath plain victimry, our ability to *saciar* (satiate) our hopes and dreams in creative and joyful ways" (163).

Thus, to mother ourselves entails doing what it takes to survive, but also to thrive by taking care of ourselves in ways that center experiences of joy and love (Gumbs, Martens, and Williams 2016). Engaging in our creativity by using our imaginations and participating in other creative acts is one such way. Moreover, as Anzaldúa reminds us, "[a] form of spiritual inquiry, conocimiento is reached via creative acts— writing, art-making, dancing, healing, teaching, meditation, and spiritual activism—both mental and somatic (the body, too, is a form as well as site of creativity)" (2002, 542).

When I asked my daughters about how they have had to mother themselves, they both shared stories that focus on the role of their imaginations. Xóchitl, however, first recounted the traumatic experience of being lost and frightened in a big store when she was about three years old. She associated being alone and not being watched over by me with having to step up and make sure she survived on her own: "I was crying in the corner. I was lost. I didn't know where I was. So, I needed to keep myself alive and tell someone." Through the sacred plática process of deep listening and raised awareness, Xóchitl was reminded by her sister of a very different, this time empowering, way in which she experienced/experiences mothering herself and later spirals back to her imagination as a resilience tool for sobrevivencia. In Belén's storytelling, she focused on being creative as the primary way in which she is "a mom to [her]self" when she needs to "figure things out by [her]self." She specifically shared her personal process of working through "dilemmas" by writing and drawing, and especially cartooning. In fact, waving her arm across the air, Belén dramatically read her own imagined cartoon banner, "On a Journey of Self-Discovery," when she began discussing how she engages in "mothering [her]self mentally." As she elaborated:

I have a strategy for thinking stuff out. And it's not exactly an imaginary friend (or actually, kind of), but I just, sometimes I'm thinking through something, or kind of dealing with stuff that kind of makes me feel a little bit split. Where different parts of me are thinking different things or think I should do different things. So I kind of, sometimes I split those parts into, I don't know, it can be instinct, um, it can be logic, it can be emotion, brain, it can be spirit. And sometimes I cartoon with that, and I just kind of put out my sentipensante process on paper, through art. . . . So I just kind of feel like each one of those, uh, parts of my body, like, they think different things, they have a different attitude or spin to whatever I'm dealing with. And I just feel like writing it out helps me better understand myself or what I'm going through. So I can see the different options, different choices, different methods for dealing with it. . . . And it's not just for problems. Sometimes they can be encouraging too.

Through Belén's self-reflection, we see how creativity can elevate the joy of sobrevivencia, of thriving while doing the oftentimes hard work of conocimiento, to "understand [one]self or what [one's] going through" as a process of discernment on the way to deciding what actions are the best to take next. Indeed, as Anzaldúa contends, empowerment can include "the bodily feeling of being able to connect with inner voices / resources (images, symbols, beliefs, memories) during periods of stillness, silence, and deep listening or with kindred others in collective actions. This alchemy of connection provides the knowledge, strength, and energy to persist and be resilient in pursuing goals" (2002, 571). Akin to several authors in *Revolutionary Mothering: Love on the Front Lines* (Gumbs, Martens, and Williams 2016), Belén celebrates the intimate labor of lovingly mothering ourselves through practicing our creativity in such embodied ways. Furthermore, intentionally occupying this generative Borderlands-nepantla space of change, suggests Belén, can help us make our way through "problems" and the negotiation of contradictory messages, as well as be an "encouraging" space.

When Belén initially quipped, "Sometimes I wish I had an imaginary friend," the attentively listening Xóchitl was moved to quickly interject, "*I* have an imaginary friend, and I always talk to her." After Belén concluded her meditative monologue on how she connects her artistic expression with self-discovery/conocimiento, Xóchitl returned to her story: "I have something to say. I have an imaginary friend, and it's there when I need her. It's a cat. She goes to school with me. And her name is Sapphire. And it's a white cat, with white paws, and it has blue eyes. And I have another cat, she doesn't have a name, it's just my friend. And . . . it's white, and it has green eyes, and it has black ears, and it has white paws, and yeah. And she always goes to school with me when I need a friend. . . . But I would rather, I would like to have a real cat." She shared—for the first time with anyone, she was sure to tell us—the role that her imaginary cats have played in mothering herself: "I always talk to her"; "It's there when I need her." That Xóchitl genders them female is striking, perhaps in recognition of the cats' maternal and spiritual feminine power. There was a lot of love and joy and pride in Xóchitl's recounting, and I—and I think Belén as well—felt the love and joy and pride of her sharing this marvelous story with us. It was a generative moment as we were wrapping up our first plática session, reminding the three of us that we have been yearning for a cat and reconfiguring the Western hierarchical human-pet relationship into the idea that there's a cat out there who wants to mother *us*. Indeed, these spirit animals are already Xóchitl's companions. They are already part of the village. We are related to all that lives.

Particularly compelling to me is that Xóchitl shared this sacred story in the context of the question, "How do you mother yourself?" and she did so after first sharing the trauma of being lost without me, her mother, who ostensibly was supposed to be present taking care of her at all times. Still, to ensure I truly comprehended these profound conocimientos, I inquired, "Are you kind of like *their* mother, or do they help mother *you*?" Xóchitl, inhabiting the borderlands between the material and spiritual worlds and the human animal world and the cat animal world, affirmed, "They [the cats] help mother me." The three of us were quiet for a moment around the altar, and then, in awe of the conocimientos shared by a child who is still able to access her interspecies facultad in this way, for sobrevivencia, I say, "Thank you for sharing that with us." (And here I thank her again for giving me permission to share this sacred story with you.) A sacred plática methodology recognizes that we all learn from one another, including potentially from the invisible yet present *ánimas*.[14]

Both Xóchitl and Belén went beyond the need to survive and elaborated on sobrevivencia with examples of ways in which they have created joy and self-nurturance, engaged with their "bodymindspirits" (Lara 2002) through their imaginations and creativity, and transformed themselves, their environment, and their reality through loving care. I am filled with humble pride, witnessing the ways my "pedagogies of the spirit" (Galván 2006) and "of the home" (Delgado Bernal 2006), be they spoken or performed through my ways of being, are being passed on, as well as spiraling back in new iterations that teach me. Within this sacred plática we co-created a mothering-daughtering space for sharing conocimientos about healing, spirituality, and creativity as integral to sobrevivencia. Although I participated in the experience of *susto* that Xóchitl initially recounts, I have also provided tools for healing and empowerment (by, for example, helping to create the brave space where she is able to disclose her experience of being lost and release it, as well as by telling my own "lo real maravilloso" cat stories throughout our lives).[15] To these conocimientos, I see Xóchitl turning to call her spirit back later on during the plática. Her curandera cats have helped ensure she never feels lost and motherless again.[16] They are her interspecies mothers too. And I honor them now, as I did out loud during our sacred plática, as my spiritual comadres.

By disclosing her private ritual of cartooning, Belén also expresses her own strategy for making herself whole, through essentially convening her own council of selves and writing and drawing from her "different parts," which embody her multiple intelligences. In our brave sacred plática space, Belén articulates her movement from feeling split by the outside to taking the process of healing into her own hands by purposefully splitting herself: from "dealing with stuff that kind of makes me feel a little bit split" to "I split those parts into . . . instinct . . . logic . . . emotion, brain . . . spirit." She listens to these multiple intelligences ("each one of those . . . parts of my body . . . [that] think different things") by "cartoon[ing] with" them. She cultivates her facultad to lovingly generate conocimiento by "put[ting] out [her] sentipensante process on paper, through art." For Belén, mothering herself looks like engaging in what Anzaldúa calls the "Coyolxauhqui imperative": "the impulse to write something down, [driven] by the desire and urgency to communicate, to make meaning, to make sense of things, to create [one]self through this knowledge-producing act" (2015, 1). Moreover, Anzaldúa, who understands writing as "a process of discovery and perception that produces knowledge and conocimiento," explicitly describes this creative impulse as "a struggle to reconstruct oneself and heal the sustos resulting from woundings, traumas, racism, and other acts of violation *que hechan pedazos nuestras almas*, split us, scatter our energies, and haunt us" (1).[17] Belén's narrative about the power to visually re-member ourselves in resistance to social fragmentation that can disempower us reminds me that m(other)work includes all the ways in which we support ourselves and others in becoming whole and working toward wellness, and thus more connected to our individual and collective power.

In Closing: From Sobrevivencia to Sobrevidencia

Opening and closing our intergenerational pláticas with our everyday ritual of abrazos, in affirmation of our relationships, as mothers and daughters, as grandmothers and granddaughters, we experienced our sacred pláticas as a generative Borderlands. "The space between" us as "individuals [did] shrink with intimacy" (Anzaldúa [1987] 2012, i.) as we bore witness to each other's profound experiences and meaning-making labors, further understanding one another and ourselves, the bodies-lands from which we come, and strengthening our interrelationships in the process. This radical intimate labor that is Borderlands m(other)work also means we did so as curandera-guerreras resisting dominant society's investment in keeping us apart from our knowing selves and from one another's intergenerational conocimientos. Through the revelations of never-before-told stories, revisiting and revising of favorite stories, and exploration of "sentipensamientos" (Rendón 2009) in our "Ceremonies of Return" (Gonzales 2012), these sacred pláticas became balms, as well as preventive medicine for the future.

When we engage in "research as ceremony" (Wilson 2009), we are creating an intentional space for conocimientos de sobrevivencia. *Videncia* is the spiritual gift to see the future or beyond the surface. Through engaging in intergenerational sacred pláticas, I have also found that *sobrevivencia* has the potential to become *sobrevidencia*—where the conocimientos that emerge from cultivating our facultades via storytelling and listening in a sacred brave space help us become "seers" lovingly guiding ourselves and one another as m(other)workers through the serpentine path of surviving and thriving. That is where you will find us—Linda, Lola, Belén, Xóchitl, and Irene—journeying alongside our plantitas, spirit cats, cartooned selves, y otras ánimas, embracing ourselves and one another as need be.

Acknowledgments

In addition to my beloved plática participants, I wish to acknowledge the audience at the Mujeres Activas en Letras y Cambio Social (MALCS) Summer Institute in July 2017, where I first presented this research. For their enthusiastic support of my scholarship and healing praxis, I also thank my writing group colleagues at San Diego State, Yea-Wen Chen and Guadalupe Ayala; my comadre-colegas Angelita Borbón, Maria Ibarra, Laura Jiménez, and Maria Figueroa; and my Curandera-Scholar-Activist students, who participated in their own "Cafecito con tu Mami" plática.

Author's Language Note

In the spirit of Chicana/Latina writers who purposefully leave Spanish, Nahuatl, Mayan, and other Indigenous languages in roman, by italicizing non-English words only at first mention and not italicizing code-switching conversations, I am recognizing that, for many of us, expressing ourselves multilingually is "normal" and part of our epistemology. Moreover, I am inviting English-dominant readers to embrace learning new words and ways of knowing.

Notes

1. See my future sister essay, "Sacred Plática Methodology: From Ceremonial Groundwork to Healing Conocimientos," in which, largely informed by Angelita Borbón's praxis of "consciencia dialogue" (2007) and "comadre consciencia" (Lara 2008), I delve into the plática's holistic health for Women of Color praxis and Indigenous talking-circle origins; relationship with Chicana/Latina feminist epistemologies and Indigenous research and healing methodologies (e.g., Wilson 2009; Chavez Arteaga 2012; Fierros and Delgado Bernal 2016; Carrillo et al. 2017); focus on cultivating our storytelling-listening facultades to create transformative and/or healing conocimientos (e.g., Latina Feminist Group 2001; Anzaldúa 2002; Keating 2007; Chabram-Dernersesian and de la Torre 2008; Rendón 2009); and implications for intergenerational research and beyond. On la facultad as linked to our spiritual ways of knowing and more, see Anzaldúa's oeuvre and her interlocutors.

2. Three generations were born in California: my maternal grandmother in Calexico, my mother in Long Beach, and my daughters in San Diego. Three generations were born in Baja California: my maternal great-grandmother in Todos Santos, my great-great-grandmother in El Pescadero, and me in Ensenada.

3. For an overview of Kumeyaay (in the United States) / Kumiai (in Mexico) history and culture, see "Kumeyaay History," Kumeyaay website, accessed August 8, 2018, https://www.kumeyaay.com/kumeyaay-history.html.

4. Nepantla theory (comadre to Borderlands theory) emphasizes spiritual epistemology and praxis; as a Nahuatl term for "in between," nepantla more directly names its Mesoamerican Indigenous philosophical foundation, including the importance of place and land. A physical and temporal space of potential conflict, negotiation, and change, nepantla is where and when the material and spiritual worlds are simultaneously experienced (Anzaldúa 2002, 2015).

5. My work is permeated with the importance of healing one's "body-mindspirit" and developing one's abilities to be a healer *and* a warrior in the face of oppression (Lara 2002). Guzmán specifically recognizes the "guerrera spirit"—"a warrior spirit that invokes resistance and resilience"—of our Latina mothering work in developing this same spirit in our children (2012, 45). As Anzaldúa offers, conocimiento is a nonlinear process of awareness, meaning making, and knowledge creation, which holds the radical possibility for personal, social justice, and ecological transformation and healing, and "urg[es] [us] to act on the knowledge gained" (2002, 577).

6. Saúco is "elderberry" and is widely recognized for its medicinal properties (http://www.botanical-online.com/medicinalssauco.htm). Yerba del manso or yerba mansa, called "vavish" by the O'otham, "has been used for centuries throughout the Southwest by American Indians and Hispanics for ailments ranging from toothaches to sinus infections" (Dabovich and Associated Press, n.d.). http://abcnews.go.com/Technology/story?id=5456546&page=1.

7. I draw from the National Latina Health Organization's list of beliefs and AnaLouise Keating's (2007) dialogue guidelines, which include Inés Hernández-Ávila's "we are related to all that lives" (2002, 532).

8. Villenas draws from Dills's theorization of "performance narratives" (1998) to document her "mother's body and everyday actions and movements [as] the narratives of her life" (Villenas 2006, 148). She then elaborates: "Life story is not only the verbal or the oral, but also the embodied. Parents transmit 'life lessons' through their daily actions and rituals, which become 'pedagogical moments' or moments of teaching and learning" (148).

9. Located less than one hour south of the San Ysidro–Tijuana border crossing, La Salina was the family's home base during weekends and summers.

10. Additional memories these plantita pláticas inspired included Lola's experience of yearning for a pomegranate tree and it suddenly sprouting in the backyard and, years later, similarly yearning for a tree to provide shade in the front yard, and voila!

11. *Merriam-Webster*, s.v. "thrive (*v.*)," accessed August 9, 2018, https://www.merriam-webster.com/dictionary/thrive.

12. See, for example, Kimmerer's (2013) and McDonald's (2017) discussion of ethnobotanist Leigh Joseph's work.

13. *Merriam-Webster*, s.v. "thrive (v.)."

14. Here I am reminded of Hernández-Ávila's powerful relationship with las ánimas, the ancestor spirits that one of her elders reminds her she can call on for strength and inspiration (2002). Also see Borbón's work on consciencia dialogues (2007), in which she recognizes the role of las ánimas and the native science teachings of her Elders in co-creating knowledge.

15. Here I am referring to Cuban writer Alejo Carpentier's concept of "the marvelous real" inadequately translated by many as magical realism.

16. On susto, soul retrieval, and curanderismo, see, for example, Castillo (1994), Ávila (1999), Anzaldúa (2002), Lara (2002), and Gonzales (2012).

17. Keating elaborates: "Drawing from the [Nahua] story of Coyolxauhqui [who is interpreted as being dismembered by patriarchy], Anzaldúa developed this theory to describe a complex healing process, an inner compulsion or desire to move from fragmentation to complex wholeness" (Anzaldúa 2015, 243).

References

Anzaldúa, Gloria E. 2002. "Now Let Us Shift . . . the Path of Conocimiento . . . Inner Work, Public Acts." In *This Bridge We Call Home: Radical Visions for Transformation*, edited by Gloria E. Anzaldúa and AnaLouise Keating, 540–78. New York: Routledge.

Anzaldúa, Gloria. (1987) 2012. *Borderlands / La Frontera: The New Mestiza*. 4th ed. San Francisco: Aunt Lute Books.

Anzaldúa, Gloria. 2015. *Light in the Dark / La Luz en Lo Oscuro: Rewriting Identity, Spirituality, Reality*. Edited by AnaLouise Keating. Durham, NC: Duke University Press.

Ávila, Elena, with Joy Parker. 1999. *Woman Who Glows in the Dark: A Curandera Reveals Traditional Aztec Secrets of Physical and Spiritual Health*. New York: Tarcher/Putnam.

Borbón, Angelita. 2007. "Conciencia Dialogue." Keynote address, Language of Spirit Conference on Quantum Entanglement and Beauty, SEED Graduate Institute, Albuquerque, NM, August 12, 2007.

Caballero, Cecilia, Yvette Martínez-Vu, Judith C. Pérez-Torres, Michelle Téllez, and Christine Vega. 2017. "'Our Labor Is Our Prayer, Our Mothering Is Our Offering:' A Chicana M(other)work Framework for Collective Resistance." *Chicana/Latina Studies: The Journal of MALCS* 16 (2): 44–75.

Carrillo, Ricardo A., Isaac Alvarez Cardenas, Ramon DelCastillo, Berta Hernandez, Jerry Tello, Concepcion Saucedo Martinez, Eliseo Cheo Torres, David Hoskins, E. Padron, Evelyn Crespo, Sal Nuñez, and Samuelin Martinez. 2017. *Cultura y Bienestar: Mesoamerican Based Healing and Mental Health Practice Based Evidence*. N.p.: Self-published.

Castillo, Ana. 1994. *Massacre of the Dreamers: Essays on Xicanisma*. Albuquerque: University of New Mexico Press.

Chabram-Dernersesian, Angie, and Adela de la Torre, eds. 2008. *Speaking from the Body: Latinas on Health and Culture*. Tucson: University of Arizona Press.

Chavez Arteaga, Alicia. 2012. "Las Mujeres de Teatro Izcalli: Transformative Stories of Healing and Resistance." Master's thesis, San Diego State University.

Collins, Patricia Hill. 1994. "Shifting the Center: Race, Class, and Feminist Theorizing about Motherhood." In *Representations of Motherhood*, edited by Donna Bassin, Margaret Honey, and Meryle Mahrer Kaplan, 56–74. New Haven, CT: Yale University Press.

Dabovich, Melanie, and Associated Press. "Yerba Mansa 'Calming Herb' May Be Next Echinacea." n.d. *ABC News*. Accessed August 8, 2018. http://abcnews.go.com/Technology/story?id=5456546&page=1.

Delgado Bernal, Dolores. 2006. "Learning and Living Pedagogies of the Home: The Mestiza Consciousness of Chicana Students." In *Chicana/Latina Education in Everyday Life: Feminista Perspectives on Pedagogy and Epistemology*, edited by Dolores Delgado Bernal, C. Alejandra Elenes, Francisca E. Godinez, and Sofia Villenas, 113–32. Albany: SUNY Press.

Delgado Bernal, Dolores, Rebecca Burciaga, and Judith Flores Carmona. 2012. "Chicana/Latina Testimonios: Mapping the Methodological, Pedagogical, and Political." *Equity and Excellence in Education* 45 (3): 363–72.

Dills, Vivian Lee. 1998. "Transferring and Transforming Cultural Norms: A Mother-Daughter-Son Lifestory in Process." *Narrative Inquiry* 8 (1): 213–22.

Fierros, Cindy O., and Dolores Delgado Bernal. 2016. "Vamos a Platicar: The Contours of Pláticas as Chicana/Latina Feminist Methodology." *Chicana/Latina Studies: The Journal of MALCS* 15 (2): 98–121.

Galván, Ruth Trinidad. 2006. "Campesina Epistemologies and Pedagogies of the Spirit: Examining Women's *Sobrevivencia*." In *Chicana/Latina Education in Everyday Life: Feminista Perspectives on Pedagogy and Epistemology*, edited by Dolores Delgado Bernal, C. Alejandra Elenes, Francisca E. Godinez, and Sofia Villenas, 161–80. Albany: SUNY Press.

Gonzales, Patrisia. 2012. *Red Medicine: Traditional Indigenous Rites of Birthing and Healing*. Tucson: University of Arizona Press.

Gumbs, Alexis Pauline, China Martens, and Mai'a Williams, eds. 2016. *Revolutionary Mothering: Love on the Front Lines*. Oakland, CA: PM Press.

Guzmán, Bianca. 2012. "Cultivating a Guerrera Spirit in Latinas: The Praxis of Mothering." *Association of Mexican American Educators Journal* 6 (1): 45–51.

Hernández-Ávila, Inés. 2002. "In the Presence of Spirit(s): A Meditation on the Politics of Solidarity and Transformation." In *This Bridge We Call Home: Radical Visions for Transformation*, edited by Gloria E. Anzaldúa and AnaLouise Keating, 530–37. New York: Routledge.

Holmes, Christina. 2016. *Ecological Borderlands: Body, Nature, and Spirit in Chicana Feminism*. Urbana: University of Illinois Press.

Keating, AnaLouise. 2007. *Teaching Transformation: Transcultural Classroom Dialogues*. New York: Palgrave Macmillan.

Kimmerer, Robin Wall. 2013. *Braiding Sweetgrass, Indigenous Wisdom, Scientific Knowledge and the Teachings of Plants*. Minneapolis, MN: Milkweed.

Lara, Irene. 2002. "Healing Sueños for Academia." In *This Bridge We Call Home: Radical Visions for Transformation*, edited by Gloria E. Anzaldúa and AnaLouise Keating, 433–38. New York: Routledge.

Lara, Irene. 2008. "Latina Health Activist-Healers Bridging Body and Spirit." *Women and Therapy* 31 (1): 21–40.

Lara, Irene. 2014. "Sensing the Serpent in the Mother, Dando a Luz la Madre Serpiente: Chicana Spirituality, Sexuality, and Mamihood." In *Fleshing the Spirit: Spirituality and Activism in Chicana, Latina, and Indigenous Women's Lives*, edited by Elisa Facio and Irene Lara, 113–34. Tucson: University of Arizona Press.

Latina Feminist Group. 2001. *Telling to Live: Latina Feminist Testimonios*. Durham, NC: Duke University Press.

Marrun, Norma A. 2016. "Queering La Familia: A Redefinition of Mothering, Immigration, and Education." *Chicana/Latina Studies: The Journal of MALCS* 15 (2): 64–95.

McDonald, Bob. 2017. "Indigenous Stories Lead Scientist to Discover that Plants Can Hear." CBC Radio. August 4, 2017. http://www.cbc.ca/radio /indigenous-stories-lead-scientist-to-discover-plants-can-hear-1.4234449.

Ochoa, Gilda L. 2011. "Transformational Caring: Mexican American Women Redefining Mothering and Education." In *Latina/Chicana Mothering*, edited by Dorsía Smith Silva, 104–21. Toronto: Demeter Press.

Rendón, Laura I. 2009. *Sentipensante (Sensing/Thinking) Pedagogy: Educating for Wholeness, Social Justice and Liberation.* Sterling, VA: Stylus.

Téllez, Michelle. 2011. "*Mi Madre, Mi Hija y Yo*: Chicana Mothering Through Memory, Culture and Place." In *Latina/Chicana Mothering*, edited by Dorsía Smith Silva, 57–67. Toronto: Demeter Press.

Udel, Lisa J. 2001. "Revision and Resistance: The Politics of Native Women's Motherwork." *Frontiers* 22 (2): 43–62.

Villenas, Sofia. 2006. "Pedagogical Moments in the Borderlands: Latina Mothers Teaching and Learning." In *Chicana/Latina Education in Everyday Life: Feminista Perspectives on Pedagogy and Epistemology*, edited by Dolores Delgado Bernal, C. Alejandra Elenes, Francisca E. Godinez, and Sofia Villenas, 147–60. Albany: SUNY Press.

Wilson, Shawn. 2009. *Research as Ceremony: Indigenous Research Methods.* Black Point, NS: Fernwood.

14

Decolonial P'urhépecha Maternalista Feminist Motherwork and Pedagogy

Gabriela Spears-Rico

Birthing the Red Woman

I am alone in a hospital room staring at the white ceiling. My labor is being induced after nine dark months of carrying my daughter in the looming fear that she would die inside me. I am considered a high-risk pregnancy because of my weight. The doctors make me feel like a grotesque science experiment; a fat wild sow with a violable vagina that can be penetrated with fingers and instruments without permission. I had requested to work with the midwives because of the PTSD I carry as a survivor of child sexual abuse, but they denied my request for care because of the gestational diabetes. The doctors succeeded in scaring the shit out of me: they filled my nightmares with images of dead babies like those that had haunted my mother when she swore La Muerte had visited her to take my sister, Suguey. They tell me that I may give birth to a stillborn, that my baby may die shortly after birth, that I will be holding the body of a dead baby if I don't get induced. I am living among my partner's people in Minnesota, thousands of miles away from my sister and my mom in California, and even farther away from where all my grandmothers' afterbirths are buried.

I am *so so* far away from Michoacán. Generationally, I am the first pregnant woman in my family to break traditions. My mom was born from a midwife on the floor of my grandfather's adobe jacal in Atapaneo; her mother had been born with a *curandera* in her grandmother's jacal in Uruertaro. I will be the first in our line to be induced, to give birth in a hospital, to possibly have a C-section. Spiritually broken during my pregnancy, I vomited and cried daily, fearing everything ahead. My spirit and body were in a coma for nine months and only awakened when my baby girl moved inside, reminding me of the possibility of life. And now, here I was facing this moment without my mom, without Suguey, without my partner, too spiritually weak and sick to stand by me—I realized I had to do this alone.

Nana Xarátanga
Luna Hermosa
Holy Mother
You who are germinated by the powers of our father of fire,
    Kurhikueri
Sacred Creatrix
Sister to our nana K'eri Echeri
Sister of the stars and the celestial gods
You who have birthed the universe
Daughter of Kuerajperi
You who give life to everything
For everything begins with you
I am alone and away from all that is sacred to me
I do not have my mom
My tías in Atapaneo do not know I am giving birth
Suguey is far away
Be with me
Help me deliver this spirit onto the earth
Be with me

The doctors cut into my womb to deliver Miskikwe unto the earth. I am bleeding profusely and coming in and out of consciousness. I keep talking to the handsome Asian American doctor to stay awake and to remind him that I am bleeding. He tries to calm me and tells me that my husband is in the hallway in a wheelchair because he fainted after witnessing the cut. As they stitch me and sow me back together, I think of Coyolxauhqui. I somehow know that all my pieces will never come back together. For I have always been severed—since I was first assaulted as a child, to this moment when they cut me open to retrieve my daughter. *I have always been severed.* Then I hear Miskikwe cry. The tears of absolute desperation I have been crying for the past nine months turn into tears of raptured euphoria. And I remember I am alive. I look into her eyes for the very first time, and I hear my ancestors harmonizing over a familiar *pirekua.*

Trineni Tzitziki sera muy cierto que tu eres naturalita.
Nos juchá pórhepechska male.
Jucha no kuatantani.
Tirineni tsïtsïki. Ikarania.

"We are always harvesting the flower of death."
"Miskikwe is here to stay," they say.
It's just me and her for that moment. I forget about the pain splitting my body. I offer her my breast. And I have every reason to fight and stay awake.

Understanding my P'urhépecha Maternalista Feminist Legacy

Upon birthing Miskikwe, I finally understood why P'urhépecha women do not separate their political activism from their maternal identities. As the now ninety-two-year-old Nana Herlinda once told me, "Ultimately, the struggle is for them—for their security and happiness. We stand against those who try to wipe the hope we see in *jóvenes indígenas*. They are our hope and we know the only way we will see their capabilities bloom is by protecting *lo suyo*—land."

In Zirahuén, a caracol community in the north-central lacustrine region of Michoacán, mothers have been involved in protecting communal land since the violent conflicts between the Indigenous community and the agrarian community emerged in the 1970s to the present, when *comunerxs* find themselves struggling against a growing tourist industry that profits off the pollution of their lake.[1] In the nearby community of San Andrés Tziróndaro, mothers have advocated for and organized around issues that ensure the community's long-term sustainability—and have done so by naming the priorities most important to their children's futures, including access to healthcare, affordable schooling, the preservation of the P'urhépecha language and culture, the protection of land, and the value of women's labor in the home *and* in the community's economic life. Mothers' participation in the defense of communal land is in sync with *maternalista* feminist theory. According to Argentinian sociologist Beatriz Schmukler, feminist maternalistas believe that "motherhood as a practice can bring elements for civic participation and re-thinking political life" (1994, 51). Maternalista feminism argues that the values typically associated with mothering, such as collective activity, reciprocity, and equality, can offer women a stronger commitment to political life. As political actors, P'urhépecha women engage in maternalista feminism. Their primary motivation for being involved in the land struggle is motherhood, which is inextricably tied to their being perceived as leaders and protectors of the P'urhépecha Nation. In this chapter, I argue that for me and for my informants, employing decolonial maternalista feminist praxis and reclaiming our savage feminist legacy in the home is inextricably tied to political work and to the pedagogy I bring to the classroom.

Before the Spanish invasion of P'urhépecherio in 1530, P'urhépecha society was matrilineal; lineage, prestige, and inheritance were passed down the mother's line.[2] Our people upheld women as the sacred bearers of creation, procreators of the nation-state, and cultural carriers responsible for passing down P'urhépecha language and cultural values. As feminist theorist Peggy Sanday explains, "Women might gain power and authority in societies where maternity is viewed as a sacred or magical function—this can occur in early agrarian communities where there is frequent association between maternity and the fertility of the soil" (1974, 204).

Like other Mesoamerican cultures, P'urhépechas conceptualized the Creator as male and female: Kuerajperi sustains all life and mothers the moon deity, Xarátanga, who in turn germinates the earth's seeds and controls the seasons with her lunar cycles (Corona-Núñez 1999). Like Kuerajperi and Xarátanga, P'urhépecha women protect life within all realms of nature. Thus, the role of comuneras is naturally to defend the community from trespassers' infractions. A recent example is the uprising in Cherán, a struggle that was initially organized and inspired by P'urhépecha women (Pressly 2016). After suffering incessant illegal logging of their forest at the hands of organized crime, elderly P'urhépecha women called for self-defense, demanding that the men in the community stop the ravaging of Cherán youth's *patrimonio* (heritage, resources, future). The community eventually overthrew local leaders; cut ties with the Mexican government; controlled access, denying entry to all political parties; gathered weapons; organized patrols and surveillance; and implemented an autonomous Indigenous government designed according to the instructions left in *La Relación de Michoacán* (the only remaining P'urhépecha historical scroll or codex). Even after the disappearance and murder of

P'urhépecha men involved in the struggle, the leadership of P'urhépe-cha women continues to sustain this movement.

As evidenced in Cherán, considerable characteristics of a P'urhépe-cha mother-centric culture have carried on into the present. Although not structurally matriarchal, the communities I did my fieldwork in, Zirahuén and San Andrés Tziróndaro, possess all the qualities of a modern matriarchy, including cyclical seasonal celebrations, commu-nalism, animistic ancestral spirituality, female control of the market, and matrilineage (Bennholdt-Thomsen 1994). Structurally, P'urhépe-cha families, and more generally, Mexican families, are mother-centric; it is not uncommon for Mexican mothers to act as heads of house-hold who control intimate family life. In San Andrés Tziróndaro and Zirahuén, motherhood has allowed women to transgress the private/ public dichotomy typically attributed to the distribution of female labor and power. P'urhépecha homes are organized around the old-est matriarch's *fogón*, where the fire emanates, and where the food is cooked; P'urhépecha mothers are the respected language keepers, cultural carriers, and decision makers within the private sphere and act as the visible breadwinners in the public sphere.

Recognizing P'urhépecha matriarchal power does not deny the intersectional oppression that P'urhépecha women experience. As the most visible representations of Indigeneity in the public eye owing to their relentless practice of donning traditional clothing, Indige-nous women are primary targets of *mestizx* racism.[3] Additionally, P'urhépecha men still hold the majority of political positions in tra-ditional governance structures. When I questioned the logic of male leadership, considering that women from Zirahuén, for example, have been at the vanguard of the land struggle, P'urhépecha women responded that strategically, P'urhépecha men have to be perceived as the speaking negotiators because the mestizo patriarchal govern-ment is more likely to listen to men. Like other Indigenous societies, such as American Indian tribal governments, those in Mexico have granted leadership roles to men as a gendered performance to appease Western governmental patriarchy. In Latin America, this practice functions alongside strategically placing Indigenous women at the front lines of demonstrations, because the state is less likely to publicly enact corporal punishment on women, while it does indeed beat, murder, and disappear Indigenous men. As Nana Herlinda explained, "We knew that if women were doing the squatting, the land owners and authorities would be less likely to beat us."

Some P'urhépecha women also face violence in the home and in intimate relationships. Mercedes Olivera, a feminist Zapatista from El Centro de Investigación y Acción Para La Mujer (the Center for Investigation and Action for Women), credits the sexist attitudes of Mexican Indigenous men to a "colonized identity—a superiority complex acquired by indigenous men after the conquest as a result of the elevation of patriarchy" (Olivera 1995, 173). In other words, because patriarchy grants Indigenous men gendered privilege, they may conveniently internalize and practice machismo even if Indigenous societies were traditionally more egalitarian. Olivera's analysis of how colonial patriarchy has redefined Indigenous masculinity can be applied in Zirahuén and in other P'urhépecha communities. The elevation of patriarchy and introduction of machismo overturned the mother-centric family structure and implemented male domination. Decolonial feminists, including María Lugones, Margarita Gutiérrez, and Nellys Palomo, have also articulated this analysis. In Gutiérrez and Palomo's earth-shaking critique of patriarchy in Mexican Indigenous communities, they propose that motherhood limits Indigenous women's agency because it places them in perpetual service to others, confines their sexuality to child-bearing parameters, and constrains their education and their ability to participate in Indigenous social movements. In "A Woman's Eye View of Autonomy," Gutiérrez and Palomo theorize autonomy from the landscape of women's bodies. They challenge Indigenous people to consider women's bodies as autonomous beings that should be free from sexual violence, reproductive expectations, poverty, servitude in the home, and traditional customs that limit girls' rights (including teenage marriage). For them, Indigenous autonomy must be articulated both in the public sphere (to mestizx society) *and* within the intimate relations of Indigenous communities (such as the relationships between Indigenous men and Indigenous women). As they state, "Autonomy begins with ourselves, in our homes, at work, in the organization, the community and the people. To have autonomy is . . . to speak without repressing everything our heart thinks and feels. . . . Although we fight and we demand the rights of our peoples, we also raise a voice for our specific rights: there will be no autonomy for any of the peoples if women, half of those people, continue subjugated and without their own autonomy!" (Gutiérrez and Palomo 2000, 79).

Reclaiming Savage Feminism

Gutiérrez and Palomo's article provided me with an introduction to what young Native women are calling "savage feminism," and what earlier First Nations and Native feminists termed red/Native feminism (Tuck, Arvin, and Morrill 2013).[4] "A Woman's Eye View on Autonomy" was the first article I read that articulated an unapologetic Indigenous feminism. In considering what it means to define autonomy from Indigenous women's perspectives, I realized that it is necessary and appropriate for me to reclaim my own original P'urhépecha feminist roots. Indigenous feminists, including Paula Gunn Allen and Ana Castillo, have been encouraging Indigenous women to decolonize feminism by understanding our own feminist trajectories as older and more "radical" (rooted) than white feminism (Castillo 2014; Gunn Allen 1986).[5] This is where I depart from Schmukler's maternalista feminism, by considering that a P'urhépecha/*xicanista* maternalista feminism is also decolonial and is unapologetically rooted in who we are as Indigenous women, while savagely working to undo the damage of colonialism and stop neocolonialism from harming the earth and our children. And so, through my own re-P'urhépechizacion (reintegration into the P'urhépecha Nation postmigration), I dug for information on my own P'urhépecha feminist foremothers. Even though there is no word for feminism in my language, I have a feminist herstory, which begins with Kuerajperi and Xarátanga and continues with my own fight against extermination and with my survival of violence.[6] I call on Quenomen.

Quenomen (She Who Is Enveloped in Water) was a P'urhépecha woman who, in the fourteenth century, became the first woman to lead the territory of Zacapu—the place that birthed the P'urhépecha Nation. A woman of humble origins, Quenomen took over the territory's leadership upon the death of her husband, Carocomaco. Donning a shield and club, with two black lines painted on her cheeks, the fierce and elderly Quenomen commanded male warriors to undertake the daily ceremonial tasks to keep the empire going—including gathering firewood for the temples and strategizing to protect the territory. She was eventually deposed by Tariácuri's sons, Hiripan and Tangánxoan Tzíntzicha, who would go on to establish the P'urhépecha empire. Even though Tariácuri was threatened by Quenomen's influence, at the time of her unseating, she had already formed a critical part of P'urhépecha history as the first P'urhépecha female governor (Uliánov Guzmán 2016).

I call on Eréndira (Morning Laughter), the P'urhépecha woman who, in the early sixteenth century, led a P'urhépecha army on horseback against Spanish conquistadores. Although she was only sixteen when the Spanish arrived in Michoacán, Eréndira defied orders to marry Nanuma because she had heard Xarátanga's calling to lead her people after Tangánxoan was said to have surrendered to the Spaniards upon hearing of the genocide they had enacted on the Aztecs.

Ashamed that Tangánxoan would surrender and allow the plunder of P'urhépecha land and the destruction of monuments for P'urhépecha deities, Eréndira captured a horse from the conquistadores, learned to ride and command the strange beast, and led an uprising of P'urhépecha warriors against the Spanish (Catlett 2007). She has become a symbol of resistance against the Spanish Conquest in Michoacán and in Mexico as a whole; P'urhépecha resistance to the conquest is coded as distinctly female because of her. Eréndira is imperative to our radically rooted savage feminist legacy as P'urhépecha *uarhis* (women).

Postcolonial Schizophrenia and the Legacy of Rape

Nothing has triggered my PTSD, associated with sexual assault, more than becoming a mother. I've wrestled with the demons of childhood sexual abuse for most of my adult life; they've fed my insomnia and tormented my paranoia as I consider how to best protect my daughter from being assaulted. I suffered from postpartum depression months after delivery, tormented by how to protect my daughter from the legacy of rape that has plagued my family since the Spanish Conquest overtook Michoacán.

In my family, as in other Mexican Catholic families, rape has been a taboo subject, even though it has happened to almost every generation. I first remember hearing about the rape of my schizophrenic aunt, Josefina, when I was a toddler being raised by my grandparents in Atapaneo; my aunt told me that "Chepina" had been raped while wandering the streets alone, during one of her bouts of *locura*, to scare me into listening to my grandparents' warnings about staying indoors. Chepina's assailant was never named, but I do remember how her firstborn was ripped from her motherly clutch and sold to a wealthy family in Morelia, whose matriarch couldn't bear any children. "All the better," my tía Berta had told me. But, there was so much evidence that Chepina would never again be okay, not even for a moment.

Soy del mar, espuma
Soy triste lamento
Yo soy basurita
Soy basurita que arrastra el viento

That is the verse from a song Chepina wailed, *a grito abierto*, as she recalled all the suffering that had led up to losing her child. She was often lost in her schizophrenic world for days at a time, sometimes weeks or a month. And the people who found her and contacted the authorities would speak of her wailing. Tía Chepina, *la llorona*, died under suspicious circumstances near Morelia eight years ago—her nude, badly decomposed body was found in a cornfield. Considered the inconsequential death of a vagrant, her exit did not merit investigation. To this day, I am sure that my tía Chepina was murdered, as so many women are in Mexico.

My daughter's paternal great-auntie Missy is also schizophrenic, and she was also raped. I saw pictures of a twenty-something-year-old Missy in an old family album once. She was draped in the elegance of the 1980s, with big hair, bright-colored eye shadow, and pink lipstick. Staring at the camera confidently and seductively, she was easily the most beautiful woman I'd ever seen. Now Missy is a shadow, even though she is physically healthy and barely fifty.

I know firsthand that it is completely possible for rape to kill a soul. In my own schizophrenic temporalities, I've perpetually wrestled with the things that happened on Otay Mountain when I crossed the border with my pregnant mother in the spring of 1985. I was supposed to forget the buzzing of helicopters overhead, hiding in the bushes from *la migra*, my soggy diaper weighing down my pace because there wasn't time for bathroom breaks: "Apúrale mija, mira que yo voy más rápido estando embarazada." These are all things I was supposed to forget. Yet, I clearly remember the coyote propositioning my mother, my young mind forced to grasp that sex was the currency women and children often pay to traverse the U.S.-Mexico border. I remember how my mama-jaguar fought to protect me.

How do *I* spare my olive-skinned Xicana/Ojibwe/Dakota daughter from rape in the times we're living in? A time when Indigenous women's bodies continue to be disposable, as alarming rates of femicide overtake the Americas? When the pillage and rape of the continent, which often affects Indigenous people first, takes shape through neoliberal and neocolonial destruction? How do I teach the girl I named Reina to thrive beyond the violence, as her Dakota grandmother and great-aunties are attempting to do in restoring their places in the *winyan oyate* (woman nation)? These are the critical motherwork questions I face. And this is also where, even in my weakest moments, I invoke our savage legacy and embrace a decolonial maternalista feminism.

Applying the Magic of Savagery to Motherwork

"Every Native born into this world is a victory against colonialism and attempted genocide. You are resistance. You are hope made flesh."

"We are the grandchildren of the Indians you weren't able to remove."

These are internet memes that I hope my daughter runs into in her lifetime. As much pain as there is in our past as Indigenous women, there is also resistance and resilience. According to the white North American anthros who have studied my people, I was born into desperate poverty in my grandfather's jacal, yet years later, as my mother revealed more and more about who we really are, I realized that *we were never really poor*. The very story of my birth is potent.

My mother fled my biological father's beatings in Oregon, returning to Michoacán to birth me in my tata's jacal with doña Pachita, Atapaneo's midwife. Doña Pachita was late that morning, and my mother birthed on her own while my grandmother, Nana Sele, caught me, and my grandfather, Tata Jose, cut my umbilical cord. Nana Sele buried the afterbirth in our backyard on the land that had been granted to my grandfather after the Mexican Revolution, leaving my spirit firmly planted in P'urhépecha territory.

Early on, I knew that Tata Jose worked the earth. He smelled of coffee, sweat, and sugar cane when he came back from his milpa at midday for the *comida* Nana Sele prepared daily. I remember my grandfather's lunchtime stories about how he met my nana during the Mexican Revolution, when she was an *adelita* and he a *federal*. My family was representative of centuries of Mexican history, and my tata could recount all of it—from Mesoamerican migration and displacement to the Mexican wars our ancestors served in to the present (which was always amalgamated with the past). *We were not poor* because my tata's milpa and my nana's chickens provided. I had enough to eat, and I loved the hand-sewn dresses my nana made me, even if the jacal's adobe and cardboard roof was falling.

My tata knew how to butcher a storm with a machete. And I recently learned that he also harvested and fermented pulque. My mother told me they sold it in Morelia. Working with Mexican Indigenous communities, I have learned about the sacredness of pulque to Mexican Indigenous people. Before the earth is broken for harvest, Mixtecos bless the earth with aguamiel to request permission. "The blood of the earth," they call it. Our own *Relación de Michoacán* attests to pulque being integral to every gathering between leaders; the visions acquired from its consumption informed our future (De Alcala [1540] 1970). A pulque knower, my tata labored in the divine. *We were not poor.* Our family was infused with magic. My *amá* recounts how my nana healed people and prayed daily with her entire body, sometimes *a golpes de pecho*, and sometimes speaking in an unintelligible language. The townspeople venerated her. Now we understand that my nana was a curandera keeper of secrets—among them, apparently, *el secreto de la juventud*, as she lived to be 106. Affluent in the holy, we were never impoverished.

Reina, remember your ancestors. Your three-times great-grandmother Many Tracks was removed from Lower Sioux in Mni Sota Makoce, imprisoned at Fort Snelling, and displaced to the Crow Creek Reservation.[7] Her daughter, Pansy, was kidnapped by the U.S. government and placed in a boarding school, as were your Ojibwe tatarabuelos. The nuns cut their braids and butchered their tongues. This is why your grandmother does not speak Dakota. This is why your father trips over his Anishinaabe. But your great-uncle Greeting still gave you their names: "Ikwemakoons," he said, "Lady Bear," and, "Wajiwebiik," he spoke, "rolling valley." You, Reina Miskikwe, are hope made flesh. This is the power you are endowed with, Daughter. The relentless capacity of xicanista savagery.

Toward a Decolonial Maternalista Feminist Pedagogy

This is also the power I want to communicate to my students as I apply decolonial maternalista feminism in the classroom. The days immediately following 45's election have been the most difficult in my teaching career. I remember lying awake the night of November 8, laden with anxiety. My PTSD was triggered throughout the election when the tapes of 45 publicly bragging about sexual assault were repeatedly played, and now it was shooting through the roof as I heard my neighbors' celebratory fireworks. I grieved for myself and for my daughter. I did not know how I was going to comfort two classrooms full of mostly Women of Color.

Earlier that semester, my students had already been triggered when the phrase "Build the Wall" covered a panel advertising for the College Republicans on our campus. Furthermore, hate incidents, including the assault of an Asian woman by a white male student and the spray painting of swastikas, happened on the campus and throughout the state in the days following the election. I garnered all the strength I could and began furiously gathering the medicine (sage, tobacco, sweet grass, *copal*, cedar) I keep in my home and the ingredients I needed to cook Nana Sele's recipe for *chokolatl* (hot chocolate) and *arroz con leche*.

"Who the hell am I if not Eréndira's granddaughter?!" I asked myself. And I connected with the curandera magic in my blood as I recalled that I had vowed to abide by Tejeda and Espinoza's decolonizing pedagogical practice of protecting the integrity of oppressed bodies in my classrooms (Tejeda, Espinoza, and Gutierrez 2003). I also retraced how Cherríe Moraga and Gloria Anzaldúa, my former *maestras*, curated their classrooms. I called on the xicanista wisdom I'd been trained with and prepared to hold my students' pain. I did not name it at the time, but I was preparing to practice decolonial maternalista feminist pedagogy by invoking the savage feminist practices that had always composed who I am. I asked my students to sit in a circle, offered them nourishment, let them cleanse with the medicine at their discretion as I asked them to share their feelings, wounds, and fears. Some cried, others drew and journaled or shared poetry, while still others held each other. Women of Color dominated the space, and my white students mostly listened. Although xicanista pedagogical praxis tends to privilege the voices of the most oppressed, my white students named listening as a cleansing practice. Hurt by the hate that had overtaken the country and keenly aware of their privilege, they expressed feelings of confusion and numbness.

In invoking my decolonial maternalista feminist praxis as pedagogy, I've realized that my motherwork does not end when I leave my daughter in the mornings; what I'm doing with my students *is* motherwork. It is the labor of sending more informed, less oppressed, and less oppressive human beings into the world. It is labor that is not discussed or named or even compensated as such. It is a labor that is unworthy for tenure at an R1. It is a labor that I am carrying out for my students and a continuance of the motherwork I'm doing for my daughter.

I know that I will constantly have to reaffirm my daughter's humanity as she grows up, questioning her self-worth because of the complete lack of respect for Indigenous people on her tierra, in Mni Sota Makoce and throughout the continent. As a Mexican and an American Indian woman in a mixed documented status family, Reina's intersectional identities are among the most attacked by 45's regime. Yet, I find hope in practicing decolonial maternalista feminist pedagogy. When I teach my students about Indian mascots or about the neocolonialism plaguing the entire continent through projects like the Dakota Access Pipeline or the Toluca-Naucalpan Highway, which will displace Matlatzinca people in Mexico (EZLN 2016), I am not only educating my students, I am also influencing Reina's future. As academic Mothers of Color, our labor is not contained in neatly categorized boxes. Motherwork becomes part of our intersectionality, as mothering and motherhood permeate our homes, writing, and pedagogy. Decolonial maternalista feminist pedagogy is integral to the legacy we're leaving our students, our sons, and our daughters.

Notes

1.   Zirahuén declared itself a caracol community in 2003, in accordance with the Ejército Zapatista de Liberación Nacional (EZLN) model of Indigenous practices of autonomy; the structure allows the community to make decisions on schooling, resource distribution, land use, and governance without external influences. Zirahuén has been engulfed

in a conflict between those who want to preserve communal land (*comunerxs*) and the agrarian community, which hopes to privatize. *Comunerxs* consist of those who identify as the P'urhépecha precolonial inhabitants of Zirahuén, while the agrarian community are *mestizxs* who were granted land through post-Revolution agrarian reform. I use "comunerxs" to include comuneras/os and gender-nonconforming people in that group. You can read more in Zarate-Vidal (1999).

2.   P'urhépecherio is how P'urhépechas refer to Michoacán and parts of Guerrero that are identified as traditional P'urhépecha territories.

3.   I use the term "mestizx" in place of "mestizo" to be inclusive of gender variance (queer, transgender, and gender-nonconforming people) among Mexican and Latinx mestizxs.

4.   Native feminism critically engages with the imposition of patriarchy and the gender binary on Native societies. It critiques the exclusion of Native women from feminism as well as mainstream feminism's appropriation of Indigenous feminism. Native feminist theories contend with Native men's heteropatriarchal colonial engagement with theories of tribal governance. Native feminist theories reframe settler colonialism by analyzing its role in the emergence of heteropaternalistic practices. The colonially imposed blood quantum system, for example, relies on Native women's bodies as vessels to reproduce, while the boarding school system promoted shame in precolonial gendered variance. For further reading, see Piatote (2005); Tuck, Arvin, and Morrill (2013); and Jaimes and Halsey (1992).

5.   In "Who Is Your Mother?" the late Laguna Pueblo literary critic Paula Gunn Allen calls on Native women to reclaim and embrace the matriarchal roots of their tribes as part of their feminist legacy. She details the matriarchal roots of Native societies and argues that British colonialism imposed the gender binary. Similarly, in *Massacre of the Dreamers*, queer Chicana writer Ana Castillo challenges Chicanas to embrace their precolonial matriarchal roots to challenge sexism in the Chicano movement and nation and to heal from the legacy of rape that tainted La Malinche.

6.   The word "history" (i.e., his-story) is problematic because it privileges men's roles and perspectives, inherently inscribing men as the agents of history without acknowledging that women have been part of history

since the beginning of time. "Herstory" privileges women's positionality in "history" and reinscribes women as agents of historical change.

7.   Mni Sota Makoce is the Dakota name of Minnesota, which translates into "Land Where the Waters Reflect the Clouds."

References

Bennholdt-Thomsen, Veronica. 1994. *Juchitán, la Ciudad de las Mujeres*. Oaxaca: Instituto Oaxaqueño de las Culturas.

Castillo, Ana. 2014. *Massacre of the Dreamers: Essays on Xicanisma*. Albuquerque: University of New Mexico Press.

Catlett, Juan M., dir. 2007. *Eréndira la Indomable*. Mexico City: Centro Universitario de Estudios Cinematográficos. DVD. 107 min.

Corona-Núñez, José. 1999. *Mitología Tarasca*. Morelia: Instituto Michoacáno de la Cultura.

De Alcala, Jeronimo. (1540) 1970. *The Chronicles of Michoacán*. Translated by Eugene R. Craine and Reginald C. Reindorp. Norman: University of Oklahoma Press.

EZLN. 2016. "Zapatista Communique: May the Earth Tremble at Its Core." *Upside Down World*, November 4, 2016. http://upsidedownworld.org/archives/mexico/zapatista-communique-may-the-earth-tremble-at-its-core/.

Gunn Allen, Paula. 1986. "Who Is Your Mother?" In *The Sacred Hoop*, 209–21. Boston: Beacon Press.

Gutiérrez, Margarita, and Nellys Palomo. 2000. "A Woman's Eye View on Autonomy." In *Indigenous Autonomy in Mexico*, edited by Aracely Burguete Cal y Mayor, 54–82. Copenhagen: IWGIA.

Jaimes, M. Annette, and Theresa Halsey. 1992. "American Indian Women: At the Center of Indigenous Resistance in Contemporary North America." In *The State of Native America: Genocide, Colonization, and Resistance*, edited by M. Annette Jaimes, Evelyn Hu-DeHart, and Delinda Wunder, 311–344. Boston: South End Press.

Olivera, Mercedes. 1995. "Practica Feminista en el Movimiento Zapatista de Liberación Nacional." In *Chiapas: ¿Y las Mujeres Que?*, edited by Rosa Rojas, 168–84. Mexico City: Ediciones la Correa Feminista, Centro de Investigación y Capacitación de la Mujer.

Piatote, Beth H. 2005. "Beyond Feminism: Toward a Theory and Politics of Kinswomanism." *WWR Magazine* 1 (2): 22–25.

Pressly, Linda. 2016. "Cheran: The Town That Threw Out Police, Politicians and Gangsters." *BBC News Magazine*, October 13, 2016. http://www.bbc .com/news/magazine-37612083.

Sanday, Peggy R. 1974. "Female Status in the Public Domain." In *Women, Culture, and Society*, edited by Michelle Rosaldo Zimbalist, 189–206. Stanford, CA: Stanford University Press.

Schmukler, Beatriz. 1994. "Maternidad y Ciudadanía Femenina." In *Repensar y Politizar la Maternidad*, edited by Cecilia Talamante Díaz, Fanny Salinas Campeas, Maria de Lourdes Valenzuela, and Gomez Gallardo, 37–51. Mexico City: Grupo de Educación Popular de Mujeres.

Tejeda, Carlos, Manuel Espinoza, and Kris Gutierrez. 2003. "Toward a Decolonizing Pedagogy: Social Justice Reconsidered." In *Rethinking Education for Social Change*, edited by Peter P. Trifonas, 10–40. New York: Routledge.

Tohe, Laura. 2000. "There's No Word for Feminism in My Language." *Wicazo Sa Review* 15 (2): 103–10.

Tuck, Eve, Maile Arvin, and Angie Morrill. 2013. "Decolonizing Feminism: Challenging Connections Between Settler Colonialism and Heteropatriarchy." *Feminist Formations* 25 (1): 8–34.

Uliánov Guzmán, Pável. 2016. "Quenomen: La Unica Gobernante P'urhépecha Prehispánica." *Michoacán 3.0*, March 17, 2016. http://michoacantrespuntocero .com/quenomen-la-unica-gobernante-purhepecha-prehispanica/.

Zarate-Vidal, Margarita. 1999. "Somos Indios de Papel." In *Bajo el Signo del Estado*, edited by José Eduardo Hernández, 113–25. Zamora: El Colegio de Michoacán.

Part IV

Loss, Reproductive Justice, and Holistic Pregnancy

15

No Gracias por la Lástima

My Chicana Mother of Adoption Truth

Corina Benavides López

Aquí Comienza Mi Historia / Here My Story Begins

I share my *testimonio* of reproductive loss and gains experienced throughout my quest to realize my dream of motherhood through adoption. I do this to resist the *lástima* (pity) I experience regarding my reproductive losses while pursuing my *profesora*-scholar-activist career. Most importantly, I work to dismantle the adoption oppression I experience when I share that my son is adopted. This adoption oppression is sometimes expressed in subtle responses of "Wow, that's wonderful." And then, silence. Other times I navigate dialogues about assumed "loss of opportunity" to have biological children and "gratefulness" expressed on behalf of society for my adopting a child, resulting in silence in responses to my family's story.

What I have learned is that people do not want to know about the pain and trauma of reproductive losses endured in isolation by many *mujeres*. For me, a Chicana mother of adoption (Pavao 2005), pain was triggered when someone would ask, "Don't you want to have babies yet?"[1] Today, that trigger is having to address gendered and racialized judgments: "Why don't you have another baby? It's so unfair to him [my son]. He's going to be alone without familia." My *testimonio* documents my journey in co-creating my family through radical love and resistance (hooks 2001) and serves as a challenge to the social construction that only "biology is family and love."[2]

Un Poema, My Fall and Winter Anniversaries

I hear you, *te siento*,
I know you (want to) live . . . in my darkness,
I struggle because you are spirits in the wings of my dreams,
My anger and sadness explode into desperation. . . *no puedo respirar*,
Four heartbeats of pain, grief, anxiety, darkness that pound into a
    headache, backache,
stiff neck, *dolor de corazón*,
I do not let you go . . . *nunca*,
I cleanse and soothe you with the scent, power and smoke of ances-
    tral *hierbas* passed
down from other mothers in grief,
You all stay alive in my *lagrimas*.

From Loss Comes Life

Welcoming my baby boy, Huitzin, was the culmination of a ten-year journey marked by reproductive losses that left me in grief.[3] Before becoming a mother, I completed my undergraduate and graduate degrees, but the years I sacrificed navigating academic rigors and acute stress had physiological repercussions. When ready to become parents, my partner and I were forced to navigate the medical indus- trial complex to learn answers. The decision to exit the labyrinth of costly medical appointments, probing, and medical history questions was a feminist choice. But the experience left me embattled.

In the fall of 2010, the same year I became *doctora*, my partner and I began our search for our baby. The journey of self-reflection consumed us. In 2012, we decided on an open adoption, in which the birth/first mother/parents, child, and adoptive parents can access each other's information.[4] Then, during our adoption process, I became pregnant in 2013, and I again faced reproductive loss. Simultaneously, I endured the academic job market and eventually received a permanent position. During my first year on the tenure track, I navigated the demands faced by early career faculty, and my partner and I worked to receive approval as a qualified adoption family.

La Corazonada: A Hummingbird Beats into Its Nest

The adoption preparation process left us exhausted and hopeless. On a Monday in mid-June 2014, my partner and I met with our social worker for counseling. During the meeting, our social worker exclaimed, "You guys, this *is* happening. . . . Have hope and faith that it will happen." We left the meeting feeling assured. We placed a sign saying, "This *is* happening!" in the bedroom we'd had cleaned out for the baby's arrival for nearly a year.

Wednesday of the same week, our social worker contacted us to ask if we would be okay with showing our adoption profile to a potential birth mother.[5] That same evening, we were selected as parents to a newborn boy. The following day, our social worker informed us that our baby boy's birth mother, Karmen (pseudonym), had decided to hand over the baby to us the following week. Overwhelmed, we began preparations. In less than one week's time, we prepared what others prepare throughout their entire pregnancy. We identified a name and set up a nursery. By Monday we were ready for the baby's arrival!

In preparation to meet Karmen, we purchased a gift as a symbol of our bond. The chosen gift was a small Mexican tin box with a *sagrado corazón* (sacred heart) at the center of the lid and silver *milagritos* (small miracles) surrounding the heart. The gift felt right as a symbol of the connection we would forever have with Karmen. We made sure to buy two boxes, one for her and one for the baby as a *recuerdo* (keepsake), representing the strong *mujer* who had carried him in her womb and consciously chose us as his parents, enduring the mental, spiritual, and emotional anguish of handing over her baby and entrusting us with his life, her m(other)work.

We chose our son's name before the meeting, but his middle name, Huitzin, arrived to us in a spiritual moment an hour before, requiring paperwork to be redrafted. Meeting Karmen, a twenty-two-year-old Salvadoran woman, was powerful. She took lead of the meeting, talking in English with a thick accent, refusing to speak in Spanish, asking us how *we* felt. She made sure to take care of my partner and me by focusing on the baby and us, not on herself. Karmen shared how necessary and important it was that we loved her son. She assured us that he, just one week old, would make us proud. I had not met our son yet, but the idea of him filled my heart with unspeakable love and pride.

My partner then asked Karmen why she chose us. She stated, "It was a *corazonada*" (a strong hunch in her heart), when she saw the picture of us on the profile cover. Viewing our carefully chosen images and messages, she felt the values of family, love, and happiness. I began crying, and we explained how throughout the years, my partner and I had gifted sacred hearts to each other on special celebrations. She paused and stopped our conversation, turned to the social workers in the room, and stated, "I am ready." Our social worker then left the room and returned with our son, Huitzin.

Karmen faced the baby as she held him for the last time, and through quiet tears of love said, "Papa, make them proud, this is now your mommy and daddy. Make sure to be good." She lovingly patted him on the chest, giving him a *bendición* (blessing), kissed his forehead, and handed him to me. My Huitzin snuggled himself in my chest, making beautiful cooing sounds. I cried in silence. My partner cried in awe of the inspiring act of love that everyone in the room experienced, *our* m(other)work.

Karmen talked directly to me, "So how do you feel?" I responded, "Like only the most important things that matter are in this room. . . . I feel love." Holding her eye contact with me, Karmen talked to only me. "You are *now* the mother. It is *your* job to love this baby. *You* are to care for him and love him. He is going to make you proud, I know it." Her elder spirit took over her soul and spoke to mine, *madre a madre*. In tears, and in awe of this powerful woman, I responded in agreement. The interaction between us as mothers became a united love that I can only explain as a birthing process.

The Burden of Loss. . . . Silencio

Because I did not receive the "God given" gift of carrying a baby in my womb to term, I carried my baby in the wings of my dreams (Moraga 1997) and endured the discomfort of my reproductive loss and alienation in silence. Instead of the traditional celebratory congratulations on a pregnancy, my partner and I received questions and judgments, deep-seated in an oppressive silence of adoption. This adoption oppression emerged in comments made by loving friends and family, like the following:

"But, why did you choose to adopt and not keep trying? You will keep trying, right?"
"But, if the birth mother knows who you are, are you not scared about her taking the baby away?"

After the baby arrived, we began enduring the judgments of being "bad" parents for not "giving" our son a sibling:

"It's just so sad and unfair to him if he doesn't have brothers or
sisters."
"Well, you know he's always going to be alone."

Then there are the judgments made by those who identify as social
justice folks, expressed in the following way:

"Well, that's good for you that you chose *that* route, but adoption is
just not the route we would ever take."
"You *are* open to babies of other races, right, or are you just open to
Latina/o babies?"
"Why are you guys only looking into adopting a newborn? You know
there are many older kids that need families and a home. You
should really consider that option."

These comments silence our family adoption story. They ignore
the experience of loss and the difficult journey to parenthood. The
process of educating our extended family and friends was, has been,
and continues to be exhausting! It is a burden those with biological
children are not required to endure.

Not My Final Comment. . . . No al Silencio

I break my silence because people don't want to know. I feel the silence
when I state that my son is adopted and the person looks away or gives
me the "que lástima" look. Or, when I attempt to share my feelings
about my losses and people quickly state, "But you never know . . . ,"
and they proceed to explain how a friend or family member became
pregnant without "trying." In sharing my family's pain and my process of becoming *mamí*, I express the radical love and resistance
that I practice each day when I look into the big brown eyes my son

inherited from Karmen. She is always with us. But I also experience me in him, as he sings the songs of my childhood back to me, passed down by my mother. I gift this testimonio to my Huitzin, who every day challenges the social construction that only "biology *is* family and love." I gift this testimonio to Karmen, because her m(other)work gifted me with the honor of motherhood.

Notes

1. I use the concept "mother of adoption" instead of "adoptive mother" because it places the identity of mother at the forefront and illustrates the familial construct and community with which I identify. The use of "mother of adoption" borrows from Joyce Maguire Pavao's construct of family of adoption.
2. See bell hooks's critical discussion on the concept of radical love and the wounds that love heals.
3. Huitzin is a derivative of the Nahuatl word for hummingbird, *huitzitzilin*. Depending on the Indigenous spiritual philosophy, hummingbirds are often seen as having healing medicinal powers.
4. "Birth mother," "first mother," and "first parents" are concepts used to refer to the biological mother and father of a child in the adoption process.
5. An adoption profile is one's story shared through pictures, highlighted facts, and a letter written to potential birth mothers/parents used to help with adoption placement.

References

hooks, bell. 2001. *All About Love: New Visions.* New York: William Morrow.

Moraga, Cherríe. 1997. *Waiting in the Wings: Portrait of a Queer Motherhood.* Ithaca, NY: Firebrand Books.

Pavao, Joyce Maguire. 2005. *The Family of Adoption.* Revised ed. Boston: Beacon Press.

16

Birthing
Healing Justice

My Journey Through Miscarriage, Healing
Conocimientos, and Decolonizing My Womb

Mara Chavez-Diaz

After many calls to my health provider, I was finally able to schedule an appointment with a gynecologist. For more than four weeks, I had been bleeding. Waiting in the medical exam room with my four-year-old daughter, Itzel Xiadani, I felt relieved that I would finally be seen. This feeling did not last. Instead of the gynecologist I expected, a registered nurse entered the room and asked me in an annoyed tone, "Do you speak English?" Hearing these words from a white body, and in a community-based health clinic serving predominantly monolingual low-income immigrant Latinx communities, startled me to the core of my being. The medical violence and intrusion of my being would not end there. As the "expert," she assumed many things about me, a twenty-two-year-old working-class Latinx, the minute she walked in. I explained that I'd had an IUD for four years, and that I had been bleeding for more than a month. I described my health condition in great detail. Yet, this did not matter. She had already made a diagnosis. Despite my explaining to her that I was in a monogamous relationship, she insisted on asking how many partners I was sleeping with. In the end, she did not bother to physically examine me. Instead, she had me tested for STDs. She did not perform a pregnancy test, even though one of the symptoms I described was sore breasts. I walked out feeling humiliated by having to endure her colonizing gaze and outraged that I had not received the proper medical attention I needed. Six days later, at approximately 3 a.m., I was awakened by excruciating abdominal pain, and in a matter of minutes, I felt my life slipping out of my body. Terrified, my partner called an ambulance, and I was taken to the emergency room. Based on my delicate condition and symptoms, they performed a pregnancy test and then an ultrasound. I was told I was pregnant but that my baby was not in my uterus. I had an ectopic pregnancy.[1] My baby had attached to my ovarian tube, and I was internally bleeding. After my surgery, the surgeon told me to consider myself very lucky, for had I arrived minutes later, I might not have made it to tell my story.

Approximately 10 to 15 percent of pregnancies end in miscarriage. Medical science understands miscarriage as the spontaneous or natural termination of a pregnancy prior to the twentieth week of gestation. In retrospect, my experience of miscarriage goes much deeper than the medical definitions healthcare professionals take for granted. While I surrender to the understanding that life and death are natural processes, I refuse to remain silent about the material reality that my experience of miscarriage was unnatural. And my painful story of miscarriage as a working-class Woman of Color is not the exception.[2] As I shared my herstory with other *muxeres*, I learned that my *testimonio* is part of a common collective experience among Women of Color, who experience violence within the "medical-industrial complex," and who are forced to go through the painful loss of miscarriage(s) in silence.[3] Most importantly, I was strengthened by the power of sharing our herstories, for I was not alone anymore.[4] Indeed, our herstories bring to the forefront the parallel links between colonization and gender violence by making visible how colonial ideology and power have inflicted and continue to inflict violence on the earth and on the bodies of women and Indigenous people (Smith 2005).

Consequently, women's reproductive health cannot be addressed without also tackling the environmental racism and other -isms present in our daily lives as Women of Color. The health of women's fertility is a mirror of how healthy our environment is. As a working-class first-generation Xicana raised in West Oakland, I experienced this firsthand. Living in a low-income community meant that our home was right below heavily traveled Interstate 580 and across from an environmentally toxic recycling company that disposed of lethal metals and chemicals, such as asbestos.[5] This toxic recycling company is one of many in my community. My entire childhood, I grew up being exposed to the toxic fumes of cars and chemicals.[6] Later, as a teen mom, medical science diagnosed me with postpartum depression, after I gave birth to my first child. Not knowledgeable of alternative methods of contraception, I succumbed to medical science's insistence that, given my postpartum depression, an IUD was my only viable birth control method.[7] Hence, this chapter begins with the understanding that making the links between women's reproductive freedom, white supremacy, and the rape of mother earth is critical to our collective struggles for liberation, sustainability, and self-determination (Ross 2016).

From this critical stance, I expand understandings of birth injustice beyond the narrow binaries that the medical-industrial complex uses to silence Women of Color who go through the painful loss of miscarriage. Birth justice is far more than critical analysis and political activism; it is life-affirming soul work that has the power to move and transform us (Oparah and Bonaparte 2016). In this spirit, I share my testimonio of decolonizing my womb as part of a decolonial and (re)Indigenizing process of healing generational womb trauma and (re)centering the spiritual energy of the feminine in my life as a mother-activist-scholar. My experience surviving three miscarriages was a turning point in my healing journey. I have witnessed firsthand the power and potential of ancestral *healing conocimientos* in acquiring a deeper understanding of how systems of oppression condition women to stay disconnected from our wombs, repressing our sacredness and power as creators.[8] Coming into motherhood as a conscious Xicana activist allowed me to root myself in the healing conocimientos of my *abuelas* to recover from my miscarriages. In the process of birthing healing justice, I (re)claimed my voice to contest the heteropatriarchal violence and silencing I had experienced going through the loss and pain of miscarriage.

Unsettling the Medical-Industrial Complex: Epistemology of Body as Earth

Medical science operates under the reductionist assumption that the doctor, as the "expert," must first diagnose the problem and then proceed to numb/cut/colonize our bodies to cure us (Duffy 1993). Not surprisingly, the medical-industrial complex treats our health and well-being in isolation and without any regard to our body wisdom or ancestral ways of healing. Unsettling this complex is much more than working to dismantle heteronormative systems of power that oppress our bodies. This work is critical but not enough. At the root of unsettling the medical-industrial complex is redefining and (re)claiming our power and abilities as Indigenous women and Women of Color to heal our communities and self. In the Bay Area, a growing and thriving birth justice movement is focused on (re)claiming and revitalizing women-centered ways of caring for our bodies by providing low-income Women of Color access to education, holistic and Indigenously rooted doula care, and spaces for women to individually and collectively heal our wombs.[9] These ways of knowing and being draw attention to how, as Women of Color, we are negotiating our positions as mothers while (re)claiming and revitalizing healing conocimientos that empower our bodies, families, and communities.

This work draws from Patrisia Gonzales's articulation of "red medicine," which she defines as a holistic system of healing that includes birthing practices, dreaming, and purification rites to reestablish personal and social equilibrium. Red medicine understands that the body is "a ceremonial site, and it is a 'place' of Indigeneity; and through it we re-place ourselves in the land and the life-giving elements" (2012, 156). Red medicine (re)centers our interrelatedness to all life, human and nonhuman, and these subjugated knowledges are critical to our survival and that of the next seven generations. It affirms our bodies as teachers. In this way, "Situating knowledge in the Brown body begins the validation of the narratives of survival, transformation, and emancipation of our respective communities, reclaiming histories and identities. And in these ways, we embody our theory" (Cruz 2001, 668).

By carving out spaces to share our birthing stories, which come from our bodies and lived experiences, Women of Color are redefining and broadening the scope of healing justice. Our herstories can serve as consciousness-raising conocimientos that aim to empower younger generations of women to decolonize from the medical-industrial complex. In my healing journey, the experience of decolonizing my womb allowed me to be guided by my womb as a source of creativity and wisdom in my life.[10] The way I move in this world is now guided by an understanding that "the womb is our first orientation on earth" (Gonzales 2012, 47) and "the birthplace of all our creative abilities" (Queen Afua 2000, 44). Diving deep into my own depths to heal my womb and then channel this energy to be of service for the world is how I have come to deploy *an epistemology of body as earth*, to counter the colonizing ways in which medical science has imposed itself on my Brown body. Knowing my body is earth and the earth is my body affirms my sacred connection to creator and the healing of past and future generations. This epistemology calls for a radical healing relationship to our bodies as earth that goes beyond the binaries attempting to fragment us. It honors and embraces the ancestral healing conocimientos of our body as critical to supporting and maintaining our individual and collective survival and well-being.

Generational Womb Trauma and (Re)claiming Healing Conocimientos de Mis Abuelas

When my mother, Idolina Castañeda Ontiveros, was born, her *ombligo* (umbilical cord) was buried in the heart of a tree in El Valle, Michoacán, by my great-grandmother Rosa Tovar Padilla. *Mi abuelita* Rosa, a powerful and respected *huesera*, *herbera*, and *partera*, buried the placenta and ombligo of all her children and grandchildren, just as my great-great-grandmother had taught her.[11] In 2004, at the age of forty-nine, my mother visited for the first time the beautiful tree where her ombligo still lives. The oldest of eight children, my mother would be the first generation of muxeres to experience the medicalized and colonized experience of giving birth in a hospital room. As a recent immigrant and monolingual Woman of Color in the United States, she experienced a painful and lonely labor—away from mi abuelita or any family. Despite more than twenty-four hours of excruciating labor pain, my mother gave birth to me, her first-born child, drug-free.[12] Eighteen years later, despite being categorized "high risk," I would give birth to my own daughter, Itzel Xiadani, with the loving support of my mother. With little medical intervention, I was blessed to give birth to a healthy child. (Re)membering and sharing our birth herstories and the womb conocimientos imprinted in our bodies are critical to healing the self, for "these birthing stories are medicine" (Gonzales 2012, 39). These healing conocimientos are in sharp contrast to the practice of obstetrics, which is founded on principles of pathology and a determination to control (Brodsky 2008).

Despite the love and healing I experienced giving birth to my first child, nothing would have prepared me for the excruciating hardship of enduring a second ectopic miscarriage and emergency surgery. The emotional and physical wounding resulting from my miscarriage and the removal of one of my ovarian tubes in the process crystallized my commitment to self-healing. Unlike Western doctors, who advised me to return to all my normal activities only two weeks after my surgery, the general wisdom of the muxeres in my family placed me on a strict regimen of self-care that lasted for forty days, or what women's knowledge of the womb refers to as the *cuarentena*.[13] I gave myself permission to receive love and wisdom from all the muxeres who unselfishly shared their time and knowledge to help me heal. During this time, I was instructed to be on full-time bed rest and to protect my thirteen joints at all times to prevent *aires* from entering my body (Roman 2008).[14] I learned to patiently and respectfully listen to and develop a relationship with these *remedios*, which included drinking teas made with *romero, ruda, estafiate*, and manzanilla to help heal and bring warmth to my womb. I drank *toronjil* and *siete azares* to help me cope with sadness and the emotional pain of my miscarriage and losing my ovarian tube. My diet included many vegetable soups, *atoles de agua con chocoloate*, and herbs, which were prepared by my mother and other women in my family to nourish me. I was blessed to count on unconditional support from a loving network of muxeres who supported my full recovery and healing.

Immense reflection and growth came from the opportunity to remain still and let the herbs heal my womb. With loving tenderness, I nurtured a healing relationship with my womb. Listening to my womb's intuition with compassion guided my process of dissolving the many wounds and conditioning inflicted by medical science to separate me from *my body as earth*. Even after my cuarentena, I continued to work on healing my womb with the guidance and support of various healers in my community. I focused on letting go of the many layers of shame and sadness that I carried in my womb from my experiences of being shamed as a teen mother and being sexually violated as a young woman. The spiritual ritual of doing an inventory with my womb of all she had been through since birth provided me the opportunity to heal my own wounded spirit and that of past generations of muxeres in my family. I learned of the generational trauma I had inherited, given that both my maternal and paternal abuelitas had endured years of physical and psychological violence from my grand-fathers. My abuelitas's pain surfaced in my own healing as unexpected periods of deep sadness and fear that I felt were not my own.

Despite my desire to run away from these emotions, I gained the courage to face the sadness and fear with loving compassion and to patiently sit with these emotions. By being receptive to my inner waters and emotions, I was able to release this generational womb pain that had shown up in the course of my own healing. In the pro-cess of emptying my womb, I experienced an overflow of love reach my heart as I found strength in the herstories of perseverance and the healing conocimientos that have also traveled with us and taken root in us over generations. In more ways than I can describe, these spir-itual and healing conocimientos passed on by my mother, abuelitas, and tías allowed me to overcome the impositions of unequal school-ing and the challenges of teen motherhood to succeed as the first and only college graduate in my large extended family, and ultimately to work toward decolonizing my womb. Inspired by generations of muxeres in my family who gave birth through ceremony, I work to (re)claim and (re)vitalize the empowering healing conocimientos that validate an epistemology of body as earth.

Embodying Miscarriage as Radical Healing Praxis

At seven weeks pregnant, I have a second ultrasound, which confirms to my doctor that I have "an embryo with no heartbeat." This news comes one day after my abuelita's birthday and six months since her death after a two-year battle with ovarian cancer. According to my doctor, I do not have a "normal pregnancy," and I am going to have a miscarriage. Options to take care of my miscarriage were discussed in medical terms, and the process was simply yet another routine medical examination. According to my doctor, miscarriages are very common, and she has become accustomed to them as part of her medical expertise. Yet, for me this was not another routine medical examination. The words "normal pregnancy" kept circulating in my mind over and over. Who gets to determine what a normal pregnancy is supposed to look like and feel like?

My grandmother passed away six months before I found out I was pregnant. Not having her physically with me during the healing process for my third miscarriage was heartbreaking. Her healing conocimientos, however, remained imprinted in my DNA. While very emotional work, my mother and I listened to my interviews with my grandmother about her womb-healing conocimientos, recorded months before her death. My mother deepened her own healing gift by piecing together what she'd learned from these interviews and from talking to other muxeres in my family. She performed some remedios on my womb for the first time. Drawing from her memories of when my grandmother conducted some of these remedies on her womb, my mother performed *sobadas* and *curaciones* with hot oils and *plantitas* to help heal and bring warmth to my womb. In addition, I was blessed to be able to access a strong network of healers, parteras, and activists within the Bay Area birth justice movement, who helped deepen my emotional and physical healing and the decolonization of my womb. Attending *temazkal*—in both Mexica and Lakota tradition—was also a critical aspect of decolonizing my womb and reconnecting with the earth's womb for healing and medicine.[15] In temazkal, I became one with the earth, and in her womb, my body was able to experience transformation, renewal, and rebirth. These spaces were also "home sites," or "places of radical healing and transformation," which led to my spiritual awakening and coming home to my own body.[16]

I also received healing from my healer/acupuncturist, with whom I worked intensively for months after my miscarriage to clear my womb and heal from the physical and emotional scars of surgery and miscarriage. From these sessions, an array of emotions, ranging from sadness to fear, resurfaced and provided me an opportunity to release additional layers of generational womb trauma, making space in my womb for creation and creativity. I came to understand my miscarriages as new transitions in my body, for after any traumatic experience, the body, like the earth, has the opportunity to heal and reach a new level of being. For each of my miscarriages, I was able to experience a huge shift in my life resulting from the opportunity to rest, reflect, and heal. The gift and blessing of being conscious through the entire process of my third miscarriage deepened my connection to mother earth and to her cries of pain when the destruction of life imprints on her soil. This time around I was able to honor my body's natural process of miscarriage and hold the sacred ritual of laying my baby to rest on the earth's soil. Rooted in the richness of the earth's fertile soil, my womb became fertile ground to water seeds of self-love, compassion, and forgiveness, and for my spiritual rebirth.

While medical science has made great advances in life-saving technologies—after all, the skillful hands of a surgeon helped save my life—these technologies cannot come at the expense of torturing and killing Indigenous, Black, and Brown bodies, or dismissing non-Western ways of knowing that honor our bodies as knowledgeable. Throughout this chapter, I argue that (re)claiming and (re)vitalizing our mothers' herstories and the healing conocimientos of the body as a source of knowing and being engender our empowerment and agency to heal ourselves and to counter the colonizing imposition of the medical-industrial complex. An epistemology of body as earth makes it possible for us to (re)center our bodies, our sacredness, and our power as creators in our world. This work unapologetically honors a way of knowing that comes from my body, a knowing that embodies *agua es mi sangre, aire es mi aliento, tierra es mi cuerpo, y fuego es mi espiritu* (water is my blood, air is my breath, earth is my body, fire is my spirit). My testimonio and the birthing herstories of muxeres in my family show how our womb conocimientos are powerful and healing medicine. I take pride in knowing that the medical-industrial complex does not define who I am as a mother-activist-scholar. Our shared experiences of exclusion in the hands of medical science are also fertile ground for the revitalization and maintenance of empowering mothering practices (Lavell-Harvard and Anderson 2014). I am living proof of the centrality of strong, powerful muxeres who redefine mothering from an Indigenous perspective, one that simultaneously disrupts the colonization of our bodies by the medical-industrial complex and (re)centers ancestral healing conocimientos imprinted in our bodies.

Notes

1. Xu Xiong, Pierre Buekens, and Elise Wollast (1995), in a meta-analysis of the literature on links between IUD use and ectopic pregnancy, conclude that current IUD use does not increase the risk of ectopic pregnancy; however, a pregnancy with an IUD in situ is more often ectopic than a pregnancy with no IUD in place. Despite this established medical knowledge, the nurse who provided me services ignored my symptoms and failed to do a pregnancy test because of her biases and assumptions.

2. The documentary series *Unnatural Causes: Is Inequality Making Us Sick?* (Smith 2008) investigates the increasing and alarming socioeconomic and racial disparities in health by exploring the root causes of health inequities. Episode two of the series highlights how racism is a determining factor in women's reproductive health. For example, African American women are at increased risk during pregnancy because of the cumulative effects of racism that they experience over a lifetime, and this is the case even for women who have achieved higher-than-average social and class status.

3. Latina Feminist Group (2001) proposes testimonios as a method for feminist research praxis. Framed by common political views, a testimonio is a way to collectively create knowledge and theory based on experiences. Ehrenreich and Ehrenreich (1971) introduced the term "medical-industrial complex" to describe the for-profit health industry

and the rise in power of the medical industry in U.S. healthcare policy. Mia Mingus, writer, educator, and community organizer for disability justice and transformative justice, in her blog, *Leaving Evidence*, defines the medical-industrial complex as "an enormous system with tentacles that reach beyond simply doctors, nurses, clinics, and hospitals. It is a system about profit, first and foremost, rather than 'health,' wellbeing and care. Its roots run deep and its history and present are connected to everything including eugenics, capitalism, colonization, slavery, immigration, war, prisons, and reproductive oppression. It is not just a major piece of the history of *ableism*, but all systems of oppression" (Mingus 2015).

4. For bodies of work that address the legacy and continual violence and inhumane experimentations medical research has perpetuated on the bodies of Indigenous people, enslaved Africans, and colonized women in the name of "scientific progress," see Gamble and Blustein (1994). The authors highlight the cruel and inhumane medical acts committed on the bodies of Women of Color and remind us that the foundation of modern gynecology is based on the sacrifices of three slave women. They quote the "father" of modern gynecology, J. Marion: "The first patient I operated on was Lucy. . . . That was before the days of anesthetics, and the poor girl, on her knees, bore the operation with great heroism and bravery" (187). Harriet Washington (2006) coins the term "medical apartheid" to describe historical and present-day racial medical abuses and exploitation of Black bodies.

5. According to the *CDC Health Disparities and Inequalities Report, 2013* (Boehmer et al. 2013), the populations with the highest estimated percentage living within 150 meters of a major highway are racial and ethnic minority communities, foreign-born persons, and persons who speak a language other than English at home.

6. While the causes of miscarriage are still not well understood, and further studies are needed, Webb et al. (2014) nonetheless show that miscarriages are associated with exposure to certain environmental agents. Scientific evidence has linked adult and early life exposure to volatile organic compounds and heavy metals to infertility, miscarriages, and birth defects, demonstrating that toxic environmental agents pose serious threats to the livelihood of future generations.

7. Zambrana (1994) and Gamble and Blustein (1994) help uncover the historical and present-day abuses Latinx women have been subjected to by

the medical profession, which forces contraceptive drugs and devices on Brown bodies.

8. My understanding of conocimientos draws from Gloria Anzaldúa's definition of them as "subversive knowledges" that provide "a form of spiritual inquiry / activism," which is "reached via creative acts— writing, art-making, dancing, healing, teaching, meditation, and spiritual activism—both mental and somatic" (Anzaldúa and Keating 2002, 542). As "subversive knowledges," *healing* conocimientos bring complexity and a more holistic understanding of knowledges that integrate emotion, spirit, and ancestral traditions for the purposes of healing the self and the collective.

9. One such example in the Bay Area is the work of the ReCLAIM Collective (Resisting Colonial Legacy and Its Impacts on Medicine). The group focuses on reclaiming traditional knowledge and sacred practices that are integral to promoting the health of individuals and communities. The birth justice movement is engaging in a groundbreaking radical healing praxis that is working to expand access to traditional childbirthing and woman-centered care. As traditional hands-on healers, *parteras* are teaching womb care for women and children and are also knowledgeable in herbal medicine for reproductive health. Most importantly, these partera activists are birthing the next generations of babies through rites that engage in birth as ceremony, and they are making the links between women's fertility health and systems of oppression to support their birth justice activism.

10. I want to emphasize that this understanding is not meant to exclude women who may not have a physical womb, for they too can still connect with the energy of their womb as source of wisdom and creativity.

11. My grandmothers' treatment of the placenta and afterbirth as sacred rituals is rooted in ancient Mesoamerican Indigenous birth rituals, which continue to be maintained among Indigenous and Mexican Indian communities in Mexico. Gonzales (2012) elaborates on the significance of this birthing and traditional medicine: "Through the ceremonies of the ombligo and placenta, people re-place themselves and become re-membered in the land—within it, among it, around it, above and below it" (56).

12. First, I want to emphasize that my mother's decision not to take drugs during her labor was rooted in an understanding of birth taught by her

mother and grandmother, which did not require taking any kinds of drugs unless your life or that of your child depended on it. Second, this position does not in any way judge women who may choose or be given drugs during pregnancy or labor. I believe in promoting traditional Indigenous rites of birthing and healing as a holistic way of treating birth as ceremony, but I also believe in making use of Western medicine technologies, especially when such advancements promote the well-being of mother and child and can help support life.

13. A *cuarentena* is an Indigenous Mexican birth ritual in which a woman who gave birth or had a miscarriage adheres to specific self-care instructions on how to heal and recover for a ritual time of forty days. These instructions could advise anything from a range of healing practices, including full-time bed rest, wearing *fajas*, eating a special diet, *sobadas*, *baños*, and drinking certain *hierbas*.

14. I acknowledge that I was privileged to be able to take these forty days, and that we need systemic change so that more people can have paid sick leave as needed. I also recognize that many women may not have access to these healing and birthing conocimientos or elders and family to assist them in their healing, given how colonialism has disrupted our women-centered ways of knowing and abilities to sustain our ancestral healing modalities.

15. Temazkal is an ancient Indigenous purification sweat ceremony that is traditional to many Indigenous peoples of the Americas. Entering the temazkal is entering the earth's womb, with the lava rocks embodying the spirit of the ancestors, and the steam from the water poured over the rocks representing the breath of the Creator.

16. In "Spirit Journey: 'Home' as a Site for Healing and Transformation," Elisa Facio deploys the metaphor of "home" to "describe physical, spatial, and temporal locations ranging from participation in inipi and *temazkalli* ceremonies to negotiation my own body as a spiritual medium" (2014, 60).

References

Anzaldúa, Gloria, and AnaLouise Keating, eds. 2002. *This Bridge We Call Home: Radical Visions for Transformation*. New York: Routledge.

Boehmer, Tegan K., Stephanie L. Foster, Jeffrey R. Henry, Efomo L. Woghiren-Akinnifesi, and Fuyuen Y. Yip. 2013. "Residential Proximity to Major

Highways—United States, 2010." In *CDC Health Disparities and Inequalities Report, 2013*, supplement, *MMWR* 62 (Suppl 3): 46–50. https://www.cdc.gov/mmwr/preview/mmwrhtml/su6203a8.htm.

Brodsky, Phyllis L. 2008. *The Control of Childbirth: Women Versus Medicine Through the Ages.* Jefferson, NC: McFarland.

Cruz, Cindy. 2001. "Toward an Epistemology of a Brown Body." *International Journal of Qualitative Studies in Education* 14 (5): 657–70.

Duffy, John. 1993. *From Humors to Medical Science: A History of American Medicine.* Urbana: University of Illinois Press.

Ehrenreich, Barbara, and John Ehrenreich. 1971. *The American Health Empire: Power, Profit, and Politics.* New York: Random House.

Facio, Elisa. 2014. "Spirit Journey: 'Home' as a Site for Healing and Transformation." In *Fleshing the Spirit: Spirituality and Activism in Chicana, Latina, and Indigenous Women's Lives*, edited by Elisa Facio and Irene Lara, 59–72. Tucson: University of Arizona Press.

Gamble, Vanessa Northington, and Bonnie Ellen Blustein. 1994. "Racial Differentials in Medical Care: Implications for Research on Women." In *Women and Health Research: Ethical and Legal Issues of Including Women in Clinical Studies*, vol. 2, edited by Anna C. Mastroianni, Ruth Faden, and Daniel Federman, 174–91. Washington, DC: National Academies Press.

Gonzales, Patrisia. 2012. *Red Medicine: Traditional Indigenous Rites of Birthing and Healing.* Tucson: University of Arizona Press.

Latina Feminist Group. 2001. *Telling to Live: Latina Feminist Testimonios.* Durham, NC: Duke University Press.

Lavell-Harvard, D. Memee, and Kim Anderson, eds. 2014. *Mothers of the Nations: Indigenous Mothering as Global Resistance, Reclaiming and Recovery.* Bradford, ON: Demeter Press.

Mingus, Mia. 2015. "Medical Industrial Complex Visual." *Leaving Evidence*, February 5, 2015. https://leavingevidence.wordpress.com/2015/02/06/medical-industrial-complex-visual/.

Oparah, Chinyere, and Alicia Bonaparte, eds. 2016. *Birthing Justice: Black Women, Pregnancy, and Childbirth.* New York: Routledge.

Queen Afua. 2000. *Sacred Woman: A Guide to Healing the Feminine Body, Mind, and Spirit.* New York: One World.

Roman, Estela. 2008. *Nuestra Medicina: De los Remedios para el Aire y los Remedios para el Alma.* Bloomington, IN: Palibrio.

Ross, Loretta J. 2016. "Birth Justice and Population Control." In *Birthing Justice: Black Women, Pregnancy, and Childbirth*, edited by Julia Chinyere Oparah and Alicia D. Bonaparte, 72–80. New York: Routledge.

Smith, Andrea. 2005. *Conquest: Sexual Violence and American Indian Genocide*. Cambridge, MA: South End Press.

Smith, Llewellyn M., dir. 2008. *Unnatural Causes: Is Inequality Making Us Sick?* Narrated by Larry Adelman. San Francisco: California Newsreel. DVD. 236 min.

Washington, Harriet A. 2006. *Medical Apartheid: The Dark History of Medical Experimentation on Black Americans from Colonial Times to the Present*. New York: Doubleday.

Webb, Ellen, Sheila Bushkin-Bedient, Amanda Cheng, Christopher D. Kassotis, Victoria Balise, and Susan C. Nagel. 2014. "Developmental and Reproductive Effects of Chemicals Associated with Unconventional Oil and Natural Gas Operations." *Review on Environmental Health* 29 (4): 307–18. https://doi.org/10.1515/reveh-2014-0057.

Xiong, Xu, Pierre Buekens, and Elise Wollast. 1995. "IUD Use and the Risk of Ectopic Pregnancy: A Meta-Analysis of Case-Control Studies." *Contraception* 52 (1): 23–34. http://dx.doi.org/10.1016/0010-7824(95)00120-Y.

Zambrana, Ruth E. 1994. "Inclusion of Latino Women in Clinical and Research Studies: Scientific Suggestions for Assuring Legal and Ethical Integrity." In *Women and Health Research: Ethical and Legal Issues of Including Women in Clinical Studies*, vol. 2, edited by Anna C. Mastroianni, Ruth Faden, and Daniel Federman, 232–40. Washington, DC: National Academies Press.

Mothers of Color
in Academia

Fierce Mothering Challenging Spatial Exclusion
Through a Chicana Feminist Praxis

Nora Cisneros, LeighAnna Hidalgo,
Christine Vega, and Yvette Martínez-Vu

Somos las Mothers of Color in Academia, MOCA.
As low-income students, mothers, fathers, queer, and gender non-conforming Parents
of Color, we face racialized, gendered, classed, and other barriers to sustain our families
and fulfill our educational aspirations.
—EXCERPT FROM MOCA STATEMENT OF
DEMANDS TO THE UNIVERSITY

Soy mamá!
Response: *Somos mamás!*

When Mothers of Color are under attack, what do you do?
Response: *Stand up, fight back!*
—CHANT FROM OUR DÍA DE LAS MADRES ACTION
ON CAMPUS, MAY 10, 2016

Somos las (we are the) Mothers of Color in Academia (MOCA), an
effort led by Women of Color (WOC) that challenges exclusion and
disrupts the silencing of our existence in academic spaces. In this
chapter, we highlight MOCA and our grassroots efforts to identify the
gaps that so many academic institutions have in providing adequate

resources for student-parents. We also showcase a form of resistance we call "fierce mothering" to demonstrate how this strategy has led to tangible changes on our campus. We are inspired by Grace Gámez's (2015) framework of fierce mothering and the possibilities it holds for mothers in oppressive contexts. Gámez reminds us that fierce mothering is intergenerational and stems from collective concerns. MOCA also offers a form of fierce mothering informed by concepts of Chicana feminist praxis (Delgado Bernal et al. 2006), spatial entitlement (Johnson 2013), and the rasquache aesthetic (Mesa-Bains 1999) to create institutional changes that support student-parents in higher education. Our fierce mothering also includes a form of Mother-Scholar activism—a call to center and to act on the power of Mother-Scholars of Color as critical members of the academic community. This chapter's first epigraph is part of a statement, including demands, that we delivered during a Día de las Madres (Mother's Day) action on May 10, 2016, in Southern California, which we describe in more detail later. These demands derived from the lack of centralized resources for all mothers in our home institution, including proper lactation spaces and timely childcare access. Our public action is but one example of the steps we've taken to manifest fierce mothering.

We define "fierce mothering" as a response to the forceful forms of institutional violence that mothers must address, such as lack of access to childcare, inadequate lactation spaces, or invisibility on campus. Fierce mothering relates to the instinct to protect our children. In fighting back against systemic violence, mothers display bold acts, which include bringing our children to spaces where they are not welcome (often for lack of childcare), breastfeeding in public (because of insufficient lactation spaces and to push back against breastfeeding stigmas), or choosing to make our identities as mothers visible when we are often told to closet those identities. We include Mother-Scholar activism as a component of fierce mothering, since our actions include activism, advocacy, and research supporting the transition of our public demands into university policy changes.

These acts of fierce mothering can not only lead to tangible change on campus but can also teach other Mother-Scholars how to engage in liberatory practices for themselves and their families. As Loretta J. Ross queries in the preface to *Revolutionary Mothering*, "How do we get from a conservative definition of mothering as a biological destiny to mothering as a liberating practice that can thwart runaway capitalism?" (2016, xv). As a collective, we challenge conservative views of mothers to fiercely liberate ourselves and others in the depth of activism for political, social, and structural change.

MOCA formed in 2014 after we shared similar experiences of overt and covert marginalization at our university as WOC who were pregnant and had our children with us on campus. MOCA comprises the spiritual daughters of the Chicana, Mexicana, Salvadoreña, Black, Asian, and Indigenous feminist *teoristas* and ancestors whose work we followed at some point in our educational trajectory and *conocimiento* (Acevedo-Gil 2017). We shared dichotomous experiences of (in)visibility as pregnant-presenting individuals on campus. Our pregnant bodies were sites of discrimination and negative stereotypes; we felt the assumptions made by our peers and professors about our perceived lack of commitment to the academy and our scholarship (Caballero et al. 2017; Téllez 2013; Gutiérrez y Muhs et al. 2013). Many of those stereotypes are racialized and gendered, such as the presumption that we would drop out of our doctoral programs (Solórzano and Yosso 2006; Pérez Huber et al. 2015), but instead of dropping out, many parent-scholars are *pushed out* by the lack of resources. As Reyna Anaya (2011) notes in her study, child-rearing responsibilities are one reason that a woman's higher education path is interrupted more than a man's. For graduate student mothers, these child-rearing responsibilities directly affect attrition rates. We believe that our children and our pregnancies should not be treated as interruptions to our academic trajectory; rather, they disrupt Westernized heteropatriarchal educational expectations.

For the last few years, MOCA has organized on campus and met with different constituents to demand changes in access and resources for student-parents. Our organizing efforts have led to several of MOCA's demands being met out of a total of ten:

1. Hire permanent full-time staff at the university wellness center to coordinate services for student-parents and hire a full-time counselor at the counseling services center who specializes in reproductive health, including parenthood, miscarriages, and abortions.

2. Provide a family center on campus, with staff to consult on returning to work, education support, program development, and evaluation. Maintain a university parent portal that disseminates breastfeeding and parenting policies, resources, and services for the parenting community.

3. Subsidize carpool parking for student-parents who drive their children to and from childcare, on or off campus.

4. Inventory and create maps of accessible and available lactation sites on our campus that meet or exceed legal requirements.

5. Provide lactation rooms and changing stations that are gender nonconforming, clearly marked, clean, unlocked, and within a five-minute walking distance of any building on our campus.

6. Require orientations that raise the visibility of parenting families during welcome week for all students, newly hired staff, and faculty.

7. Provide affordable insurance coverage for our dependents.

8. Adjust financial aid packages to account for additional costs of having dependents, regardless of academic enrollment.

9. Provide more early care facilities on campus that provide evening and weekend childcare to serve student-parents, particularly low-income Title V – subsidized families.

10. Allow students to select placement for their children in their preferred early care facility.

While we have had some success with these demands, we could not have done all this work on our own. All parenting students require alliances, accomplices, and support from nonparenting students, faculty, administration, and staff. Our fierce mothering is a call to action for change, visibility, and an end to practices that push out of the academy People of Color who make informed, critical decisions to raise children in this world.

Literature Review

Mothers in the Academy

MOCA acknowledges several academic publications on mothering that do not account for issues of race. For instance, in *Mama, Ph.D.* (2008), edited by Elrena Evans and Caroline Grant, contributors offer a series of personal narratives that discuss how pregnant, childbearing, or nursing mothers share experiences of struggle in a workplace that does not provide on-site childcare, flexible leave policies, or lactation spaces. Several essays make suggestions for improving academic settings to be more supportive of mothers. The authors acknowledge the dismal number of women who secure tenure and the even fewer who are WOC. Nevertheless, this anthology perpetuates the lack of diversity in academia by publishing few essays by WOC and even fewer on the experiences of queer mothers. Another example, Mary Ann Mason, Nicholas H. Wolfinger, and Marc Goulden's *Do Babies Matter? Gender and Family in the Ivory Tower* (2013), provides a look into the experiences of parents in the University of California (UC) system. The authors acknowledge that even though women's representation in undergraduate and graduate education has increased since the 1960s, their employment in the professoriat does not show similar progress. Mason, Wolfinger, and Goulden argue that gender-related family dynamics are partially responsible for the lower tenure rates for women. While their study does not account for racialized differences, the gender imbalance is critical to note and is an issue that MOCA aims to address through our activism.

Additionally, Reyna Anaya's study (2011) centers the experiences of Mothers of Color (MOCs) in graduate school. She employs the intersectional framework used by Kimberlé Williams Crenshaw (1994) and Patricia Hill Collins (1994) and discusses the complex experiences of MOCs in graduate school. Anaya claims, "Access and support are not the same for all women. Women of Color experiences (i.e., Graduate Student Mothers of Color) are often silenced on university campuses by the dominant white culture's socially constructed ideals of gender roles and ethnic/race assumptions." Anaya also states that "understanding intersectionality, therefore, validates and creates visibility of individual, Women of Color experiences" (2011, 15). She points out that the way motherhood is written about does not include the experiences of MOCs and critiques the lack of intersectional, racial, and gendered identities in the literature by noting that the invisibility goes beyond the physical experience of motherhood.

Spatial Entitlement and Rasquachismo

Processes of spatial domination produce the exclusion that MOCs experience in academic institutions. Examples of spatial domination include insufficient accessible lactation rooms, parking, and breastfeeding supplies, which are important to analyze in the university since the university is a microcosm of social inequalities in the city. In *The Production of Space* (1991), Henri Lefebvre critiques the modern city, arguing that the struggle over space is grounded in capitalism and at its core is deeply geographic.[1] Lefebvre calls for a revolutionary "critique of space" (92), in which the people from below "confront the state in its role as organizer of space" and begin creating "counter-spaces and counter-plans" to resist hegemony (383).[2] In university settings, MOCs are "the people from below," and it is our duty to question how universities produce space to maintain male dominance. We build on theories of space by also using theories of WOC and *rasquachismo* to inform our organizing efforts, as well as by analyzing how university spaces exclude MOCs.

Our organizing efforts as MOCA build on a well-established tradition of Black and Brown activism in Southern California, which Gaye Theresa Johnson writes about in her book *Spaces of Conflict* (2013). Johnson introduces two concepts important to our discussion: spatial immobilization and spatial entitlement. By spatial immobilization, Johnson refers to racist policies toward Black and Brown communities, such as residential segregation, employment discrimination, police brutality, the militarization of Communities of Color, mass incarceration, detention and deportation, and anti-immigrant policies—all of which exclude People of Color from full social citizenship (Johnson 2013). Conversely, spatial entitlement refers to how marginalized People of Color have historically challenged immobilization by forming new political collectivities to make claims on the right to public space.

It is important to note that before entering the university setting, WOC have shared histories of spatial immobilization, and we argue that within the institutional setting, MOCs continue to face persistent spatial immobilization, whereby, for example, they are excluded from access to on-campus childcare facilities. WOC are often excluded from access to equitable childcare because they shoulder the burden of denouncing institutional policies regarding campus childcare that are only seemingly race and gender neutral. For example, some universities advertise accessible childcare for their incoming students but offer minimal or no support in securing a space or in accessing financial aid to assist with the elevated cost of such care. Oftentimes, the few childcare spots allotted to low-income student families are in facilities with lower-quality amenities, higher teacher turnover, and physically separate buildings from the higher-quality childcare facilities, which are reserved for the children of professors as well as middle- and high-income student families. Denouncing institutional policies takes tremendous labor for WOC, who may already be vulnerable in academia as first-generation students, student workers, and underrepresented bodies across various sectors of academia.

To fight back against classist institutional policies that affect student-parents, we draw on the rich history of interracial social movements to focus on the Black, Native, Chicana, and Central American collectivities that have formed around the battle for upholding the rights of mothers on university campuses. To build student-parent power, we collaborate across interracial student groups on and off campus. Each of these collaborations allows us to voice our demands, grow support, and gain momentum for our movement. In doing so, MOCs are reimagining public universities as democratic spaces, where our children are part and parcel to our work (in fact, we actually bring our children to MOCA events with collaborators). Including our children in spaces where they are not welcome is but one way to challenge spatial entitlement, to reclaim space, and to create an alternative expression of belonging.

Past studies on race and space found that poor Communities of Color often reclaim spaces meant to divide them (Latorre 2008; Cockcroft and Sanchez 1993; Sanchez-Tranquilino 1995; Johnson 2013). The imposition of freeways and the concrete channel of the Los Angeles River parceled off the land, splitting up neighborhoods. Through artist interventions, communities practice spatial entitlement; for instance, the concrete walls in the LA River were reappropriated through community-based murals to tell the histories of the marginalized communities who live there (Sanchez-Tranquilino 1995; Johnson 2013). In that same vein, our demonstrations make an intervention in university spaces that were designed to privilege white males at the expense of mothers. Our demonstrations make an intervention in "public" space by making our mothering visible on campuses that exclude us, where institutions violently and inhumanely neglect the rights of mothers. We do this by opening up our actions in ceremony, acknowledging our ancestors, and calling them in to the space that existed long before the university campus. At every demonstration, we make a point of bringing our children, breast pumps, strollers, diaper bags, and toys, which are parts of our everyday mothering experience that go unseen in the dominant experiences of campus life. Our analysis connects MOCs to these well-established traditions of spatial entitlement within Communities of Color, where we reclaim spaces meant to exclude us and repurpose them as spaces where we can nurture our children.

For us, the process of reclaiming space is a performed hustle, similar to the rasquache aesthetic. *Rasquachismo* is a concept well-known among the Chicanx art community, and it has been theorized as a Chicanx art sensibility. We build on rasquachismo by adding a spatial dimension to what Tomás Ybarra-Frausto (1987) and Amalia Mesa-Bains (1999) have addressed as a phenomenon present in Chicanx visual art, theater, music, and poetry, which is an "underdog perspective" (Mesa-Bains 1999, 157). Mesa-Bains argues that rasquachismo is a working-class sensibility with a "dual function of resistance and affirmation" (158). As such, rasquachismo is an aesthetic expression that "is both defiant and inventive," that comes "from discards, fragments, even recycled everyday materials," and that is "a combination of resistant and resilient attitudes devised to allow the Chicano to survive and persevere with a sense of dignity" (157). In response to the dearth of lactation rooms on campus, MOCA relies on resourcefulness to repurpose, appropriate, and reinvent campus space by subverting the original intent of grad lounges, group study areas, and conference rooms into creative improvisational lactating or childcare spaces that meet the mothering community's needs.

Our Work: Toward a MOCA Framework

Our mother-scholar-activist work centralizes Chicana feminist theory (CFT) as praxis (Delgado Bernal et al. 2006). For us, CFT unsettles the dominant inquiry of Western education by employing and centralizing the lived experiences of Chicana and Latina PhD mothers, specifically those of our "bodymindspirit" (Lara 2003), especially pregnancy and birthing. Our everyday activism is informed by CFT and unsettles deficit perspectives of what is "known" and "expected" of MOCs. Indeed, CFT serves as a bridge for Chicanas and Latinas to produce and contribute as practitioners of inquiry. Therefore, for MOCA, to engage in Chicana feminist praxis is to engage in a form of spiritual activism (Anzaldúa 1987; Delgado Bernal et al. 2006; Rojas Durazo, Silvestre, and Zepeda 2014) that resists and challenges the heteropatriarchy and sexism that MOCs experience in the academy.

Cindy Cruz reminds us in "Towards an Epistemology of a Brown Body" (2006) that the location of the Brown body "must be acknowledged in its centrality in creating new knowledges. . . . [U]nderstanding the Brown body and the regulation of its movement is fundamental in the reclamation of narrative and the development of radical projects of transformation and liberation" (657). Within MOCA, we understand that our mothering bodies are producers of life, knowledge, and resistance. Our decision to bring the next generation of children into this world is revolutionary and a manifestation of our mother-scholar-activist identities as well as our identities as fierce mothers. We, the authors, also self-identify as Chicana, Indigena, and Salvadoreña agents of social change, magnifying the voices of MOCs' herstories in the development of critical praxis that "propels the Brown body from a neocolonial past and into the embodiments of radical subjectivities" (Cruz 2001, 658). Our Día de las Madres action is an example of fierce mothering and Mother-Scholar activism because of the acts of resistance we perform against hostile institutional spaces.

Día de las Madres: Our Day of Action and Demands

On May 10, 2016, we gathered with fellow student-parents, Mother-Scholars, families, friends, and allies inside and outside our campus's main administration building to begin our Día de las Madres action. We opened with an Indigenous ceremony, led by our spiritual uncle, who began by asking our ancestors and earth mother permission for our day of action.[3] Embodying a rasquache aesthetic and acknowledging the Indigenous lands of the Gabrielino-Tongva, we offered tobacco while burning medicine in a community circle.[4] We call these *movidas* (hustles) rasquache because they attempt to repurpose a white heteropatriarchal space to serve the needs of Students of Color with ceremony, medicine, and song. Our actions reinsert the Indigenous and reinscribe the feminine into the academic landscape, reminding us that this land is Indigenous. Our spiritual uncle sang a warrior woman's song and talked about the importance of resistance. The action began in front of the academic affairs building, where many of us had experienced discrimination. We marched and ended at the research library (where we pumped many times through clear glass windows, exposing ourselves) to highlight the lack of lactation space. With megaphones, strollers, children, families, and a crowd of more than one hundred people, we read MOCA's ten demands through a large speaker and microphone.

After closing with our demands, we opened the floor for the community to share their *testimonios* as student-parents at the university. Some individuals walked out of the library, complaining about the noise, but we responded with "No justice, no peace!" until the grumbling students gave up and walked away. We made it clear that if our needs were not met, we would not be silenced. We reclaimed the front steps of the library with a speaker, roaring songs of justice and liberation. Our children danced, ate snacks, and played together. Others hugged, took pictures, and slowly trickled out after an eventful day of action. Acknowledging Black mothers, Black feminism, and our cross-campus interracial alliances, we closed our action by chanting the poem by Assata Shakur:

It is our duty to fight for our freedom.
It is our duty to win.
We must love and support one another.
We have nothing to lose but our chains.

Our day of action emboldened us and generated many future meetings with community members, students, and stakeholders.

Actions for Access and Equity

Breastfeeding and Pumping

Currently, none of our campus libraries hold official lactation rooms or policies to accommodate lactating scholars. The historical prominence of men in universities, while outdated given the higher enrollment of women across higher education, remains visible in the physical structures and policies of most libraries. As Jane Juffer (2006) reminds us in *Single Mother: The Emergence of the Domestic Intellectual*, many universities are keen on critiquing nuclear family norms in larger society, but they fail to critique structures that reinforce male-centric spaces. MOCA have persisted in claiming spatial entitlement (Johnson 2013) through rasquachismo (Mesa-Bains 1999) and the everyday practices of pumping in public. This spatial resistance demonstrates our fierce mothering, the political consciousness we have developed, and the alliances we have built to collectively make demands of the university.

The spatial structure and practices of the university reflect a campus climate that excludes student-parents. For instance, when several members of MOCA requested a room for lactation at the main research library, we received a key to a dirty basement closet. We began booking library study rooms every week to pump and study. The rooms were less than ideal, as we were exposed through the glass walls and took turns shuffling seating arrangements while pumping to cover each other. We often relied on one another to secure lactation pump accessories as they were not available for purchase at the university student pharmacy nor at any of the university convenience stores. In appropriating university locations as pumping spaces, we created spaces of congregation where we could share our knowledge of natural remedies and strategies for overcoming generational trauma. This support was the difference between continuing in our academic trajectory, taking a leave of absence, or dropping out. Thus, a rasquache working-class student-parent aesthetic was born out of circumstances in which the university environment failed to include the biological needs of mothers. We transformed these exclusions into alternative spaces where MOCs gathered to tend to physical, emotional, spiritual, and academic needs.

Through our fierce mothering, Mother-Scholar activism, and coordinated acts of resistance, we transformed male-dominated spaces into sites of nurturance. These appropriated pumping spaces on campus effectively became organizing spaces, which birthed MOCA as an activist group. We began seeking connections across campus and allied with undergraduate and graduate Student of Color collectives. We leveraged our research and activist skills to communicate our lactation needs with administrative stakeholders. Most MOCA are active members on committees that examine student health insurance policies and the university's built environment. Our work with these committees has prompted large-scale research projects that are underpinning policy changes to increase official lactation sites on our campus. Each of these alliances generated more spaces of interracial congregation, where MOCA were able to make audible and visible the plight of mothers on campus.

Childcare

Another focus of MOCA's fierce mothering is increasing access to affordable childcare both on and off campus to accommodate the particular needs of student-parents and working mothers. This requires that we challenge our university's current early care policies, which discriminate against low-income student-parents as Title V recipients.[5] According to our university's records, more than two hundred undergraduates and six hundred graduate students have dependents. These numbers are conservative since many graduate students are not required to complete Free Application for Federal Student Aid (FAFSA) forms. Three existing childcare centers are available to serve the academic community at our campus, with only one center open to student-parents that is located off campus. Some of us have been on a waitlist for one and a half to three years. We are often advised to place our unborn children on a waitlist as soon as we know we are pregnant. In 2016, the off-campus childcare center served fifty-four families, with more than one hundred families awaiting care. That means only 30 percent of families at most are having their childcare needs met. The waitlist jeopardizes student-parents' futures, as many students lack the financial capital and familial networks to secure alternative forms of childcare while they wait to be placed. As working mothers seeking subsidized childcare, we are burdened with additional paperwork and bureaucratic procedures that further delay our children's placement.

The off-campus daycare center for student-parents is located thirty minutes away from campus, within family housing. Geographically segregating student-parents, particularly for subsidized families, is discriminatory. The additional stops in the commute affect our children's dinner and evening routines, which we all feel the next morning. As fierce mothers, we have advocated for the needs of student-parents, especially Title V recipients, in town halls, graduate student associations, and orientations. For the last few years we have organized and met with on-campus administration and staff to discuss the existing gaps and inequities. We have been placed in committees for student-parents to be heard and to advocate for all students with children. Since then, our efforts have moved this work toward changes and open conversations for change with undergraduate student-parents, staff, faculty, and policyholders to accommodate the needs of the student-parent community. These needs include

- more spaces available for student-parents on campus
- integration of all children with faculty and medical staff, which will decrease the ludicrous waitlists
- more childcare centers on campus, which will also decrease waitlists (e.g., UC Davis has eight childcare facilities on campus and does not have childcare waitlists)
- transparency of funds and allocation, ensuring equitable access for all children
- inclusive, safe, shaded, clean, and green spaces for all children
- equitable pay for all educators in on- and off-campus daycare

Our Children's Play Is Political

MOCA have disrupted academia's erasure of mothering students on our campus by engaging in actions that bring attention to lactation and childcare barriers. The Día de las Madres action disrupted traditionally male-centered quiet campus spaces (such as administration offices and the main research library) with our children's presence and sounds. MOCA and allies have intentionally brought our children to academic spaces, meetings, and events. This has been a practical decision, because many campus events take place after childcare hours. Many mothers have expressed not wanting to be away from their children in the evenings, so they have brought their children to meetings, often prompting organizers to adjust meetings to more family-friendly locations and times. Some of our mothers brought their children to daytime campus events and meetings because of the shortage of affordable childcare. Our actions and events have been marked by the presence of strollers, toys, children's books, diapers, and breast pump supplies. We view our children's presence and play as a part of our fierce mothering in academia.

Our children's play has deeply shaped the planning and execution of our projects related to student-parents. At the early stages of our work, we were often invited by campus entities to partake in research on student-parents at times and places that were inaccessible for mothers of young children. After numerous conversations in which we had to explain to campus entities why they were failing to reach out to student-mothers, we created recommendations for working with mothers on campus. One of the most pragmatic requirements is that child-friendly spaces and childcare be provided for student-mothers. Other recommendations include securing (1) accessible parking, (2) child-friendly foods, (3) children's books and toys, and (4) lactation time and accommodation. Taking our children to some of these research-related projects highlighted the importance of creating an environment in which children can play and feel welcome. As a result of the exhaustion we felt encountering campus entities' constant failure to meet minimum requirements, we decided to collaborate with another student organization to design and collect data that are centered on student-parents' needs. Our children's presence and play are prioritized and sustained at each stage of our ongoing research projects.

Additionally, our children's individual and collective play have presented us with opportunities to understand how they are making sense of the contexts they encounter. On one notable occasion, our children's play revealed that adults in their childcare facility had ignored an incident in which children in a predominantly white classroom expressed racist views during storytime. Teachers and administrators had failed to communicate this incident to us as the mothers of the few Children of Color in those facilities. Play was the time and space in which our children tried to make sense of the hurtful event. This knowledge led to a formal investigation, and we voiced the need for integrating equity and diversity into the training and curriculum of these facilities. Our observations of their play have led to civic action in which our children's play was political, such as MOCA investigating and denouncing inequities in these institutions. By centering our children's presence and play in how we design and execute actions, meetings, and research, we shift play toward a political act that is foundational in our fierce mothering.

Conclusion

As of June 2017, we have leveraged our activism to expand breast-feeding access and childcare on campus. In response to our demands, the following changes have been implemented. We collaborated with the School of Public Health to inventory and access current university lactation sites. We worked with the student health center to train three on-call lactation consultants, who are available for students needing lactation support. We also worked with the admissions office to ensure MOCA is present in orientations for undergraduate and graduate students and for newly hired staff and faculty to raise awareness of parenting families. We collaborated with undergraduate parents to expand the evening drop-in childcare on campus. We are in touch with student health services about creating an online portal that displays resources for parenting students. Likewise, we are partnering with parenting groups and government service representatives from Medi-Cal and Women, Infants, and Children (WIC) nutrition programs to ensure that parenting students can access these services.

We learned that working alongside external community members also grounds us as a collective of mothers whose histories are rooted in communities older and more life giving than any ivory tower. This reminds us of the importance of reaching beyond the academy. Our acts of fierce mothering allowed us to disrupt the spatial exclusion we faced as mothers on campus. We continue to organize so that all parents can have access to lactation rooms, equitable childcare, and child-friendly spaces. Although our work is successfully leading to institutional changes, we are still confronted with many challenges. We negotiate completing our dissertations, applying for fellowship grants, and centering the care of our children, among other responsibilities. Our accomplishments are not cause for celebration so much as reminders of the injustice in low-income Students of Color being charged with the task of making the institution equitable, while middle-class tenured professors and wealthy administrators maintain the status quo. In our everyday activism, we end with a call to action for faculty, staff, and other allies to be accomplices in supporting MOCA and all student-parents.[6]

Sin mamás no hay . . .
Response: *Revolución*

Sin mamás no hay . . .
Response: *Profesión*

Notes

1. We borrow Henri Lefebvre's definition of space. In *The Production of Space*, he argues that space is not simply a container for matter or bodies but rather that bodies produce and are produced by space.

2. The production of abstract space is inherently violent because it seeks to generate profits for itself regardless of the human toll on others (Lefebvre 1991). Lefebvre argues that the wealthy elite, who control the social production of space, reproduce space to maintain their dominance and power over others. Nonetheless, space cannot stay stagnant, and what Lefebvre calls "trial by space" is the dramatic moment when "capitalism or socialism, state or community is put radically to question" (417).

3. A spiritual uncle or aunt is a community relative, elder, or person of wisdom who is a leader or spiritual and ceremonial knowledge keeper. Usually, a spiritual uncle or aunt will assist in the opening and closing of Indigenous and Native ceremonies.

4. The Gabrielino-Tongva are the original peoples of the Los Angeles Basin and Southern California.

5. Many graduate students are low income and qualify for a California Department of Education grant if they make thirty thousand dollars or less, as well as qualify for Title V programs to pay daycare on a sliding scale.

6. For literature on undergraduate Mother-Scholars, please see Vaidya (2016).

References

Acevedo-Gil, Nancy. 2017. "College-Conocimiento: Toward an Interdisciplinary College Choice Framework for Latinx Students." *Race, Ethnicity, and Education* 20 (6): 829–50.

Anaya, Reyna. 2011. "Graduate Student Mothers of Color: The Intersectionality Between Graduate Student, Motherhood and Women of Color in Higher Education." *Intersections: Gender and Social Justice*, no. 9, 13–31.

Anzaldúa, Gloria. 1987. *Borderlands / La Frontera: The New Mestiza*. San Francisco: Aunt Lute Books.

Caballero, Cecilia, Yvette Martínez-Vu, Judith Pérez-Torres, Michelle Téllez, and Christine Vega. 2017. "'Our Labor Is Our Prayer, Our Mothering Is

Our Offering': A Chicana M(other)work Framework for Collective Resistance." *Chicana/Latina Studies: The Journal of MALCS* 16 (2): 44–75.

Cockcroft, Eva Sperling, and Holly Barnet Sanchez, eds. 1993. *Signs from the Heart: California Chicano Murals.* Albuquerque: University of New Mexico Press.

Collins, Patricia Hill. 1994. "Shifting the Center: Race, Class, and Feminist Theorizing About Motherhood." In *Mothering: Ideology, Experience, and Agency*, edited by Evelyn Nakano Glenn, Grace Chang, and Linda Rennie Forcey, 45–66. New York: Routledge.

Crenshaw, Kimberlé Williams. 1994. "Against Women of Color." In *The Public Nature of Private Violence*, edited by Martha Albertson Fineman and Roxanne Mykitiuk, 93–118. New York: Routledge.

Cruz, Cindy. 2001. "Towards an Epistemology of a Brown Body." *International Journal of Qualitative Studies in Education* 14 (5): 657–69.

Delgado Bernal, Dolores, C. Alejandra Elenes, Francisca E. Godinez, Sofia Villenas, eds. 2006. *Chicana/Latina Education in Everyday Life: Feminista Perspectives on Pedagogy and Epistemology.* Albany: SUNY Press.

Evans, Elrena, and Caroline Grant, eds. 2008. *Mama, PhD: Women Write About Motherhood and Academic Life.* New Brunswick, NJ: Rutgers University Press.

Gámez, Grace. 2015. "But Some of Them Are Fierce: Navigating and Negotiating the Terrain of Motherhood as Formerly Incarcerated and Convicted Mothers." PhD diss., Arizona State University, Tempe.

Gutiérrez y Muhs, Gabriella, Yolanda Flores Niemann, Carmen G. González, and Angela P. Harris. 2013. *Presumed Incompetent: The Intersections of Race and Class for Women in Academia.* Boulder: University Press of Colorado.

Johnson, Gaye Theresa. 2013. *Spaces of Conflict, Sounds of Solidarity: Music, Race, and Spatial Entitlement in Los Angeles.* Berkeley: University of California Press.

Juffer, Jane. 2006. *Single Mother: The Emergence of the Domestic Intellectual.* New York: New York University Press.

Lara, Irene. 2003. "Decolonizing Latina Spiritualities and Sexualities: Healing Practices in Las Américas." PhD diss., University of California, Berkeley.

Latorre, Guisela. 2008. *Walls of Empowerment: Chicana/o Indigenist Murals of California.* Austin: University of Texas Press.

Lefebvre, Henri. 1991. *The Production of Space.* Oxford: Blackwell.

Mason, Mary Ann, Nicholas H. Wolfinger, and Marc Goulden. 2013. *Do Babies Matter? Gender and Family in the Ivory Tower*. New Brunswick, NJ: Rutgers University Press.

Mesa-Bains, Amalia. 1999. "Domesticana: The Sensibility of Chicana Rasquache." *Aztlán* 24 (2): 157–67.

Pérez Huber, Lindsay, María C. Malagón, Brianna R. Ramirez, Lorena Camargo Gonzalez, Alberto Jimenez, and Veronica N. Vélez. 2015. *Still Falling Through the Cracks: Revisiting the Latina/o Educational Pipeline*. CSRC Research Report 19. Los Angeles: UCLA Chicano Studies Research Center.

Rojas Durazo, Ana Clarissa, Audrey Silvestre, and Nadia Zepeda. 2014. "Chicana Feminist Praxis: Community Accountability Coalitions in the University." *Chicana/Latina Studies: The Journal of MALCS* 13 (2): 284–303.

Ross, Loretta J. 2016. Preface to *Revolutionary Mothering: Love on the Front Lines*. Edited by Alexis Pauline Gumbs, China Martens, and Mai'a Williams. Oakland, CA: PM Press.

Sanchez-Tranquilino, Marcos. 1995. "Space, Power, and Youth Culture: Mexican American Graffiti and Chicano Murals in East Los Angeles, 1972–1978." In *Looking High and Low: Art and Cultural Identity*, edited by Brenda Jo Bright and Liza Bakewell, 55–88. Tucson: University of Arizona Press.

Solórzano, Daniel G., and Tara J. Yosso. 2006. *Leaks in the Chicana and Chicano Educational Pipeline*. Latino Policy and Issues Brief 13. Los Angeles: UCLA Chicano Studies Research Center.

Téllez, Michelle. 2013. "Lectures, Evaluations, and Diapers: Navigating the Terrains of Chicana Single Motherhood in the Academy." *Feminist Formations* 25 (3): 79–97.

Vaidya, Anjanette N. 2016. "Treatise for My Mamas: On Young Mothers, Higher Education, and the 'Myth of Lost Opportunity.'" Undergraduate research paper, Rutgers University, December 11, 2016.

Ybarra-Frausto, Tomás. 1987. *Rasquachismo: A Chicano Sensibility*. Phoenix, AZ: MARS Artspace.

My Forever Sleeping Baby

On Research, Stillbirth, and Remembrance

Rose G. Salseda

I cannot recall the gifts I received from my family for Mother's Day 2016; however, I distinctly remember the card my husband included with them. The artwork for the card comprised a smiling Brown-skinned woman with wavy black hair gathered in a loose bun. She wore a funky yet stylish dress paired with cowboy boots and, tied around her waist, an apron with "best mom" written across. In one hand, she held a *cafecito*, and in the other arm, she cradled a swaddled sleeping baby. On either side of her stood two small children who looked at her adoringly. I was instantly taken by this image, not only because I, a curly-haired, bronze-skinned Chicana, resembled the mother, but also because the number of children represented my own. My husband's unique find was so impressive that I immediately posted a snapshot of the card on social media with the declaration "Daniel found the most perfect card!"

A few moments later, I received a comment from a professor: "All you need is a third baby!" The remark, although innocent and meant to be playful, felt like a jab deep within my belly. This colleague had only met my two daughters. She did not know about Sebastian, my first baby and only son, who had passed away six years earlier. I did not expect her to be aware of him. Those who do know about Sebastian only became familiar with him through my pregnancy, a handful of photographs, and the experiences that my husband and I have shared. In fact, besides Daniel and me, only hospital staff and our parents were able to see him in person; but, even then, he was not alive. Sebastian was stillborn. He died from complications caused by trisomy 18, a severe chromosomal disorder, when I was thirty-six weeks pregnant. In the card, I saw him as the sleeping baby. He is forever my sleeping baby, born silent with eyes closed.

Rarely do we discuss pregnancy loss in our society, even though miscarriage and stillbirth are not uncommon. For those who experience pregnancy loss, sharing their stories can be incredibly difficult. For bereaved parents of stillborn babies, like my husband and me, our stories are woven with the unfathomable. While parents of healthy newborns get to take their babies home, parents like us see ours taken to the hospital morgue. Instead of tending to the needs of a newborn, we contend with overwhelming grief and our baby's interment. As those other parents watch their babies grow, ours are fixed within memories of pregnancy and, if we are lucky, a few sonogram images or postmortem photographs. Our stories are difficult to tell because they are painful to remember. This pain is intensified by the anxiety or shame some of us may feel from what we understand to be the failure of our bodies to produce a healthy or "normal" child—or a child that is simply alive. Then, after we come home from the hospital and reenter the world, how do we account for our dead baby? How do we explain that our still swollen belly only *appears* pregnant? How do we explain the unused car seat strapped into the van, the unworn baby clothes hanging in the closet, the empty crib in the nursery? If we do at all, it is often done with tears.

Despite the difficulty of talking about and explaining my stillbirth experience to others, I strive to openly share my story. Thus, the professor who made that unfortunate comment in 2016 would eventually learn of my son, as would other new friends and colleagues who have entered my life since his death. I do this because, for me, remaining silent is more painful. It equates to a form of erasure that negates my experience and Sebastian's existence. As an academic, speaking about life in the first person is uncommon and can often feel taboo. As a Chicana and a first-generation college student in an overwhelmingly white, privileged, and Eurocentric discipline, this taboo felt intense at times in my struggle to be taken seriously as a young scholar. Indeed, a few colleagues could not or were unwilling to acknowledge my "private" life experience with pregnancy, loss, and bereavement. Yet, ironically, my training as an academic provided me with the research skills I used to prepare for and contend with these experiences. Thus, this *testimonio* bears witness to Sebastian and my experience being pregnant with him, while it also points to how my research background helped me cope with the life-altering experiences of pregnancy, birth, and death.

I became pregnant with Sebastian during my last year in the master's program in art history at the University of Texas at Austin. Becoming pregnant, however, had been more difficult than Daniel and I had expected. We had tried for six months before an at-home kit gave us the news we'd hoped for. We were ecstatic. I would be able to finish the master's program during the first trimester and then have the baby during the year I planned to take off before beginning a doctoral program. Yet, during our first prenatal visit at six weeks pregnant, our OB/GYN could not find a heartbeat and warned us that we could possibly miscarry. I cried, and Daniel almost fainted. For the next two weeks, as I began writing my thesis for graduate school, I came into the clinic for blood tests to measure my pregnancy hormone levels. Writing the thesis provided some respite from the worry, but I still feared the prospect of miscarrying. Although I am not religious, I began to pray to St. Jude, the patron saint of hope, after a Chicana friend and colleague made the suggestion. So, I wrote my master's thesis during the day, and at night, I lit a *vela* and prayed for life in my womb.

After a couple of blood tests, which showed a steady increase of hormones, I went in for another exam. Daniel and I were hopeful but braced ourselves for the worst. Then, on the sonogram monitor, we saw our *frijolito* with a rapidly beating heart! We were relieved and took an image of our little bean home to show our parents and closest friends. Yet, we did not know then that this early pregnancy scare would foreshadow events to come.

For the next several months, our pregnancy seemed, happily, ordinary. Morning sickness was a terrible experience, but I battled through the nausea to complete my thesis and finish the last course in the master's program. As I entered the second trimester of pregnancy, we sent pregnancy announcements to family and friends, and my parents, grandmother, and aunt traveled to Texas from California to attend my graduation ceremony. Life seemed perfect.

Then, several weeks later, Daniel and I learned that something was wrong with Sebastian's development. During a routine anatomical screening at the eighteenth week of pregnancy, the ultrasound technician found anomalies in the umbilical cord and heart. Certain body parts also measured shorter or smaller than average. Our OB/GYN thought it was possible that our baby had trisomy 21, also known as Down syndrome. For my husband and me, this possibility did not distress us. His career centered on advocating for people with developmental and physical disabilities, including those with Down syndrome. I also grew up in a family who actively volunteered at an advocacy organization for the developmentally disabled, which provided my aunt with services. Though raising a child with Down syndrome would be difficult, our backgrounds made us feel confident in our ability to provide care and find resources for our child. Although my OB/GYN was relieved by our response, she cautioned us about the uncertainty that still existed and scheduled us with a specialist for a definitive diagnosis.

In addition to the findings of the previous technician, the specialist at the high-risk pregnancy clinic noticed clenched fists with overlapping fingers, a cleft palate, and a smaller-than-average brain size among other physical signs. Together they pointed to a condition that excluded Down syndrome. The specialist was certain that our baby had trisomy 18. The expedited results of an amniocentesis would confirm his diagnosis a couple days later.

The specialist explained that trisomy 18, also known as Edwards syndrome, is a chromosomal disorder that affects the usual development of a fetus. It causes an array of abnormalities, such as defects to the heart and other vital organs that are life threatening. Fifty percent of fetuses with trisomy 18 die before birth. Of those that survive, most die within the first month of being born. Due to the severity of their medical conditions and developmental delays, only 5–10 percent of infants with trisomy 18 live past their first birthdays (U.S. National Library of Medicine 2017; Trisomy 18 Foundation, n.d.).

The specialist then listened to and answered all our questions. Yet, despite all the information, I felt compelled to go straight from the clinic to the university's library to research and read more about the condition. Although I understood the diagnosis, the severity of the disorder and the seeming inevitability of death overwhelmed me. The act of researching had always been a process in which I could retreat to focus, reflect, and make sense of questions or findings. I needed that right then—a space to let all this information sink in. Then, with compassion, the doctor said to us, "It's a wonder any of us are born." The statement slowed my racing thoughts, and together the three of us reflected on this truth. So much could and does go wrong in pregnancy.

Because of abortion restrictions in the state of Texas, Daniel and I had to decide quickly whether to terminate the pregnancy. We had just a couple of weeks before that decision would be lawfully taken from us. The only nearby doctor who could perform the procedure at this point in the pregnancy was located two hours away in Houston. It would require me to stay in the city as an outpatient for up to three days. Although doctors had overwhelmingly determined the abortion procedure safe, I read in journal articles about slight risks that could affect my health, and in very rare cases, the procedure could lead to death. Our only other option was to continue the pregnancy knowing that I would have to go through the labor and birth experience whether or not our baby was alive. If he survived birth, he would not live for very long because of the severe malformations of his vital organs. I did not want my baby to suffer, but if he lived, he would struggle with the most basic of bodily functions, such as breathing and eating, until one of them led to his death.

Daniel and I discussed our options and all possible outcomes. Although we are strongly pro-choice, we decided to continue the pregnancy. It seemed like the lowest-risk option to my health, and because we were still young, with no fertility issues, we also had the time to wait before trying again. In addition, if our baby lived, we had access to resources for the developmentally disabled and health insurance that could cover many of the costs of specialized care; if we needed help with medical bills, we knew we could rely on both sides of our extended families to pitch in. Simply put, our decision was largely influenced by our privileges in age, fertility, health insurance, insider knowledge, access to services, and financial support. Experiencing the time pressure to make such a significant decision, and realizing all the privileges we needed to continue our pregnancy, simply deepened our understanding of the need to further protect women's rights to choose. As the activist Loretta Ross forcefully reiterates in her preface to *Revolutionary Mothering*, the reproductive justice framework includes the human right to have *and* not to have a child (Ross 2016). Yet, such justice cannot be attained by all women until medical care, social services, and financial support among other resources are extended to and made accessible to everyone during both the prenatal and the postpartum periods.

After speaking with my doctors, we began the arduous task of telling our family and friends. We called our parents, grandmothers, and siblings, asking them to help us share the devastating news with extended family. Daniel sent a mass email to our friends, and I sent individual emails to colleagues. Then, we shared the emailed letter online via social media to notify everyone else in our lives. As news regarding our pregnancy circulated, we began to receive condolences and prayers. Unexpectedly, a few family and friends—Chicanas from different generations—opened up to us about their firsthand experiences with miscarriage and fetal death. Pregnancy loss had occurred to more people in our lives than we had previously realized. The intergenerational and cultural silence is something I still do not fully understand, but I quickly recognized that sharing our situation encouraged others to open up about their pregnancy loss experiences.

Immediately, we began planning for Sebastian's delivery and preparing ourselves for his death. We met with a neonatologist and his team of specialists, who would deliver our baby if he were to survive the pregnancy and labor experience. We chose not to undergo any medical interventions for Sebastian, so we also met with a palliative care specialist who would help relieve his discomfort and any pain until his death. I then began seeing my OB/GYN more regularly, beyond the typical schedule of prenatal visits, to monitor the baby's condition more closely.

In addition, I began to heavily rely on my research skills as a way to cope with the experience of my pregnancy and to prepare myself for its outcome. Having time off from graduate school and being unemployed, I spent hours reading about trisomy 18, late-term miscarriage, and stillbirth in medical journals and on trusted internet resources. I also scoured forums where I could read firsthand accounts written by bereaved parents who shared their stories of losing children with trisomy 18 specifically, and those who experienced pregnancy loss in general, avoiding overly religious and emotional posts in favor of those with more detailed information. After I felt I had gained a solid understanding of the medical condition and had surveyed a wide array of experiences, I then prepped myself by looking at medical photographs of babies with trisomy 18 and those with the particular physical abnormalities common with the condition. Eventually, when I felt brave enough, I began looking at medical photos of stillborn fetuses. I needed to prepare myself for everything, so that nothing would be a surprise. This was my way of not only thoroughly educating myself, but also ensuring that I could mentally survive this experience. If graduate school prepared me for anything, it was for this.

While this research and preparation was grim, Daniel and I tried our best to enjoy the time we had with Sebastian, knowing that even if he did survive birth, his severe medical conditions would make that enjoyment extremely difficult. My womb protected him from the discomfort; it nurtured him—breathed for him and fed him. We often lay in bed together, with Daniel's hands and face pressed against my belly to feel Sebastian's movements. A friend, who was a former midwife, suggested we begin listening to Sebastian's heartbeat and taught us how to use a fetal stethoscope. Each day, Daniel put the contraption on his head and listened to the baby.

As it got closer to our due date, Daniel and I increasingly prepared for the possible survival of our baby. We purchased some clothes and a car seat. A few sweet friends sent us some gifts, too. We made arrangements for both of our parents to drive from California to Texas to provide support. At the thirty-fifth week of pregnancy, however, Sebastian's movement became irregular. We knew he would not be with us much longer. On October 5, 2009, when I was almost thirty-seven weeks pregnant, Daniel was able to hear his heartbeat one last time.

We called our doctor, and after confirming the death with a sonogram, we made arrangements to induce labor the next day. We called
our parents, and they began a carpool to Texas, determined to make it
to the birth even though the baby had died. We then told a few friends.
One brought us a hot meal, and others made plans to meet us once
we came back from the hospital. Sebastian was born two days later.

I was worried I would be inconsolable at the sight of my dead baby.
When Daniel handed him to me, however, I instantly felt a rush of
intense love. Sebastian was so beautiful. He was tiny, weighing just
over three pounds and measuring sixteen inches long. He had a full
head of black wavy hair, a round nose, and my long toes. Because
of his slight cleft palate, his lips were in the shape of an upside-down
heart. The research and preparation I had done in the months leading
to his birth enabled me to experience this moment without tears. For
that, I am grateful.

Our parents then came in to take turns holding Sebastian. When
we were all ready, we had a priest come pray for and bless him. As
keepsakes, we took his footprints and a lock of his hair, and a professional photographer came to take pictures of him. We spent seven
hours with our son before saying our final goodbyes.

Occasionally, our eldest daughter comments about a framed black-
and-white photograph that we have of Sebastian. Taken by the professional photographer on the day of his birth, Sebastian looks like
he is sleeping. Out from under a crocheted cap are curls that, along
with swirls of lanugo on his forehead, frame his closed eyes. His heart-
shaped mouth appears relaxed and is slightly open, revealing his
tongue. His tiny hand wraps around the tip of my index finger, as my
hand and that of my husband lies across the bottom half of his body.
Our hands and the aforementioned cap, which is too big for his head,
emphasize Sebastian's smallness. Yet, his cheeks were still somehow
chubby. His sister often refers to him as her "baby brother," although

technically, he would have been older than her if he had lived. So, when she saw the card my husband gave to me on Mother's Day 2016, it was no surprise that, like me, she understood the baby in the art-work to be a representation of Sebastian. Born sixteen months after Sebastian's death, she has been raised with stories about her brother. Now, my youngest daughter is beginning to learn his story, too. My hope is that they never feel the stigma to keep quiet about the dead. I also hope that their brother's story will help them in the future if they, or those close to them, ever experience pregnancy loss.

Through sharing my experience of Sebastian with others, I hope they become sensitive to pregnancy loss and the need to expand and protect women's rights. My hope is guided by the refusal to participate in the professional silence surrounding pregnancy and death, or the intergenerational and cultural silence surrounding miscarriage and stillbirth. The experience of my first child and his death was devastat-ing; however, remembering him with others provides the opportunity to increase awareness of pregnancy loss and the importance of repro-ductive justice, especially for Women of Color.

References

Ross, Loretta J. 2016. Preface to *Revolutionary Mothering: Love on the Front Lines.* Edited by Alexis Pauline Gumbs, China Martens, and Mai'a Wil-liams, xvi. Oakland, CA: PM Press.

Trisomy 18 Foundation. n.d. "What Is Trisomy 18?" Accessed July 8, 2017. https://www.trisomy18.org/what-is-trisomy-18/.

U.S. National Library of Medicine. 2012. "Trisomy 18." *Genetics Home Refer-ence: Your Guide to Understanding Genetic Conditions.* Published March 2012. https://ghr.nlm.nih.gov/condition/trisomy-18.

Contributors

Trina Greene Brown is a Black feminist mama-activist who founded Parenting for Liberation. With fifteen years in the feminist movement, Trina is a national capacity builder for Resonance Network and Move to End Violence. Recognized as the 2017 Black Feminist Rising, Trina is a leader on the rise, bringing Black families with her.

Cecilia Caballero is an Afro-Xicana mother-scholar, speculative fiction writer, essayist, poet, and consultant. Cecilia was born and raised in the San Francisco Bay Area to formerly undocumented immigrant parents from Michoacán, Mexico. Her father worked as a farmworker, and her mother worked in the fast-food industry. Her parents also sell homemade *pan dulce, tamales, tortas,* and *fruta* as street vendors. Their hustle equipped Cecilia with the *ganas* to pursue higher education, and she is the first person in her family to graduate from high school, college, and soon a PhD program. Currently, Cecilia is a PhD candidate in the Department of American Studies and Ethnicity at the University of Southern California. She also holds BAs in English and Chicanx studies from UC Berkeley and an AA in liberal arts from Los Medanos Community College. Her dissertation focuses on narratives of Chicana/x Latina/x feminism, mothering, gender, sexuality, and spiritual activism in literature, cultural production, and digital storytelling. Cecilia's academic work has been supported by the Mellon Mays Undergraduate Fellowship, the Woodrow Wilson National Fellowship, and the Social Science Research Council, among others. Her critical and creative writing has been published by *Chicana/Latina Studies: The Journal of MALCS*, *Third Woman Press*, the *Acentos Review*, *The Body Is Not an Apology*, and more. Cecilia is the mother of a nine-year-old, Alonzo, who was born during her time as an undergraduate student.

Sandra L. Candel received her doctoral degree from the University of Nevada, Las Vegas, with an emphasis in cultural studies, international education, and multicultural education. She works with deported mothers and their U.S.-born children living in the border city of Tijuana, Mexico, and focuses on transnational feminism, transnational students, and border pedagogy.

Mara Chavez-Diaz is a mama, daughter, sister, healer, activist-scholar committed to building a better world for the next seven generations. She received a BA in ethnic studies from Mills College, and her MA/PhD from the University of California, Berkeley. Her focus is on youth of color, decolonizing methodologies in education, and healing.

Nora Cisneros is a doctoral candidate in the Graduate School of Education and Information Studies at UCLA. Nora's teaching and research address how and why Indigenous young women use multimodal writing as a critical medium for identity formation. Nora's two semillas—Tlalli and Antonio—are everything to her.

Gabriela Corona Valencia is a doctoral student in the Graduate School of Education and Information Studies at UCLA. Her work focuses on (de)constructing the educational and cultural oppressions experienced by young Brown girls within the South and East Los Angeles areas. She enjoys binge watching true crime shows and eating golden, crispy french fries.

Victoria Isabel Durán is a doctoral candidate at the University of San Francisco. Her research is centered in critical race theory, revolutionary mothering, Indigenous knowledge, and education for liberation. Her heart beams with love and, justice for her children, Emiliano, Amara, and Maceo. Together they restore her hope for a better world. She gives thanks to the MALA MADRES, who inspire and radiate love.

Shahla Fayazpour is a doctoral candidate at the University of Nevada, Las Vegas. As a multicultural educator, she focuses on diversity and social justice. Her dissertation focuses on identity development of immigrant parents and their roles in the U.S. educational system. She is also interested in women's studies.

Alma Itzé Flores is an assistant professor in the College of Education at California State University, Sacramento. Her research examines the educational experiences of Chicanx/Latinx first-generation college students and Chicanx/Latinx (im)migrant families, as well as the development and analysis of Chicana/Latina feminist pedagogies and research methodologies.

Grace Gámez is the program coordinator of the Reframing Justice Project (RFJP) at American Friends Service Committee, Arizona. Through RFJP she works to shift social assumptions around what justice requires in the state of Arizona, from models rooted in punishment toward ones that embrace radical community making and healing.

Andrea Garavito Martínez is a doctoral candidate in the Department of Education, Culture, and Society at the University of Utah.

Her research and teaching interests include multicultural education, Chicana/Latina feminism, and teacher education research. She enjoys sharing her "foodie adventures" and running and hiking with her four-year-old son, Emiliano Jose.

Monica Hernández-Johnson is a Central American doctoral student in curriculum and instruction, with an emphasis on multicultural, cultural, and international studies. Her research focuses on Latinas' higher education experiences using standpoint theory. Her use of testimonios offers new perspectives and challenges Western epistemological frameworks, which ignore and silence marginalized voices.

Cristina Herrera is a professor and chair of Chicano and Latin American studies at Fresno State. She's published widely on Chicana literature and authored the 2014 book *Contemporary Chicana Literature: (Re)writing the Maternal Script.* Cristina is currently working on multiple projects related to Chicana and Latina young adult literature.

LeighAnna Hidalgo is a doctoral candidate in UCLA's Department of Chicana/o Studies. She holds MAs in Chicana/o studies and applied anthropology. She's a cofounder of MOCA de UCLA and is mother to Paloma and Mateo. She researches street vending, self-employment, panracial movements, urban space, and visual research.

Hortencia Jiménez earned her PhD from the University of Texas at Austin. She is a professor of sociology at Hartnell College and the editor of *Readings in Race, Ethnicity, and Immigration.* Hortencia is a proud mother of three children: Luis, Itzel, and Elena.

Irene Lara teaches at SDSU's Women's Studies Department. Her teaching, scholarship, and mamihood are inspired by Indigenous knowledge, Anzaldúan thought, curandera praxis, and living in the

Borderlands. She's the coeditor of *Fleshing the Spirit: Spirituality and Activism in Chicana, Latina, and Indigenous Women's Lives* and *Women in Culture.*

Corina Benavides López is assistant professor of Chicana/o studies at the California State University, Dominguez Hills. As a FemCrit educational scholar, she promotes transformative and emancipatory scholarship on how systems of oppression affect Chicanx and people of color in the United States. Her son challenges, teaches, and grounds her every day.

Katherine Maldonado is a doctoral student in the Department of Sociology at the University of California, Riverside, and a single mother of three boys. Her areas of specialization include race and class inequality and critical criminology, focusing on gangs, gender, Chicana motherhood, and barrio youth survival strategies.

Dr. **Yvette Martínez-Vu** is a first-generation PhD Xicana mama. She was born and raised in the San Fernando Valley, California, to immigrant parents from Jalisco and Sonora, Mexico. Dr. Martínez-Vu has a BA in English and a PhD in theater and performance studies from UCLA. Her dissertation examines how Mexican, Chicana, and indigenous women use theatrical objects as a medium for resistance and empowerment within post-1990s performances in Mexico and the United States. Dr. Martínez-Vu has organized regional and international conferences. She is the recipient of various awards, including the IUPLR Mellon Fellowship, Ford Dissertation Fellowship, UCLA Dissertation Year Fellowship, a multiyear UC Cota-Robles Fellowship, and the Mellon Mays Undergraduate Fellowship. Dr. Martínez-Vu also has experience providing freelance academic coaching and editing services for undergraduate and graduate students. She is the cofounder of two activist collectives, including the multi-institutional

Chicana Motherwork Collective and Mothers of Color in Academia de UCLA group. Dr. Martínez-Vu enjoys advocating for undergraduates to pursue higher education while working on their self-care. Since completing her PhD, Dr. Martínez-Vu accepted a position as assistant director for the UCSB McNair Scholars Program. This position is a combination of advising, teaching, grant writing, research, and project management.

Larissa M. Mercado-López is an associate professor of women's studies at Fresno State, a member of the advisory boards for the Society for the Study of Gloria Anzaldúa, and coeditor of five collections of scholarship, including three volumes on the life and work of Anzaldúa. She is a mother to four children.

Nereida Oliva received her PhD from the Department of Educational Leadership and Policy at the University of Utah. She teaches ethnic studies at Hartnell College and hopes to continue supporting students in higher education through teaching, learning, and research. Nereida is also the mother of Anabelle Sade Oliva.

Judith C. Pérez-Torres is a first-generation Chicana scholar and teacher born and raised in the Los Angeles area to immigrant parents from Mexico. She is a mother of three: Luna (seven), Tino (five), and Joaquín (three), all born during her ABD status. Her children are the three main reasons she was able to push through and complete the doctoral program. Judith entered the CSU system as an undergraduate, receiving her BA in human communication, with a minor in service learning student leadership, and her MEd and PhD in educational leadership and policy from the University of Utah. Her research interests include exploring Chicana/x and Latina/x racialized educational leadership. Judith enjoys teaching and learning from all her students—from undergraduates to graduate students—and aims to instill the importance of equitable education through a CRT lens to improve the educational experiences for students of color. She is currently an adjunct professor at CSU Fullerton in the Department of Educational Leadership and the Office of First Year Experience.

Rose G. Salseda is an assistant professor of art and art history at Stanford University. She specializes in U.S. Latinx and African American art. She is the associate director of the U.S. Latinx Art Forum, an academic and advocacy organization dedicated to Latinx art and art history.

Ravijot Singh is a field coordinator and program management team member for AC/OP under MESA at University of Nevada, Las Vegas. Her conceptual and theoretical frameworks draw from critical multicultural education, language affirmation, postcolonialism, and social justice education, all of which seek to dismantle English-only education policy and its neoliberal underpinnings.

Gabriela Spears-Rico is a cultural anthropologist and an assistant professor of Chicanx/Latinx studies, with a joint appointment in American Indian studies. A P'urhepecha/Matlatzinca scholar and poet, Spears-Rico's BA is from Stanford University, and her PhD in comparative ethnic studies is from the University of California at Berkeley.

Dr. **Michelle Téllez**, an assistant professor in the Department of Mexican American Studies at the University of Arizona, is an interdisciplinary scholar trained in community studies, sociology, Chicana/o studies, and education who specializes in ethnic and women's studies. A graduate of UCLA (BA, 1996), Teachers College, Columbia University (MA, 2000), and Claremont Graduate University (PhD, 2005), her writing and research projects seek to uncover stories of identity, transnational community formation, cross-border labor organizing, gendered migration, autonomy, and resistance along the U.S.-Mexico Border. Dr. Téllez has published in several book anthologies and in journals such as *Gender & Society, Feminist Formation, Aztlán, Chicana/Latina Studies, Violence Against Women*, and in online forums such as *The Feminist Wire, Truth Out*, and *Latino Rebels*. In her twenty years of community engagement and activism, she has been involved in multiple projects for change at the grassroots level, utilizing critical pedagogy, principles of sustainability, community-based arts, performance, and visual media. Dr. Téllez is a founding member of the Chicana M(other)work Collective and the Binational Artist in Residency project. She is on the editorial review board for *Chicana/Latina Studies: The Journal of Mujeres Activas en Letras y Cambio Social* and on the board of directors for the Southwest Folklife Alliance. She is a single mother to her twelve-year-old daughter, Milagro. To find out more about her work, please visit www.michelletellez.com.

Christine Vega is a PhD mother-scholar activista and *maestra* born and raised in Pacoima, California. She is a first-generation college student and transferred from Los Angeles Mission College to UCLA, where she received BAs in Chicana/o and women's and gender studies. She is the mother to her five-year-old s(u)n, Janitzio Itztlaloc, born during her second year of doctoral studies. Currently, she is a doctoral candidate in the Graduate School of Education and Information Studies at the University of California, Los Angeles. Christine is a founding mother of another collective, Mothers of Color in Academia de UCLA. Christine has published with UCLA's *Regeneración Tlacuilolli* and the *InterActions Journal*; most currently her "Othermotherwork: 'Testimonio' and the Refusal of Historical Trauma" has appeared in the *International Journal of Qualitative Studies in Education*. She is a Dissertation Year Fellow (DYF), completing her dissertation on a critical race *feminista* analysis of first-generation doctoral mother-scholars and their everyday *movidas* "hustle." She is currently an editor for *InterActions*, a peer-reviewed journal at UCLA, and has worked for the Equity and Diversity Committee for the School of Education and Information Studies. She is an artist, indoor cyclist, foodie, and coffee connoisseur.

Verónica N. Vélez is an associate professor and founding director of the education and social justice minor and program at Western Washington University. Her work focuses on Latinx migrant mother activism in school reform, community-based participatory action research, and digital mapping technologies to explore the spatial dimensions of educational (in)opportunity.

Gretel H. Vera-Rosas is an assistant professor in the Sociology Department at California State University, Dominguez Hills. Her research and teaching interests include decolonial feminisms, visual culture, theories of motherhood, critical race theory, and immigration. She enjoys running and gardening with her three-year-old son, Raymi.

Index